Fine WoodWorking *on* Chairs and Beds

Fine WoodWorking
on Chairs and Beds

33 articles selected by
the editors of
Fine Woodworking
magazine

 The Taunton Press

Cover photo by Rick Mastelli

for fellow enthusiasts

First printing: January 1986
Second printing: October 1987
Third printing: October 1990
Fourth printing: September 1994
Fifth printing: February 1997
International Standard Book Number: 0-918804-45-0
Library of Congress Catalog Card Number: 85-51878
Printed in the United States of America

A FINE WOODWORKING Book

FINE WOODWORKING® is a trademark of The Taunton Press, Inc.,
registered in the U.S. Patent and Trademark Office.

The Taunton Press, Inc.
63 South Main Street
Box 5506
Newtown, CT 06470-5506

Contents

Introduction

Of all the types of furniture, chairs are most like people. They mimic our own sizes and shapes, and temperaments, as they wait to receive our bodies. They're at the heart of every interior landscape, for the chairs sit where we ourselves intend to sit. We see chairs all the time, omnipresent sculpture-in-the-round. We spend many of our waking hours perched upon, or sunk into, chairs. Then we spend our sleeping hours in their horizontal analogs, beds.

No one would buy pants that don't fit, but every day we sit in chairs designed for the theoretical average body, ill-matched to our own short, tall or lumpy selves. Yet a chair can be tailored as closely as a suit of clothes, to match the person and the decor. This is the chairmaker's art and craft, which many consider the pinnacle of furnituremaking. In 33 articles collected from the first ten years of *Fine Woodworking* magazine, authors who are also craftsmen tell you exactly how they design and make stools, chairs, sofas, cribs and beds. There are even plans for making everybody's favorite, the rocking chair.

John Kelsey, editor

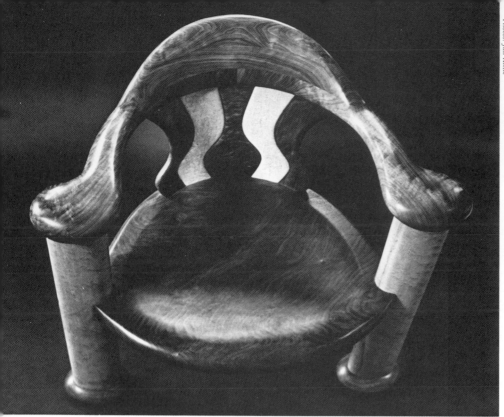

Photos: Jim Kittle

Throne chair, curly and crotch walnut, bird's-eye maple, $5,800. Right, underside of seat shows pinned tenons, Whitley's signature.

Right:
Whitley rocker,
figured walnut, $975.

Far right:
Continuous-line rocker,
crotch walnut, $5,500.

Have a seat

For more than 30 years, Robert C. Whitley's bread and butter has been restoring and reproducing antique furniture. He's become good enough to be named master conservator at Independence Hall in Philadelphia, and to be commissioned to reproduce the Oval Office desk for the Kennedy Foundation

What's rare about Whitley is his ability to design and make contemporary furniture along with the antique, and to be happy with both. His walnut rocker, center, was designed about 15 years ago and Whitley makes several dozen a year, in batches of ten. (All 1979 prices.) In 1978 he showed three new chairs at the Maker's Gallery in Manhattan. The curving parts of the chariot chair and the continuous-line rocker are carved from solid wood, with mortise and tenon joints at each hairpin turn. The webbing at the inside of each bend is part of the tenon. The legs of all three chairs are notched to receive the seats, and the joints are held by tapered dowels that penetrate 7 in. into the seats. The trick is to drill a tiny hole into the dowel hole from below, so glue can be injected and air can escape as the dowel is driven home. The back pedestal of the throne chair is fastened to the seat by a complex assembly of through pinned tenons, top right.

Chariot chair, curly maple, $5,200.

From *Fine Woodworking* magazine (January 1979) 14:84

Five Chairs: One View
A critique of design, craftsmanship and comfort

by Robert DeFuccio

The designer and maker of wood chairs is confronted with several major problems that must all be solved equally well for the piece to be wholly successful. The design must be esthetically pleasing, well executed and fit the average adult body as well as possible. The chair must also function in the area for which it was designed. One also hopes it will be durable, safe to sit in and fresh in appearance. All this is not easy to achieve. The history of wood chairs from ancient Egyptian, Greek and Roman times shows that chairmaking has changed little and that solutions to problems are limited. The weight, strength and density of a piece of ebony cut today are the same as they were in ancient Egypt. Basic construction details of chairs found in Tutankhamen's tomb, such as the pinned mortise and tenon, are exactly the same as mortise and tenon joints used today. Because the physical limitations of wood have led to such a refinement of form over the past 3,200 years of chairmaking, today's designer-craftsmen are confronted with the added challenge of being original in competition with a vast and rich global design heritage.

The design of chairs hinges on certain anthropometric data available from libraries and publishers of design books. Also useful are charts and diagrams illustrating the ideal average dimensions necessary to achieve seating comfort. Important considerations for the design of a conventional side chair or armchair are: seat height, 17 in. to 18 in.; seat pitch, 3° to 5°; arm height, 7 in. to 9 in. above seat; back pitch, 9° to 11°; minimum distance between arms, 18 in. It is possible that these dimensions may change for different types of chairs. They are also based on averages, but are nevertheless a reliable guide.

In critiquing the chairs shown in the photographs on the following pages, I measured each chair and made comparisons to what is considered average for men between 17 and 45—69½ in. tall, 163½ lb. These measurements are given in *The Measure of Man: Human Factors in Design,* by Henry Dreyfuss (revised, enlarged ed. 1967, Whitney Library/Watson-Guptill, 1 Astor Plaza, New York, N.Y. 10036). I also sat in each chair for my own reaction. (I am a bit slighter than average.) All five chairs command healthy sums (all 1979 prices) and all five pieces exhibit fine and exacting craftsmanship, yet the design and comfort of all the chairs is not, in my opinion, up to the existing level of craftsmanship.

Robert DeFuccio, of Spinnerstown, Pa., is an industrial design consultant for the Gunlocke Co., Wayland, N.Y., and Thonet Industries, York, Pa. He's designed chairs that have been produced by Knoll International and Stow/Davis Furniture Co. DeFuccio is also a craftsman—he makes his own prototypes of chairs for production—and teaches woodworking and furniture design at Philadelphia College of Art. The chairs discussed here were shown together at the Richard Kagan Studio, 326 South St., Philadelphia.

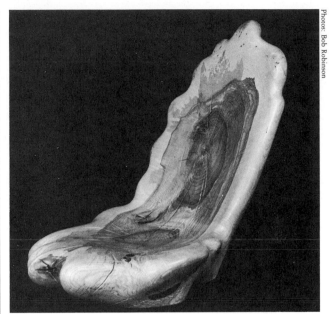

Photos: Bob Robinson

Lounge chair is white ash finished with oil. Overall height is 34 in.; overall width is 25 in.; seat height is 8 in. Price is $1,200.

Is this carved lounge chair by Jon Brooks, New Boston, N.H., a piece of sculpture or a functional low chair? Decide for yourself. This weighty and voluminous trunk of white ash has been carefully carved and shaped to yield an unusual lounge chair. Its continuous form, when related to conventional chair design, suggests a bucket or shell without upholstery. It probably possesses an optimum seating position, though I was unable to find it. All the ones I tried, whether off to one side, or with a leg tucked under me, or sitting with my legs straight out in front of me, were less than comfortable. I found myself slipping out of the chair because of the absence of pitch to the seat; a greater seating angle and more scooping of the seat would help prevent this. This chair will probably work for a select few only—those who would be pleased to own an object whose derivation is so evidently a tree trunk, complete with its beautiful grain, natural character and drying checks, and those whose physical stature is probably not unlike that of its creator, since I assume the chair fits Jon Brooks better than it does me.

A seat height of only 8 in. destines the chair to be owned by people under the age of 30. It is difficult to get into and even more difficult to get out of. Its lack of padding will also limit its appeal, because the wood is unyielding to the body and its form will not easily permit the use of pillows.

Working within the confines of the given log had to be somewhat limiting, yet Jon Brooks has created an interesting form and executed it with care and expertise.

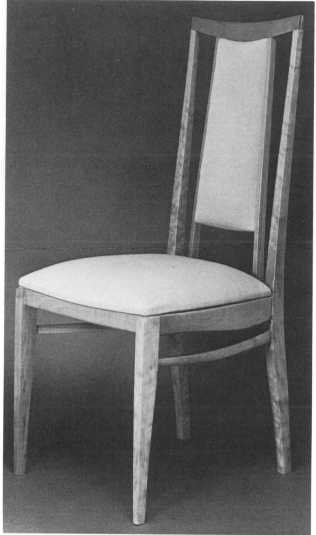

Side chair is cherry finished with oil. Overall height is 39¾ in.; seat height is 19⅛ in.; seat depth is 16¼ in; seat pitch is 2½°; back pitch is 5½°. Price is $2,500 for a set of six, excluding upholstery fabric.

The side dining chair made by Jere Osgood, Somerville, Mass., is pleasing to look at and slightly reminiscent of the Scottish architect Charles Rennie Mackintosh's high-back chair designs of the early 1900s. It is delicately scaled and nicely proportioned, although the seat is slightly short and not pitched enough. The heavily padded back upholstery, which places the person too far forward on the seat, shortens it even more. The crown of the seat seems too high and the at-rest dimension of 19⅛ in. from the floor is actually higher than necessary. The suspension for the seat is a Pirelli-type rubber webbing. I don't think a webbed seat is really necessary to provide the comfort expected from this type of chair.

Structurally this chair is sound, though I would recommend more lateral support for the front legs by increasing the depth of the front rail where it joins the front legs.

Game-table chair is 28½ in. high and 23¼ in. wide. Depth is 21¾ in.; seat height is 19 in.; seat depth is 19½ in.; seat pitch is 11°; back pitch is 14°. The finish is oil. Price is $500, excluding upholstery fabric.

This game-table chair by Wendell Castle, Scottsville, N.Y., is neither an armless chair nor an armchair. The extensions of the legs that join the back don't function as arms, yet they prevent the usual freedom of sitting positions offered by any armless chair. Sitting sideways or even off center in this chair is difficult or altogether impossible. The dimension between the arms at seat height is 17¾ in.—confining for a normal-sized person. The quick tapering of the seat from front to back accentuates this narrowness.

The back rail of Castle's chair, a beautifully executed curve, is carved to fit the small of the back and is very comfortable. It is the nicest element of the chair, though it is slightly overpowered by the large seat, which is upholstered in suede, a material that collects dust, lint and dirt. After considerable use, the area experiencing the most wear will lose its nap and contrast sharply with the unworn areas. The seam lines in the seat seem unnecessary, as they are not technically essential to the upholstery, and the seat appears puffy, its relationship to the frame awkward.

Construction details include a curved laminated veneer arc at floor level connecting the legs. The legs are splined to the curved floor rail and pinned with maple dowels. The seat frame is tongue-and-grooved and tenoned into the legs. The back is stacked and tongue-and-grooved into the legs.

Mariabronn chair is white ash finished with oil. Overall height is 28 in.; overall width is 29 in.; depth is 23¼ in.; arm height is 22¾ in.; arm width is 5½ in.; arm height above seat is 7 in.; distance between arms is 17¾ in.; seat height is 16 in.; seat pitch is 6½°; back pitch is 11½°; actual seat depth is 14½ to 15 in. Price is $850.

It is ironic that Richard Kagan, Philadelphia, Pa., selected beautiful curly white ash for his Mariabronn chair. This form relies upon a certain bulk from its wood members to achieve the necessary strength to support the seat and arm cantilevers. The visual result is a chair that appears heavy. His design might be more suited to steel tube, which would produce a flexible, stronger and lighter frame.

Kagan has filled the upper part of his chair frame with a continuous 10-oz. cowhide sling to provide a seat and back platform. I like the way Kagan has cut away the sling, providing straps to wrap around the supporting wood members. The negative spaces created work well with the rest of the chair, but the ¼-in. thick sling tends to push the occupant out of the chair because of a lack of space for the posterior—a common problem with most sling chairs. The leather will stretch after a period of frequent use, making the entire sling sag. As a result of the leather stretching, the seat and back rails will telegraph through to the finished top surface. Because the leather arrives from the tannery with only one surface finished, the craftsman must then finish the back surface and all exposed edges to a degree that is compatible with the level of craftsmanship exhibited on the rest of the chair. This is not easy to accomplish, but Kagan has done a reasonable job in trying to deal with this problem.

A unique feature of the design is the double-member arm. The space between the members is visually appealing, but I found my own arm movement limited when I sat in the chair. I also feel the chair would be more comfortable if the curve of the back rail were more pronounced. All of the joinery, which is superbly executed, is of the single joint or open mortise-and-tenon variety. Kagan has taken into account the unevenness of most floors, and has relieved the underside of the leg members so the chair rests only on four points. He has created a chair that strives to be minimal, but is not because of the nature of the wood. His chair makes demands for cross-sectional size and bulk that do not help the overall design.

Wing chair is cherry show wood covered with cotton velvet. Overall height is 43½ in.; overall width is 34 in.; seat height is 15⅝ in.; arm height is 21 in. Price is $1,500.

The idea of a contemporary wing-chair design is a good one, and Alphonse Mattia, Belmont, Mass., has made a fine attempt at a workable solution to the problem. There are, however, some difficulties. The first impression is that it should be very comfortable. It is not. The vertical wings, too deep where they meet the chair arms, restrict the user's arms and push them too far forward. Another problem is the lack of heel room. Upon rising from a chair it is natural to pull your legs in under you, but the cherry trim pieces and the lack of space between the floor and underside of the chair prohibit such movement. I found the seating area of the chair generally too confining. The seat dimension at the rear, 17½ in., is not enough for a roomy lounge chair. The allotted seating area needs enlarging.

The amount of foam, padding and cushioning material in this chair should make the seat and back more comfortable than they are, but the foam is hard. The limited durability of cotton velvet makes it a questionable upholstery. I believe that every effort should be made initially to use the best grade of fabric possible. Some factors determining selection include color, texture, fiber content, durability, type of backing, ability to resist stains and price. A wool blend would probably be more suitable. It would cost between $15 and $30 per yard, adding considerable cost to the overall price of the piece, but well worth it. This is especially significant when the cost of reupholstering such a chair is considered. □

Seat-of-the-Pants Chair Design
A scrapwood mockup solves basic problems

by Jeremy Singley

For me, chair design is a choreography of happy accidents. Since I've never "thought up" a design that didn't turn out to be pretentious, I've learned to stumble onto new ideas gracefully. Thus my most trusted guide is the seat of my pants. That's how it should be. After all, my head may be the seat of my thought, but I don't sit on my head.

I usually begin with nothing particular in mind—rarely even so much as a sketch—but start right in by experimenting with scrapwood, cordwood and leftover chair parts to create various combinations of forms. I see—or, rather, feel—what works and what doesn't work. With perseverance (and a little luck), I may discover the means to bring together a tree and a human body in a way that is pleasing to both.

The best way to encourage this sort of serendipity is to build the design around a person, so I invariably start with a living, breathing body (my own or a helper's) and sit it on a crate. Then I proceed like a tailor to cut, tack together and try my scrapwood pattern against this live model. Patterns that work I earmark for subsequent reproduction in fine hardwood. Those that don't work return to the firewood pile. This way, only my posterior or my model's suffers my mistakes, and the public is spared yet another "—uh . . . very nice" chair. My firewood pile receives the majority of the shapes I try.

A wooden apple crate is my starting point. On this I might place a 20-in. by 20-in. square of plywood as a seat. I position the crate near a wall to give my model something to lean against, but for now this is all the back my chair-in-progress has. By shimming the plywood with blocks and wedges, I can create a variety of heights and cants for the seat. By moving the crate closer to the wall or farther away from it, I can adjust how far back my model leans. If I'm designing a dining or writing chair, I pull a table up to the crate to see how the two work together. This method lets me interpolate a set of comfortable and functional overall dimensions.

Once I have a seat position that seems comfortable for my first model, I retest the seat by using other models or by "altering" the one I have. To see what would happen if my model were a different height, I put blocks under the model's feet to simulate longer legs, or under the crate to raise the seat so that the model's legs seem shorter. Often I find I must adjust the dimensions to develop a compromise that will be reasonably comfortable for a wide range of people.

At this stage, I begin to play with specific contours for the seat. To determine a cross-sectional contour that will cradle my model's derrière comfortably, I experiment with bandsawn scrapwood blocks taped to the plywood's top surface, as shown in figure 1.

When I've found a shape that seems to work, I ask more

Jeremy Singley is a full-time woodworker in East Middlebury, Vt.

questions. What if my model were fatter or thinner? And—the question often overlooked by chairmakers—what if my model were the opposite sex? A healthy woman could hardly fit into some chairs I've seen. Others, where a woman apparently was the model, are so spacious that a slender man could get lost in them. Once again I collar a variety of different size models, or make the one I'm using seem thinner by spreading the bandsawn shapes apart, or fatter by pushing the blocks together (making the seat seem wider makes the model feel smaller, and vice versa). Pushing the shapes together across the width of the seat, but not in its depth, approximates how a woman's hips would fit the seat. Spreading the shapes across the seat width will make the seat fit a woman as if she were a man. Next I run through the slouch test: Can the model shift about upon the seat and still be comfortable?

I follow a similar procedure to determine the form of the chair's back. Without worrying about how the back will be attached to the chair, I hand-hold strips of bandsawn or bent scrapwood, or bent lengths of electrical cable, plastic water pipe, metal strapping, cardboard or other materials against my model's back. Since a chair back must support people in a variety of positions as they shift, lean or slouch, I avoid a literal interpretation of my model's back, looking instead for gradual, grand sweeps that support the back over broad areas.

When a likely back form has been found, I cobble it to the prototype seat firmly enough to be leaned against (sometimes I just nail it to 2x4s leaned against the wall). I then test it with models who are taller, shorter, wider, narrower, or bent more or less than the original model, or I again use shims or other tricks to simulate more sitters. In this way, I make sure that no part of the back will bother the backbone, shoulder blades or hip bones of a wide range of individuals. This test also helps me determine the tilt of the chair's back and the distance between the chair back and the seat's front edge.

Once I've evolved a set of functional seat and back forms,

Fig. 1: Seat mockup

Bandsawn blocks can be shaped and moved to fit model.

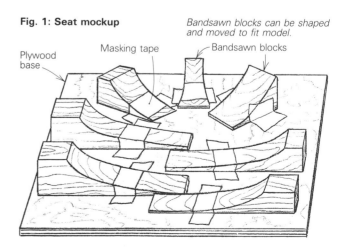

Masking tape

Bandsawn blocks

Plywood base

From *Fine Woodworking* magazine (May 1984) 46:72-77

Singley's Wainscot chair began as a trial splat leaned against a wall and a seat supported on a paint can.

Simplicity is the key in this Cheshire chair—turned tenons in round holes, and a sawn rather than steamed crest.

I've reached the end of the piecemeal stage of design, when the chair has only the most nebulous structure. The next step is to choose from among my forms (some forms won't work, but these may find their way into future designs) and see if any suggest a particular mode of construction. Whether my precarious pile of scraps will end up a Windsor, a Wegner or a what's-it must now be decided.

This is the hard part for me. I can't seem to accept that the decision is not mine to make: it's up to the chair. Sometimes this isn't a problem because the parts I've tacked and leaned together make themselves into a chair before I have a chance to meddle with them. In a case like this, I haven't found the chair, the chair has found me. The Wainscot chair shown in the photo at left above, for example, is hardly more than the original scrap board that was leaned against the wall as a trial splat (drawing, right), with the seat and crest— parts from a different chair that were  pirated from my inventory shelves—balanced, respectively, upon a five-gallon paint can and the top of the trial splat.

At other times I may undertake a more traditional chair type. My goal here is to make an existing chair design more attractive, or simpler, or more functional, or, if possible, all three. My version of the fan-back chair, the Cheshire chair shown in the photo at right above, is such a case.

Both the Wainscot and Cheshire chairs show my way of hooking the parts of a chair together: from functional part to functional part via the most direct route. Thus turned tenons in round holes, sawn curves rather than steamed bends, and simple, machine-cut joints predominate. Wherever a part or a process can be eliminated, I do so. I follow this standard most

rigidly for dining chairs, which must be affordable in multiples, and which tend to look cluttered around a table unless each is rather austere.

At the other end of the scale is the personal chair—such as the rocker or the executive's desk chair—where the cost of the additional comfort and visual appeal that can be attained with complex steambends and joints is justifiable. I have never found complexity a virtue in itself, however. The fact that a technique is difficult or different is no reason to include it in a design; it's usually a good reason to leave it out.

Getting from the apple crate to the finished hardwood chair is a matter of recording the relative proportions, locations and angles of the protochair's scrapwood parts so that they can be reproduced. The specific procedure for determining the chair's dimensions varies with the particular type of chair, the individual designer, and the situation. To outline them all would require a book. A look at how one chair might evolve, however, will give a general idea of this process and the thinking and experimenting that precede it.

Let's say I've decided to build a fan-back chair. This decision determines the general form of the chair: since the fan-back is a Windsor, we know we're talking about a scooped seat of solid wood, as opposed to a slatted, upholstered or webbed seat. Since in this case the seat is the part of the chair I'm most interested in improving, I begin here. After drawing a centerline on the plywood trial seat, I make tape-on contours, like those shown in figure 2 on page 8, adjusting their shapes and their positions on the plywood seat until I've developed a seat scoop that works.

Because the chair back largely determines the seat's outline, I resist the temptation to fool with the seat any more at this stage and I go right to the back. I cut out a flat cardboard or scrapwood crest, stick dowels (to serve as spindles) onto it with glaziers' putty or tape, and lean the works against the wall behind the seat. Then I re-arrange the parts until they look right.

I use a generous number of dowels to determine the spindle layout. If a chair has too few spindles, I've found that they end up being spaced too far apart to act as a team, and will instead be felt as individual edges digging into the sitter's back. I also use an even number of dowels, since an odd number will put a center spindle where it is unlikely to get along well with the sitter's spine.

Once I've found a back that looks right, I make a firmer version that I can have models try to see if it feels right. To keep the bottoms of the dowel spindles from being forced off the seat when the model leans back, I make a shallow, oversize hole in the seat at each spindle's proposed location. Then I bandsaw a scrapwood crest, drill holes for the tops of the two outermost spindles (called post or king spindles), and cut notches for the inner (pawn) spindles. I fit the king spindles into their shallow seat holes, add the crest, and lean the whole assembly against the wall. I insert the pawn-spindle dowels, cut somewhat over-length, into their seat holes and into the crest notches. The "chair" is then sat in (figure 2A).

The advantage of this lackadaisical method of non-construction now becomes apparent. Say the curve of the crest is wrong. I can throw it away and bandsaw another. If the seat holes are wrong, I can bore new ones. If the holes start to overlap, I make the new ones deeper than the ones they intersect, to keep the dowels from wandering.

Eventually my "chair" will look like figure 2: one old crate, one chunk of used plywood with a million holes in it, a lot of odd scrapwood affixed to the plywood, a rough bandsawn crest cut from an old 2x6, perhaps ten dowels, at *least* a mile of tape, and a variety of blocks, shims, wedges and reject parts everywhere. But when I sit in it, it feels good. Voilà! Now to make it pretty (and portable).

First, I bandsaw a scrapwood crest rail with the front view of my first, flat trial crest and the top-view curve of the second, notched trial crest. I tape this new crest in front of the notched crest, so that it appears to be mounted on the spindles. The seat's plan view comes next. This is fairly easy to determine. The back edge is a curve ⅞ in. or more behind and usually (but not always) parallel to the curved centerline of the spindle holes, the width is whatever looks good with the back, and the shape will usually suggest itself from the former two dimensions and from the seat's scoop. I label the scoop blocks, trace their positions onto the plywood, and remove them. I cut out a paper pattern (figure 3) in the shape suggested by the back and scoop, with a slot or hole for each spindle, and I lay the pattern over the mockup's plywood seat. With the pattern and the back in place together, I stand back and take a look. If the pattern looks bad, I burn it. If it looks good, I laminate a trial seat blank by edge-gluing softwood scraps together.

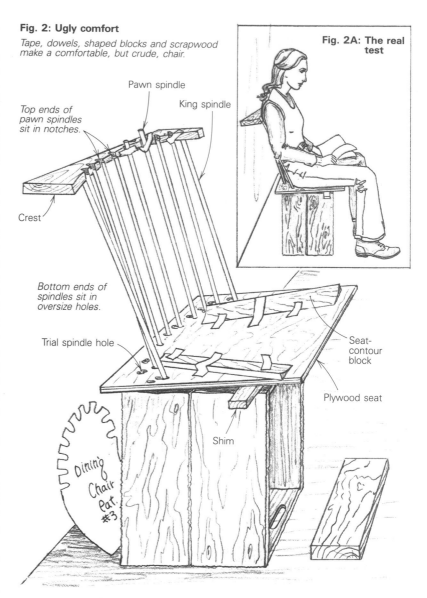

Fig. 2: Ugly comfort
Tape, dowels, shaped blocks and scrapwood make a comfortable, but crude, chair.

Pawn spindle
King spindle
Top ends of pawn spindles sit in notches.
Crest
Bottom ends of spindles sit in oversize holes.
Trial spindle hole
Seat-contour block
Plywood seat
Shim
Dining Chair Pat. #3

Fig. 2A: The real test

While the glue is drying on the scrapwood seat blank, I follow the procedure outlined in the box on pages 10-11 to transfer the position and angle of the king spindles onto a duplicate paper seat pattern, but without spindle notches. Each spindle has an angle at which it tilts, and an axis along which this angle is aligned and measured.

At this time I also make a paper pattern of the crest's shape, and record on it both the spacing between the king-spindle holes and the number of pawn spindles. Then I kill time by roughing out stock for the legs and spindles, leaving the dimensions oversize, since I don't yet know exactly what size these members will be.

By now the glue on my scrapwood seat blank is dry, and the real fun begins. I trace the pattern of the proposed seat shape onto the scrapwood blank, transferring the pattern's centerline and the king-spindle locations to the wood as well. Then I bandsaw out the seat. I may later bevel the edge, but for now I cut it square.

Next I scoop the seat using an adze, an inshave and a fish-tail gouge, with the scrapwood tape-ons derived in the first step serving as guides. I place the seat on my apple-crate test stand at the altitude and cant I settled on previously, and

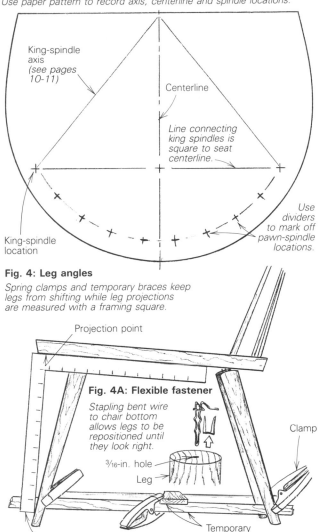

Fig. 3: Paper pattern

Use paper pattern to record axis, centerline and spindle locations.

King-spindle axis *(see pages 10-11)*

Centerline

Line connecting king spindles is square to seat centerline.

King-spindle location

Use dividers to mark off pawn-spindle locations.

Fig. 4: Leg angles

Spring clamps and temporary braces keep legs from shifting while leg projections are measured with a framing square.

Projection point

Fig. 4A: Flexible fastener

Stapling bent wire to chair bottom allows legs to be repositioned until they look right.

Clamp

³⁄₁₆-in. hole

Leg

Framing square

Temporary braces

shape, taper its ends, or make its top edge thinner; I turn thinner spindles; I turn fatter spindles; I throw it all in a corner and forget about it for a week.

Finally, like birthing pains, just at the point when it seems hopeless, it all comes together. I'm ready to build a real chair. Using my scrapwood parts and paper patterns as models, I laminate a hardwood seat blank and either steam-bend a hardwood crest blank or, as I did with the Cheshire chair shown in the right-hand photo on page 7, saw and smooth a hardwood crest. While the glue is drying on the seat blank—and the bent crest blank, if one is needed, is seasoning in its form—I set the softwood protochair back on its pedestal and think about legs. I cut four lengths of 1-in. dowel to approximate length, and wedge them with wads of glaziers' putty between the chair seat's bottom and the floor. This gives me something to look at that I can easily shift around.

Once I have an idea of leg positions and lengths, I turn some softwood or green-wood prototype legs to suit, shaping their contours in a way that I hope will be pleasing. These legs are hooked to the softwood chair bottom with staple-nails and bent lengths of wire coat hanger as shown in figure 4A.

Now the chair can stand on its own (but I don't dare sit in it yet!). If it looks right the first time, I can expect to wake up at any moment, because I'm dreaming. Most likely it won't seem right until I've pulled the staples and shifted the leg positions, bent the wires to change the splay of the legs, and/or turned new legs and refined their contours.

When I've arranged the legs so that they look right, I tie them together with braces and spring clamps, measure the distances between their bottom ends, and take a projection of the front legs' splay (figure 4). Then I turn the chair over. With the splay measurements just taken, I check that the legs haven't shifted, then I lay out the leg positions and axes on the bottom of the seat, using the same method I used for the king spindles. These positions and axes are recorded on the back side of the paper pattern, along with the leg angles. Now I turn a set of hardwood legs, bore tenon holes in the softwood seat bottom, and dry-assemble the complete protochair.

Even at this stage, I'm not committed. If the chair with real spindles and legs leaves me only lukewarm, I can plug the offending tenon holes with dowels, rebore at another position or angle, and try again.

Despite the lack of glue, the chair can now be sat in if blocks are nailed to the floor around the leg bottoms to keep the legs from spreading outward. Often this final test leads to some sawing-off of the ends of the front or back legs.

The rest, for the woodworking half of me, is denouement. The hardwood seat and crest are worked up, finished, bored, test-assembled and checked for accuracy. The tenons are kerfed with a veining tool to prevent air-lock as the parts are driven home, a small dab of glue is spread on the walls of each hole but not on the tenon (to eliminate the chance of excess glue bead) and the chair is glued up. That's when, for the designer half of me, the excitement becomes a fever. What began as a vague possibility waiting to be discovered in my firewood pile now exists: a chair.

Is it perfect? After all the previously described fussing and tinkering, I must confess it's not. But that doesn't dampen my enthusiasm, it only makes me itch to build another chair that's a little different, and then another. For me, chair design is not a process with an end. Good design, after all, cannot be created; it evolves.

(continued on next page)

sit in it. If it feels good, I go on to the next step. If it doesn't, I make adjustments. If it's still not right, I put it aside for future reference—somewhere within reach of the woodstove—and make another.

By now I generally have enough information to get a feel for the chair's overall proportions. Judging from the bulk of the seat and crest, I gauge the spindle diameters that should look right. If I'm not sure, I cut out a couple of trial spindles, square in cross section, on the bandsaw and see how they look when tried against the seat and crest. Then I turn a set of finished hardwood king spindles. I lay out the seat's spindle holes according to my pattern and bore the holes, using the method described in the box on pages 10-11.

Finally, I insert the king spindles in the seat and crest, measure how long the pawn spindles need to be to span from seat to crest (allowing for tenons), and turn these spindles. I dry-assemble the chair seat and back, and try the whole thing out on the test stand.

I have never reached this stage and been happy with the result on the first try. I make adjustments: I chamfer the seat bottom to make the seat appear thinner; I cut the seat smaller, or glue on stock to make it bigger; I change the crest's

Boring angled holes

When the novice chairmaker gets out his drill bits and protractor, it usually isn't long before he's stumped. How do you get the spindle and leg holes at the correct angles? It can be puzzling, because each of these chair parts involves a compound angle—an angle at an angle—as shown in figure 5.

We could measure the two angles with a protractor, but I find that it's better to do as loggers do: consider a compound angle as one angle leaning in a particular direction. To a logger, the direction in which a tree leans is the axis along which it will fall, at least on a windless day. To determine that direction, the logger walks around the tree at some distance, sighting its trunk against an object hanging plumb from his fingertips, such as a key chain. When the tree appears to be perpendicular to the ground, he is standing on the fall line.

I apply the same trick when making a real chair from a scrapwood prototype, like the one described on pages 6-9. On the prototype, I sight the axis line of the spindle—its "fall line." Perpendicular to the axis, I sight the lean-angle of the spindle. Then I set a drill press to bore the lean-angle, align the spindle axis with the bit, and bore the hole. I use a radial drill press because the head, not the table, tilts, making it easier to hold and align seat blanks on the table. When you understand the principles, however, you can adapt the method to a regular drill press by making an auxiliary table that tilts the work.

To determine the spindle axis, I set up my trial plywood seat and mark on it a centerline. Then I add the trial king spindles in the position I want.

I now stand a try square on the flat plywood seat and slowly move it to the left or right until the vertical edge of the square's tongue is parallel to the king spindle's centerline. I mark the point where the tongue's edge meets the seat (figure 6). The process is repeated for the other king spindle. Then I draw the spindles' axis lines—corresponding to the direction in which each spindle leans—as shown in figure 7. The two lines should either meet at the seat's centerline, or run off the front edge of the seat at points equidistant from the centerline. If they don't, I check whether the back is on straight, measuring the crest's height from the plywood at each end and comparing the back's diagonal measurements from the top of one king spindle to the bottom of the other one. If that's not the problem, I check the

crest for twist by sighting the side view of one king spindle against the other (they should line up), and by sighting down from above to see if the crest is symmetrical to a line connecting the two king-spindle holes (line A–B in figure 7). If none of this resolves the error, I split the difference. One has only so much patience.

Now, to determine the lean-angle, I hold a protractor along a sight line perpendicular to a spindle's axis line (figure 8). The protractor's hairline should split the centerline of the spindle (I use a protractor with a clear plastic tongue). It's best to hold the protractor dead-upright and read with your eye at the same level as the protractor's base—sighting across the seat's horizon. The lean-angle shown on the protractor, which will be the same for both king spindles, is the angle at which the drill press will be set.

I use Powerbore bits for spindle holes. To set up for drilling, I transfer the centerline, the crossline A–B, the

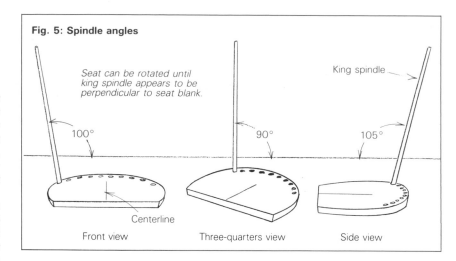

Fig. 5: Spindle angles

Seat can be rotated until king spindle appears to be perpendicular to seat blank.

King spindle

100°

90°

105°

Centerline

Front view

Three-quarters view

Side view

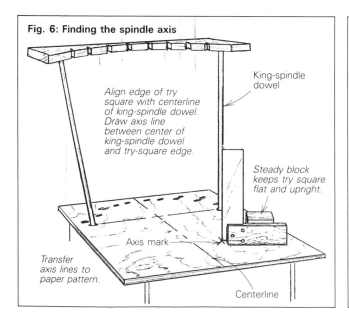

Fig. 6: Finding the spindle axis

King-spindle dowel

Align edge of try square with centerline of king-spindle dowel. Draw axis line between center of king-spindle dowel and try-square edge.

Steady block keeps try square flat and upright.

Axis mark

Transfer axis lines to paper pattern.

Centerline

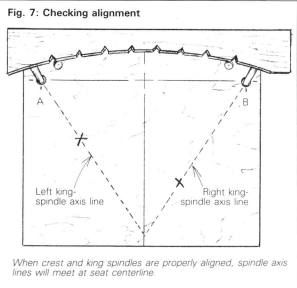

Fig. 7: Checking alignment

A

B

Left king-spindle axis line

Right king-spindle axis line

When crest and king spindles are properly aligned, spindle axis lines will meet at seat centerline.

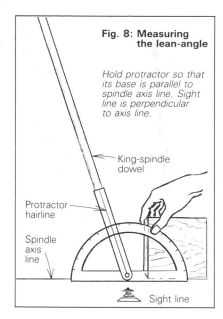

Fig. 8: Measuring the lean-angle

Hold protractor so that its base is parallel to spindle axis line. Sight line is perpendicular to axis line.

King-spindle dowel

Protractor hairline

Spindle axis line

Sight line

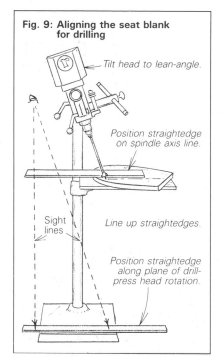

Fig. 9: Aligning the seat blank for drilling

Tilt head to lean-angle.

Position straightedge on spindle axis line.

Sight lines

Line up straightedges.

Position straightedge along plane of drill-press head rotation.

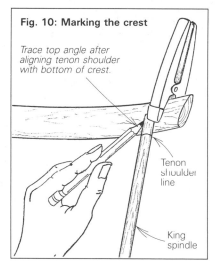

Fig. 10: Marking the crest

Trace top angle after aligning tenon shoulder with bottom of crest.

Tenon shoulder line

King spindle

hole locations and the axis lines from the prototype seat to the seat blank. One critical adjustment remains: the axis line on the seat must be set on the table in the exact plane in which the head of the drill press tilts. This plane should be parallel to the front edge of the press base, but to be sure I check by chucking an eyebolt in the press and tilting the head all the way to one side. I drop a plumb line from the eyebolt and mark the point on the floor. The process is repeated in the other direction. Connecting the points with a straightedge placed on the drill-press base shows the plane in which the head tilts, and along which the axis line must be set. If this plane doesn't correspond to the front of the press's base, I rotate the head assembly about the column until it does. Then I mark the position with matching scratch

marks on the column and head. After that, I just use the scratch marks to check press alignment.

After setting the press at the spindle's lean-angle, I place the seat on the press table and align the spindle's axis with that of the press. To do this, I lay a straightedge along the spindle axis line of the seat and, with the machine turned off, I lower the quill until the tip of the bit's center brad pierces the hole location on the blank. Then I rotate the seat blank until the top straightedge is parallel to the bottom straightedge (or, on my drill press, to the front edge of the base), as in figure 9. When everything lines up, I bore the hole, then I move the seat to the other spindle location, align that axis, and bore that king-spindle hole.

At this point, I have a seat blank with two king-spindle holes. I make the king spindles, based on the trial ones from the prototype, and plug them into the seat. Now I can set up to drill the rest of the spindle holes in the seat and in the prototype crest rail. (With these parts assembled, I can refine the design, including the outline of the seat itself.) To find the angles for the spindle holes, I clamp the crest rail to the king spindles and trace off the angles of their top tenons, as shown in figure 10. Then I bore the holes as shown in figure 11. Now I can mount the crest on the king spindles and drill the pawn-spindle holes with a hand-held electric drill (figure 12), eyeballing the drill's alignment from point to point.

To drill the seat's pawn-spindle holes, I use a bit extension with the power drill. I set up the notched crest made before the model sat in the prototype, as explained on page 8, and run the extension in the notches (figure 13). —*J.S.*

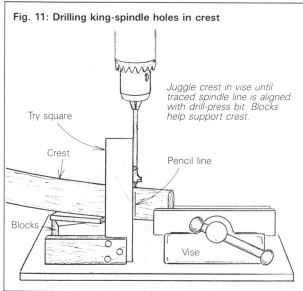

Fig. 11: Drilling king-spindle holes in crest

Juggle crest in vise until traced spindle line is aligned with drill-press bit. Blocks help support crest.

Try square

Crest

Pencil line

Blocks

Vise

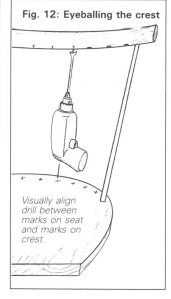

Fig. 12: Eyeballing the crest

Visually align drill between marks on seat and marks on crest.

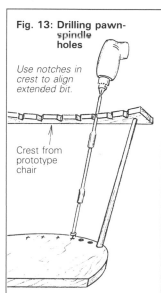

Fig. 13: Drilling pawn-spindle holes

Use notches in crest to align extended bit.

Crest from prototype chair

Five More Chairs: One View
Does traditional seating meet contemporary comfort standards?

by Robert DeFuccio

EDITOR'S NOTE: In January and February 1979, Woodcraft Supply Corp. (now Woodcraft) of Boston (Woburn, Mass.) inaugurated a new display space at its retail store with a show of five traditional chairs made by contemporary craftsmen. Three of the chairmakers—Dunbar, Moser and Alexander—have written books about their techniques. (Dunbar's *Make a Windsor Chair* is available from The Taunton Press.) So we asked Bob DeFuccio to go there and have a sit, and to give these five chairs the same rigorous scrutiny he had earlier applied to five contemporary designs (see pages 3-5). DeFuccio, of Spinnerstown, Pa., is an industrial design consultant for chair manufacturers and has designed chairs produced by Gunlocke Co. and Stowe/Davis Furniture. He designs and makes full-scale prototypes, and teaches woodworking and furniture design at Philadelphia College of Art.

In the following discussion and photo captions, all angular measurements of seat and back pitch relate to the horizontal floor and to a vertical line, respectively, not to the included angle formed by the seat and back. All 1979 prices.

Whether one's own tastes run to traditional or contemporary furniture, these chairs certainly merit attention. All five have been made with care and great technical expertise. The joinery is uniformly well done, the finishes are good. The choice of woods reflects a long tradition of craftsmanship and detailed lore. The forms are familiar to everyone: Their creators have made no effort to challenge our preconceptions. To many people, these chairs will evoke comfortable images of what chairs should be like. But they all seem to sacrifice comfort for historical accuracy. Their scale reflects people who weren't the same size as people today, and sometimes other modes of sitting. Many people will feel that these problems are overshadowed by what these chairs offer in the way of craftsmanship and esthetics. Others will feel that a chairmaker should heed the physiological needs of the sitter as well as his psychological need for the familiar.

Continuous-arm Windsor chair, made by Michael Dunbar of Portsmouth, N.H. Overall width: at arms, 21¾ in.; at seat, 17 in. Overall height: 35½ in. Seat height: 17 in. Seat pitch: 3½°. Back pitch: 14°. Seat depth: 20⅛ in. overall, 15⅜ in. usable. Seat width: 17 in. Height of arms above seat: 9¼ in. Longest back spindle: 19¼ in. Weight: 9 lb. Price: $350.

Michael Dunbar's continuous-arm Windsor chair is a fine example of a well-proportioned, lightly scaled, lightweight chair, whose heritage dates back to early 18th-century England. Dunbar made it by hand, using 18th-century methods and tools. (The procedure is described in his book *Windsor Chairmaking,* Hastings House, 1976, currently out of print).

The seat is New England white pine, the spindles and arms are red oak, and the leg turnings and stretchers are maple. The pine seat ensures a lightweight chair, and also carves easily and quickly. The maple is close and straight grained, strong and turns easily. Rived red oak is strong and when shaved to thin sections, resilient. Red oak is also right for the bow back because it can be readily steam-bent. The chair is finished with two slightly transparent coats of green milk paint, which obscures the differences of the several woods and allows one to visually read the form as a unified whole.

In studying the size and sectional dimensions of the parts,

one soon realizes that these dimensions make structural sense and probably evolved by trial and error. The spindles are thin enough to flex, but strong. The bow back is square in section, measuring ¹³⁄₁₆ in. by ¹³⁄₁₆ in. where the spindles enter, and becomes a flat rectangle ½ in. by 1 in. where it bends into the arm. This shaping provides good engagement for the spindles, yet reduces the chance of breakage during bending. The arm post turnings are heavier than the other spindles, for strength and support. The seat is 1¹³⁄₁₆ in. thick at the rear, plenty of bulk for the spindle mortises, and thick enough for pronounced scooping—visually appealing and comfortable to sit upon. The unsanded turned legs are substantial and look crisp. The side stretchers swell to increase the amount of wood around the joint where the center cross-stretcher enters.

A key to the strength of this chair is assembling the bow under tension, done by compressing the spindles down into

From *Fine Woodworking* magazine (May 1979) 16:58-61

Photos: Mike Germer, Intramedia

place with the bow. This construction permits the chair back to flex under the load of someone leaning against it, but not to weaken. The back is significantly strengthened by the two spindles that connect the upper part of the bow to the rear extension of the seat. From the side view, a sturdy triangle is formed. All the spindles are wedged from above as they go through the bow back, and from the bottom as they penetrate the seat. The four legs are also wedged through the seat.

The chair is logical and elegant, and its scale and proportions are very appealing. The combination of thin spindles, pronounced saddling of the seat, sharp, crisp turnings and changes in section as the back bow becomes arms, all contribute to visual interest. Both the shape of the parts and the residual tool marks on them reflect the tools of the chairmaker, and these traces of manufacture do not look out of place. A small asymmetry results from the way the holes were bored in seat and back. The form of the chair accepts this irregularity and is even enhanced by it. One gets the impression of complete control of the material by the craftsman, and of a form that has evolved over time. Dunbar has burned his name ¼ in. deep into the bottom of the seat, which is not painted. His intent is to discourage anyone who would plane the name off and present the chair as an antique.

As far as meeting contemporary seating needs, this chair has problems. The major one is the narrowness of the seat. The usable distance across the seat at the rear is only about 12 in., limiting the number of people who could use it. The back is comfortable, even though its pitch is too much at 14°. Modern designers consider 9° to 11° ideal for a pull-up chair. It is admirable that Dunbar has revived the old method of making American Windsor chairs, but to me the value of chairmaking of this sort is to understand yesterday's technology and joinery in an effort to make better chairs today. To make his Windsor chairs more effective, I feel Dunbar should proceed one step further and rescale to fit today's people.

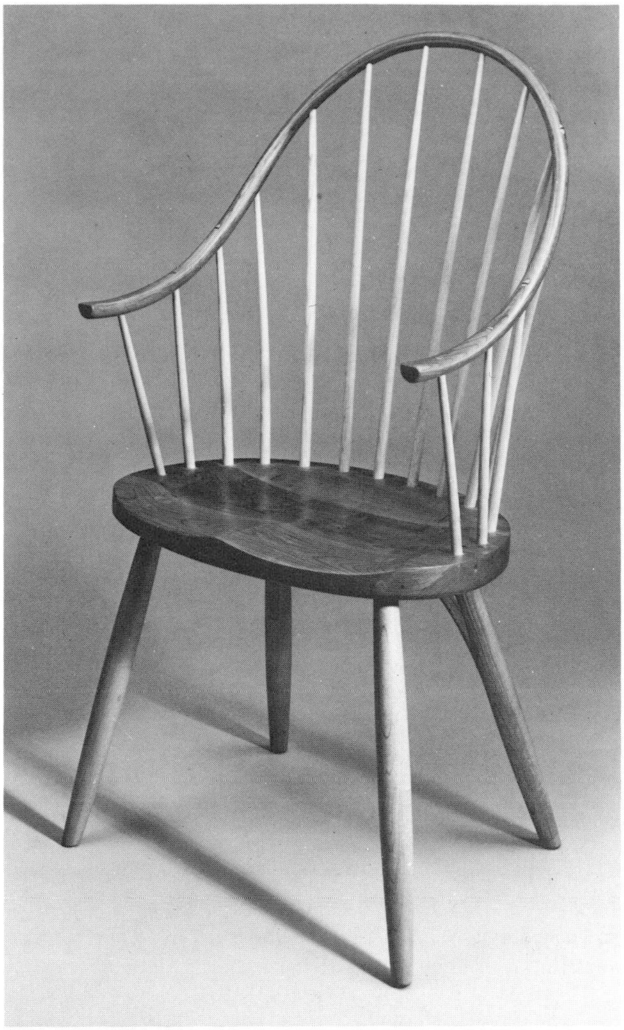

Continuous-arm Windsor chair, made by Thomas Moser of New Gloucester, Maine. Overall width: 22⅜ in. Overall height: 41¾ in. Seat height: 17½ in. Seat pitch: 2°. Back pitch: 12° (at two center spindles). Seat depth: 15⅝ in., 14⅛ in. usable. Seat width: 22¼ in. Height of arms above seat: 10 in. Weight: 11¾ lb. Price: $295.

Thomas Moser's armchair is strongly influenced by traditional Windsor chair design. He has taken many of the standard elements to create his own contemporary version of an established design. (Moser's *How to Build Shaker Furniture,* Drake/Sterling, 1977, out of print, includes four ladder-back chairs and a bench, but not the chair shown here.) Moser's chair is interesting for its delicacy but disturbing because of proportioning flaws absent from historical models. The back seems too high (41¾ in.) and the seat too short (14 in.). The chair looks compressed. The short seat provides no thigh support and is easy to slide out of because the pitch is only 2°. I put a ¾-in. spacer under the front legs, which almost eliminated the problem. The pitch was then 4½°. The seat is made from three pieces of edge-glued cherry, with the grain running side to side. It is nicely carved and scooped.

The continuous back rail and arms is bent from laminated cherry veneers. It is an eight-ply construction, with the veneers twisted during bending to permit the change of bending planes. The 14 back spindles are turned white ash. They all penetrate the back and arms, and are wedged with cherry wood. They also penetrate the seat and are wedged from the bottom. The contrasting color of the ash spindles cut flush with the cherry back and arms creates a strong graphic pattern that changes from almost perfect circles at the top of the back to long ellipses at the "elbow." This calls attention to the joinery but is also a distraction. The width of the arm is only 1⅛ in.—a wider arm would be more comfortable.

The entire back assembly flexes and adds to the general comfort of the chair. However, I doubt its strength, since the longest spindle is 24 in., 3¾ in. longer than the longest one on the Dunbar chair, and without that chair's triangulating back braces. The arm-supporting spindles are the same diameter as the other 12 spindles. A heavier arm support has to be stronger, and would be preferable.

The turned maple legs are joined to the seat with the standard wedged dowel joint. Moser has eliminated the conventional leg stretcher system and replaced it with two curved laminated braces. The braces are mortised into the back legs and doweled into the seat. This approach provides ample support for the rear legs, although I think it is visually unrelated to the rest of the chair. The front legs remain unsupported and rely solely upon their round tenons into the seat.

Moser has made an admirable effort to adapt design and structural elements from the past to create his own version of the Windsor. It is delicate and well-made, well worth the effort it would require to refine it and overcome its problems.

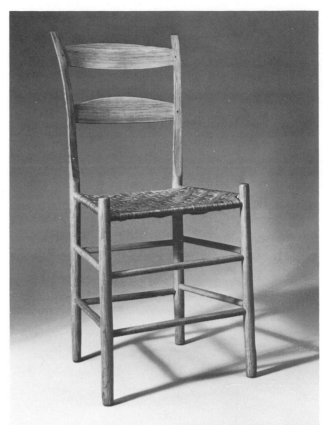

Thumb-back Windsor sidechair made by David Sawyer of East Calais, Vt. Overall width: 15½ in. Overall height: 32¼ in., 30½ in. to top of back rail. Seat height: 16¾ in. Seat pitch 2½°. Back pitch 19½°. Seat depth: 15¼ in. overall, 14 in. usable. Seat width: 15½ in. Weight: 7½ lb. Price: $110.

Bent-back sidechair by John D. Alexander Jr. of Baltimore, Md. Overall width: 17 in. Overall height: 35¼ in. Seat height: 18 in. Seat pitch: 3°. Back pitch: 15½° (at lower back rail). Seat depth: 13 in. Seat width: 17 in. Width of back: 15 in at top, 13¾ in. at seat. Weight 5½ lb. Not for sale.

David Sawyer's sidechair is called a thumb-back Windsor because of the shape of its back posts. It has a scooped cherry seat, with hickory legs, spindles, stretchers and back rail. It is well proportioned and crafted—visually, very fine. Sawyer is a serious student of traditional methods, who works mainly by splitting and shaving green wood.

Joinery details include legs that penetrate the seat and are wedged, back posts that neck down to dowel ends, penetrate the seat and are wedged from the bottom, stretchers that dowel into the legs and back spindles that dowel into the seat and back rail. The steam-bent back rail is tenoned into the back posts and held in place with four small pins.

The splay of the legs from both the front and side views makes the chair sturdy and stable. The height of the front stretcher in comparison to the side stretcher prevents kicking it while sitting. The angle of the back, 19½°, first seemed comfortable, but it is much too much deviation from the standard 9° to 11°. It offers little or no support when used as a dining or work chair. The back rail is only ½ in. thick at its heaviest, and the back spindles reduce to a scant ⁵⁄₁₆ in. diameter to join its lower edge.

All the corners and edges of the chair are eased and pleasant to touch, with the exception of the tops of the back posts. They discourage leaning one's arms against them, and could well be blunter and softer.

The chair is well engineered, though I see a potential problem with the strength of the back. The back posts are not a continuation of the back legs, and depend wholly for strength

upon their dowel joints into the seat. The back spindles do add some strength, but after a year in a centrally heated house, the back posts might shrink. The dowel joints would loosen and the back could be vulnerable. The back currently flexes—comfortable, but not reassuring.

The seat is too small—the usable depth is only 14 in., minimal, as is the width, 15½ in. More shaping of the seat in the form of saddling or scooping would also make the chair more comfortable. The seat height, 16¾ in., is a little low and this would be evident if the chair was used at a dining table—normally 29 in. high or more.

John D. Alexander Jr.'s chair is a post-and-rung construction, with a woven seat and bent back posts and slats. The chair's posts are riven white oak, with rungs and back slats of riven hickory. The seat is hickory splint webbing. It is a marvelous chair, like Sawyer's and Dunbar's made entirely by hand in the old way. An appealing feature is its light weight. a mere 5½ lb. Easily lifted with one finger, the chair could probably support a 300-lb. person. (Alexander, like Dunbar, has devoted an entire book to his chairmaking methods. It is *Make a Chair from a Tree*, The Taunton Press, 1978.)

The chair is resilient and reasonably comfortable, although the severely bent rear posts provide more back pitch than is necessary—15½°. It is relatively stable, even though the rear legs tilt in 3° from the side view. There is an obvious limit to how far back one can lean without upsetting results.

The hickory-splint seat is made from strips of inner bark ¹⁄₁₆ in. thick and ¾ in. wide. When woven this material is strong, yet flexible enough to yield slightly when one sits.

All 12 rungs dowel into the legs in a staggered configuration. Their mortises don't interfere with one another except for an intended small tangential overlap, which mechanically locks half of the rungs in place. The bent back slats are only ⁵⁄₃₂ in. thick and lead directly into the back post mortises, where they are pinned in place. The joinery derives its strength from the green front legs and rear posts shrinking around the drier rungs.

The woven seat has a center depression to it, a result of the side rails being higher than the front and rear rails. This dished effect provides a more comfortable seat than a flat one. The seat, at only 13 in. deep, is severely short and its 17 in. width is also minimal. The front legs protrude above the seat rails, interfering with the sitter.

A fine individual effort by Alexander, this chair is an excellent example of using early craft. But like the other chairs, it is not an answer to properly seating someone of average size in today's society.

A rmand La Montagne's Brewster chair is a duplicate of one he made about 10 years ago that found its way into the permanent collection of the Henry Ford Museum in Dearborn, Mich. The earlier chair was an almost perfect replica of a chair made in the 1600s by John Alden for William Brewster, elder of the Pilgrim Church, who came to America aboard the Mayflower.

There are two known authentic Brewster chairs. One, believed to be Brewster's own, is in Pilgrim Hall in Plymouth, Mass. The second, made after Brewster's death in 1664, is in the Metropolitan Museum of Art in New York City.

La Montagne's first bogus Brewster was purchased by the Henry Ford Museum in the early 1970s for $9,000. La Montagne made this reproduction to document the first hoax. His objective was to construct a historically accurate chair, with enough consistent variations to be accepted by experts as authentic. In 1977 he achieved nationwide recognition when the Brewster chair in the Ford collection was discovered to have been made by him.

La Montagne made no money from the hoax and says he never tried to obscure what he was doing. His choice of chair was influenced by Wallace Nutting's statement in his *Furniture Treasury* that one or two more Brewster chairs might exist, other than the two already documented. In adapting the original design, La Montagne varied the number of spindles and changed the wood from white ash to white oak.

Most of La Montagne's work went into aging the completed chair. This included scratching and gouging the wood, burning the parts with an acetylene torch and removing all traces of carbon by scraping and bleaching. The chair was stained black, painted red, smoked for several days, coated with an emulsion of household dust and dilute vinyl glue, and waxed. It had aged 300 years in a matter of months.

The chair was then placed where it could be seen, and sold by a friend of La Montagne to a local antique dealer. A series of buyers bought and resold it until the chair was "discovered" by the Ford Museum. With its authenticity ac-

Brewster chair made by Armand La Montagne of North Scituate, R.I. Overall width: 24¾ in., at back: 18¾ in. Overall height: 47½ in. Seat height: 18½ in. Seat pitch: 0°. Back pitch: 0°. Seat depth 15¼ in. Seat width: 23½ in. Height of arms above the seat: 9½ in. Overall height of front legs: 30⅛ in. Diameter of legs: 2⅜ in. Width of back between arms: 15½ in. Weight: 31 lb. Not for sale.

cepted, La Montagne next set out to prove the chair actually was a fake. He began to circulate rumors about its recent heritage, which the museum at first ignored. But in the summer of 1977, the museum re-examined the chair and for the first time X-rayed it. La Montagne had said X rays would reveal that the holes in the leg posts had been drilled with a modern bit. So they had been. The museum admitted it had made a costly and embarrassing mistake.

All parts of the chair are turned, except for the flat slab seat. A series of inscribed lines on the leg turnings help locate the hole positions for the ends of the round rungs. All the cross-rails are doweled and pinned into the legs. From above, the seat is a trapezoid tapering quickly from front to back.

Two of the vertical spindles are missing from the lower front of the chair. La Montagne made them, then removed them, as a logical alteration by some imaginary owner who wanted a space for his feet to rest.

The Brewster is not comfortable to sit in. The legs are perpendicular to the floor, the back has no pitch, the seat is parallel to the floor. The seat height, 18½ in., indicates that the chair was used with a low footstool which kept one's feet off cold, drafty floors. □

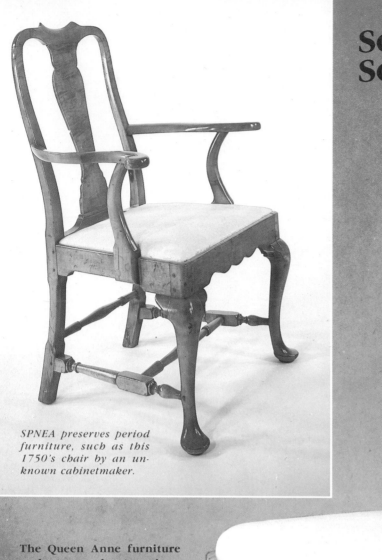

SPNEA preserves period furniture, such as this 1750's chair by an unknown cabinetmaker.

SOMETHING OLD, SOMETHING NEW

The Queen Anne furniture style swept the American Colonies in the beginning of the 18th century and evolved into its most refined form by about 1750. And, despite the changes in fashion since that time, Queen Anne has never really gone out of style—many consider it to be the perfect blend of function and beauty. The chair above was in constant use for almost 200 years before being acquired by the Society for the Preservation of New England Antiquities in Boston. The one at right was made just last year at the North Bennet Street School, whose students specialize in period reproductions. Both were on display recently in two related shows in the Boston area, the old work at the DeCordova and Dana Museum in Lincoln, the new at SPNEA's Harrison Gray Otis House.

Ron Morin built this Queen Anne reproduction at the North Bennet Street School, where students can learn the essentials of the old styles and acquire the old skills.

Photos: J. David Bohl/SPNEA

From *Fine Woodworking* magazine (September 1985) 54/128

Adventure in Chair Design

In which a student discovers some limits

by David Veleta

Straight, flat and square had been the staple diet of my first year as a student of furniture design and construction, so I was anxious to try curves when I began my second year with my first chair design. I started out wanting an upright chair suitable for reading and conversation. I had in mind an upholstered tall-back and curves and tapers that would give the chair a light and elegant look.

These initial ideas reined-in my imagination somewhat, but the constraint was helpful. It seems that the more indefinite the design parameters, the more difficult it is to focus the design process; the diversity of possibilities becomes a distraction. Within these still roomy boundaries, my design evolved in a "see-saw" manner. The "see" mostly involved looking at classic chairs, but it also meant taking a fresh, close look at the lines and shapes of anything else that caught my attention. The "saw" was sketching side and front elevations: drawing by drawing upon what I had seen.

Eventually I came up with a freehand perspective drawing (which, as it turned out, proved to be pretty close to the final form). I attribute its curved rear legs and parallel arms to an adjustable armchair adapted by Phillip Webb from a traditional design for Morris and Co. (c. 1865). The extra-tall back and the piercing crest rail were inspired by a Charles Rennie Mackintosh chair. In general, I feel that the design reflects my attraction to Japanese forms, but the association here is more vague. In fact, although you can attribute certain aspects of a design to historical precedents, original designs invariably incorporate some unpredictable and unidentifiable leap of imagination on the part of the designer.

To bring this idea for a chair down to earth, I had to make a working drawing. In addition to satisfying structural integrity, I wanted to make sure that the chair would be comfortable. Trying to figure this out on paper before anything was constructed proved to be baffling. I consulted the textbooks, but found a vast tangle of heights, depths and angles. These floating figures brought home the fact that because of the endlessly varied shapes, sizes and proportions of people, no non-adjustable chair can be really comfortable for everyone. So, using myself as a model and with tape measure in hand, I sat in a lot of chairs and discovered what I liked about how they felt and then measured them. These clues were enough to make a full-scale side-elevation working drawing, though the only way to confirm or reject my guesses was to build a mock-up.

Working from my drawings, I quickly bandsawed the parts in poplar, then half-lapped and screwed them together. Quarter-inch Masonite screwed to the seat and back and topped by an

Veleta's first chair taught him that designing doesn't end on the drawing board. The finished chair is walnut with velvet upholstered over foam and webbing on maple frames.

inch of foam completed the mock-up. I sat down. Naturally, something was not right. I cut some scrap strips of plywood into a slightly different back curve, screwed these pieces directly to the existing frame, and reattached the Masonite. This felt better. Next, I adjusted the tilt of the back by blocking up the front legs. Finally, I was satisfied.

Unfortunately, the motley looking mock-up I now had was not true to my working drawings. The abundance of curves in my three-dimensional design provided no ready reference point, so the dilemma was how to transfer the changes I had made on the mock-up to a final side-elevation working drawing. The solution, provided by a teacher, was to drop a plumb line from various points on the chair (upright and laid on its back) to a grid drawn on the floor. When connected, the points on the grid defined the curves and their relationships. Measurements up from the floor helped too, filling in any missing details.

After completing the working drawing, I began construction by form-laminating the rear legs. If excessive springback occured it would be possible to alter the other parts to fit. I tapered the laminates for strength and appearance using Jere Osgood's method (each laminate is individually tapered before gluing up). Twin mortise and tenons (side by side) connect front and rear legs; I found the full-scale drawing indispensable for laying out the shoulder lines accurately. By laying the rear leg on the drawing I could tick-off two points of the shoulder and then scribe around at the appropriate angle. I cut the shoulders shy of the line, then trimmed them to fit with a Record 073 shoulder plane.

The inside taper of the front legs begins just below the front rail so joining the rail and legs was straightforward. Joining the rear stretcher to the rear legs, however, was an entirely different matter. First, I made a simple jig for mortising the rear legs. I laid a leg on a scrap of 8/4 poplar, aligning the long layout lines of the mortises parallel with the jointed edge of the poplar. I then traced the inside curve of the leg on the poplar. Bandsawn to the line and clamped to the leg, as shown in the drawing, the jointed edge of the poplar provided a true guide for the fence on a plunge router.

So far so good. Looking at my drawing, I assumed that the shoulder angles of the rear stretcher were the same as those for the rear legs, so I proceeded to cut them with confidence. When I dry-assembled the lower frame, however, everything fit closely except the rear-stretcher shoulders. After a little head scratching, I realized that because the stretcher is canted to be flush with the curve of the leg, its shoulder angles are different than the drawing led me to believe. The only solution was to take the correct angles directly off the clamped-up frame and make a new piece. Orthographic drawings are immensely helpful, but they can sometimes obscure what is really happening in three dimensions. No matter how long and hard you look for trouble spots in a complex drawing, making the piece is the only way to work everything out. Only then can you truly finish the rest of the plans.

Now that the base frame was together I could start building up. This work was straightforward enough, until I came to the arms. These were a three-strip, straight lamination, and I used the male inner half of the rear-leg laminating form to repeat the curve. A single finger joint attaches the arm to the front leg; the full thickness of the arm is mortised into the side of the back stile and screwed from inside. Laying out these joints was a Catch-22 situation. In order to know where the final lines would be, the joints had to be home, but the joints would have to be cut already in order get them home. Caution, trial and error, and one veneer

shim yielded success. It had been so easy to draw!

Now I made the upholstery frame. I chose maple for strength and joined the pieces with bridle joints. Using the existing seat and back curves as templates I bandsawed the frame pieces so that they would sit ½ in. back from the front edge of the chair frame, as shown in the drawings. I also left a gap of ⅛ in. between the chair frame and the upholstery frames to allow for webbing and fabric. (It is better to be a little generous here since it is less trouble to pack the upholstery than to remove more wood from the frames). With the frames glued up, I beveled their faces toward the middle with a spokeshave so that someone sitting in the chair would not "bottom-out" and feel the frame through the upholstery. The seat frames are screwed in place, as shown on the drawing. Finally, since no structural cross-member supports the back of the seat frame, I mortised and screwed metal L-brackets into the rear legs beneath the frame.

Many of the techniques, procedures and pitfalls that I encountered building this chair were new to me, but they were all still woodworking, so at least somewhat familiar. However, when it came to upholstery I felt completely naive. Exploring fabric samples was overwhelming. The choice of color, texture, material and pattern was vast. I finally chose conservatively, picking a traditional burgundy velvet. Before upholstering, it was necessary to finish the chair completely to eliminate the risk of getting finishing materials on the fabric. I chose a rubbed oil-varnish mix. It was a lot of work, but the results were worth the effort.

Now it was finally time to go to the upholsterer. Not being fond of over-stuffed furniture, I had designed the chair for a minimum of padding, just enough to be comfortable. I explained this to the upholsterer and he agreed to do as I bid. But I was shocked by the completed job, which was overly stuffed compared with my expectation. My disappointment wounded the upholsterer's professional pride. He explained that he had tried less stuffing but the fabric did not "lay right"; it looked "flat," so he adjusted things as he saw fit. In retrospect, I believe he was probably correct, and I am pleased with the firm feel of the upholstery. Viewed from the side, however, the thin back uprights look imbalanced next to the generous stuffing. Fortunately, this imbalance is not noticeable from any other view. The main point is this, before going to an upholsterer be sure that you know what you want and can explain it clearly, and be sure that you are consulted if the upholsterer decides that what you want won't work.

Now that I have some distance from this project, I feel capable of criticizing it. As far as comfort and fidelity to my design are concerned, I feel the chair is a success. However, the design process itself had some drawbacks. Working with side-elevation drawings is useful, but you can end up with a "cookie-cutter" design: two side-elevation outlines held together with rails. Using parts that are rectilinear in section reinforces this feeling, and side elevations alone don't suggest how various members might be otherwise shaped.

The other thing that I learned is the importance of simplifying construction. The amount of time it takes to hand-fit joints through trial and error adds up quickly. This can also be seen as a fault in the design. On the other hand, most pieces of fine furniture require some careful hand work, and I am happy for that. I hope my next chair can be made a little more efficiently, now that I have plowed through the first one. □

David Veleta, a graduate of Leeds Design Workshop, makes furniture in Northampton, Mass.

From *Fine Woodworking* magazine (September 1985) 54:79-81

Armchair

Plan view

Detail: Leg-mortising jig

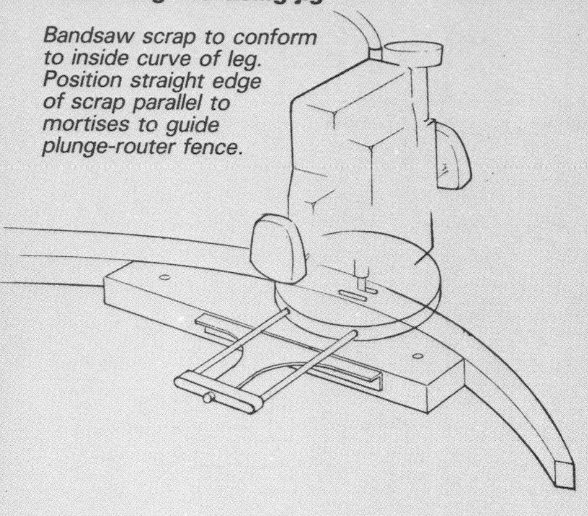

Bandsaw scrap to conform to inside curve of leg. Position straight edge of scrap parallel to mortises to guide plunge-router fence.

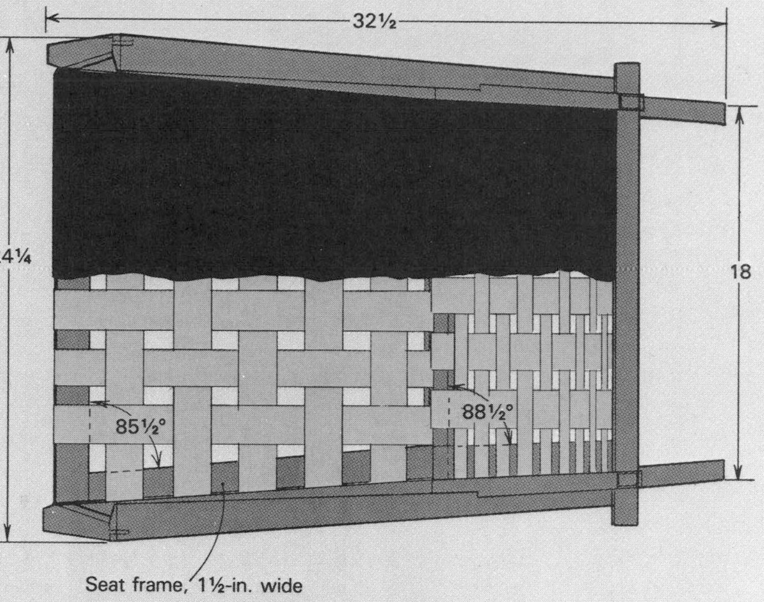

32½

24¼

18

85½°

88½°

Seat frame, 1½-in. wide

Front elevation

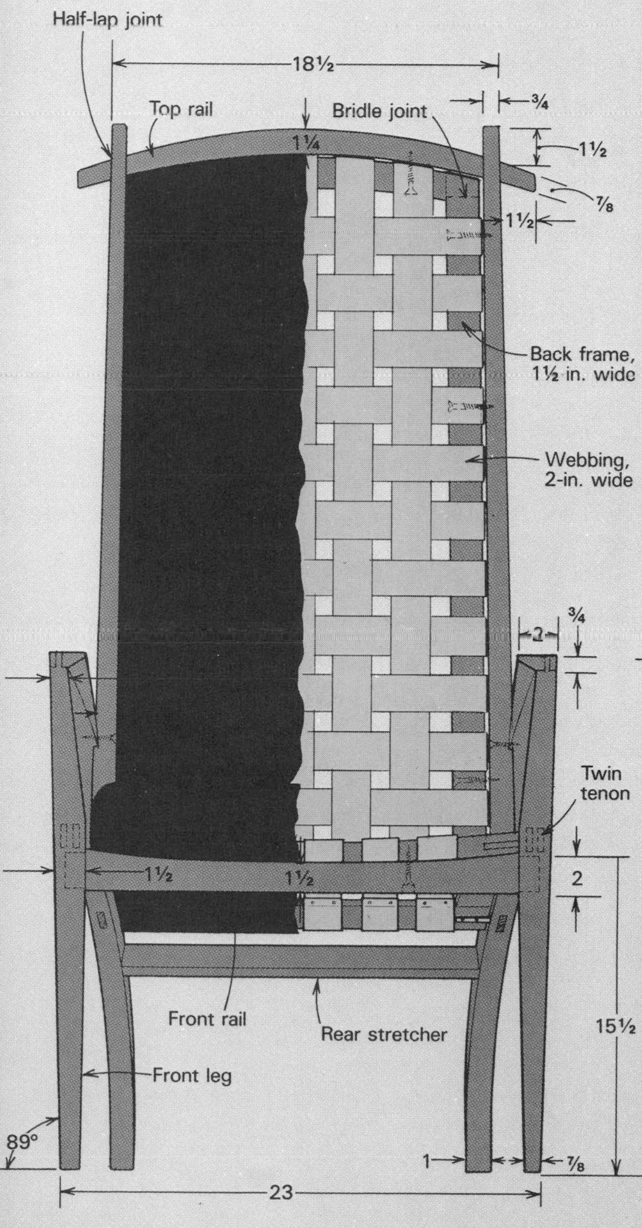

Half-lap joint

18½

Top rail

¾

Bridle joint

1¼

1½

⅞

1½

Back frame, 1½ in. wide

Webbing, 2-in. wide

¾

2

Twin tenon

1½

1½

2

25

Front rail

Rear stretcher

Front leg

89°

15½

1

⅞

⅞

23

Screw upholstered back and seat frames to chair frame. Handsew fabric to back frame after frame is installed.

Side elevation

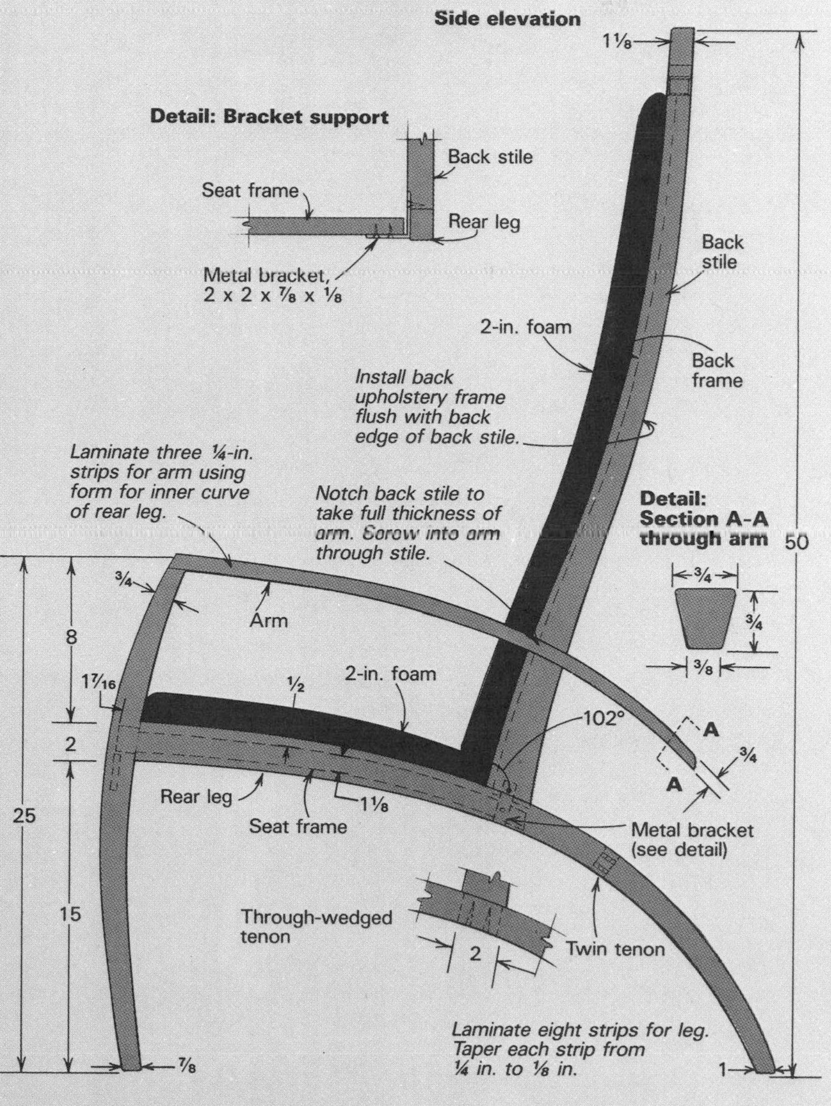

1⅛

Detail: Bracket support

Seat frame

Back stile

Rear leg

Metal bracket, 2 x 2 x ⅞ x ⅛

Install back upholstery frame flush with back edge of back stile.

Back stile

2-in. foam

Back frame

Laminate three ¼-in. strips for arm using form for inner curve of rear leg.

Notch back stile to take full thickness of arm. Screw into arm through stile.

Detail: Section A-A through arm

50

¾

¾

⅜

A

¾

A

¾

Arm

8

1⁷⁄₁₆

½

2-in. foam

102°

Metal bracket (see detail)

2

Rear leg

Seat frame

1⅛

15

Through-wedged tenon

2

Twin tenon

1

Laminate eight strips for leg. Taper each strip from ¼ in. to ⅛ in.

1

Chair Woods
Lessons from the past on choosing the right woods

by Robert C. Whitley

I stared at one hundred fifty chairs, every one of them so loose as to be dangerous to sit in. "I have tried everything to no avail," the owner said. "Do you know the glue they advertise on TV where one drop between two blocks of wood holds a car suspended in the air?" he asked me in exasperation. "Well, I must have used half a pint on each chair, and they still came apart." I nodded. "I'll admit you cabinetmakers have some secrets. Will you fix the chairs for me?" I said no, explaining that the chairs were made out of the wrong kind of wood and that they would never hold together for any length of time. He stalked off, obviously convinced I was out of my mind.

The preceding is a true account of a conversation between myself and the owner of a large, beautiful restaurant located on the banks of the Delaware River. The chairs in question are normally referred to as "captain's chairs." The original chair from which these were copied has proved to be a sturdy and practical design, made since the early 1800's. Why then were the chairs I was asked to repair not only falling apart, but incapable of restoration? Because the complete chair—legs,

seat, spindles and back—was all of soft white pine!

It seems impossible that a large manufacturer would devote great sums of money and many man hours of work producing chairs with such an obvious fault. And yet, hardly a week goes by that I don't come in contact with chairs made with the wrong choice of wood.

A chair, especially the plank-seated chair, takes greater stresses, strains and shocks than any other piece of furniture used in the home because of its everyday use in kitchens, dining rooms and general living areas.

Imagine the stress placed on the legs and back of a chair that a 200-pound person sits in three times a day while eating. First, the chair is dragged across the floor, then the body lowers into the seat, shoving forward a few inches with the full 200 pounds of weight on the base. Finally, the squirm and the wiggle to settle in! During serving and passing food to others, the weight is constantly shifting back and forth on the different legs of the chair. Now comes the balancing act! 200 pounds are thrown entirely onto the two back legs. Next is the coming down with accumulated speed to an abrupt

The author making a reproduction (right) of the chair Thomas Jefferson sat in when writing the Declaration of Independence. All woods are the same as the original: maple legs and arm posts, poplar seat and mid-arm back, hickory spindles, white oak arms and crest rail.

From *Fine Woodworking* magazine (Spring 1976) 2:50-51

stop, then the shoving of the chair to the rear with all the weight intact, and the final dragging to a place of rest.

Isn't it a wonder that these chairs have held up as long as they have? Here are the reasons why.

The Legs. Early chairmakers invariably used hard maple. It was easy to come by, but more importantly it is very hard, will resist impression, and does not splinter. Its fine, dense grain makes it easy to turn on the lathe. It also has tremendous resistance to abrasion, a quality especially needed where the legs of a chair meet the floor.

Stretchers. Base stretchers, too, were generally made of maple, only occasionally with white oak or hickory. In those cases I believe the chairmaker took into consideration a possible bending stress on the middle of a stretcher caused by the weight of feet that might be placed there. Whether the amount of stress was enough to put up with the more difficult turning qualities of the woods is debatable. In any event, although the stretchers are not to be considered as important as the legs in terms of abrasion, they too must be of a very hard wood.

The Seat. Here the craftsman's choice was influenced a great deal by the way the seat had to be contoured and shaped. Structurally he could have used a hardwood, but he knew that scooping out a comfortable seat would require at least a two-inch-thick plank to allow for ample depth to receive the legs, back and arm posts. The scooping-out process was done with an adze, a large chisel and shaped scrapers. It was laborious and time-consuming, so in the interest of ease and economy he chose softwoods to make the seat. The craftsman knew that the greater thickness of softwood would allow the legs and spindles to be deeply seated and, at the same time, weigh less, so he chose either pine or poplar, and only quite rarely a hardwood.

The Back. There were many types of chair backs, but for this discussion let me make two categories: the low back and the tall back. The low-back chair is called a "captain's chair," the type I referred to in the incident with the restaurant owner. This chair is very comfortable because of the large rolled and contoured shape which forms the back and the substantial arms. I have seen no exception to the use of either pine or poplar for this purpose. However, the short-turned spindles were always of either hard maple, oak or ash. The great dimension of the softwood back and arms allowed the hardwood spindles deep penetration.

The earliest type of low back was a Windsor chair which used pine or poplar for the back rail only, and here again it was thick enough to allow deep penetration of the spindles. The arms, which were thinner and therefore did not allow the spindles to be deeply seated, were either of white oak or maple.

The tall-back plank-seated chairs which have spindles that run from the seat to the top or crest are almost always of split-out hickory (wood split rather than ripped to rough size to ensure straight grain). A wood is needed that allows for movement—a wood that will give and spring back. Because of the small diameter of the spindles, the wood must have resiliency and an ability to resist fracture. Hickory is the only wood I know of which combines all these qualities.

When there is a thin, bent piece of wood incorporated into the back structure, it is almost always of split-out white oak, a wood which can be steamed and bent to rather small radii without fracturing. It also has great resiliency and hardness.

Bent mid-arm rails, cresting rails and backs are invariably made of split-out steam-bent white oak.

The decision regarding what woods to use for a specific chair part was to some degree made easier for the earlier craftsman because most of his chairs were painted. Or perhaps they were painted because the craftsman used various woods. In any event, craftsmen today may want to use other woods than those used by the earlier craftsmen for esthetic considerations. There's no reason why not as long as one follows these guidelines:

• Use hardwood where there will be shocks and abrasion.
• Use softwood only in great thicknesses.
• Never join softwood to softwood.

In other words, do not use a wood for a purpose for which it is unsuited. Following is a list of some available woods and the purposes to which they are suited, in my opinion. Others may disagree on specific points. For instance, hickory could be used to make a chair seat and structurally it would stand up. However, its density and hardness make it extremely difficult to sculpt to shape, and its weight would be a disadvantage.

Walnut, Cherry: Good for all parts but has limited steam bendability.

Birch: Good for most parts, but the wood is very hard to sculpt.

Beech: Same as for birch, but fractures too easily when making thin spindles.

Sycamore: Great grain for seats, but has a tendency to warp. All right for legs and stretchers, but do not use for spindles.

Red Oak: Has a very coarse, unattractive grain, but may be used for most parts.

White Oak: Perfect to use for parts that are to be steam-bent; also good for spindles and other parts. Too hard and heavy for seat.

Maple: Perfect for legs, stretchers and posts, but too hard and heavy for seats. Can be used if desired.

Poplar, Pine: For seats in thicknesses of two inches or better, and for heavy back and arm sections. Do not use for any other parts!

Ash, Hickory: All parts except seats.

Mahogany: Great for most cabinet furniture, but really not suited for plank-seated chairs except as pine and poplar are used.

Spruce, Fir: No use. □

Robert C. Whitley has been restoring and reproducing antique furniture for more than three decades. He's become good enough to be named master conservator at Independence Hall in Philadelphia, and to be commissioned to reproduce the Oval Office desk for the Kennedy Foundation. His specialty has been filling out sets of fine chairs—the client inherits one superb antique and wants five more. It would take an expert to sort the originals from the copies, were Whitley not scrupulous about signing and dating his work.

What's rare about Whitley is his ability to design and make decidedly contemporary furniture along with the antique, and to be happy with both. In contrast to the delicacy of Queen Anne and Chippendale, many of his own, modern designs have a massive feeling; pinned mortise-and-tenon joints and long, tapered dowels attach legs that are solid columns, or carved in a continuous line with hairpin turns, to hefty seats.

To make ten of Sawyer's chairs, left, one for each of us in the workshop, we started with a 6-ft. length of an 18-in. dia. white oak log. After quartering this with wedges to see the lay of the grain, we bucksawed lengths for chair parts. At top, two students saw a bolt for rungs. Steadying the log are Country Workshop sponsor Drew Langsner and his daughter Naomi. Above, teacher Dave Sawyer demonstrates drawknifing a rung on a dumbhead shaving horse.

Green Woodworking
How I split and shaved a chair at Country Workshops

by Rick Mastelli

Last summer, amid the Blue Ridge Mountains of North Carolina, I attended a week-long chairmaking workshop that changed my ideas about working wood. Ten of us had come because we were interested in learning to make chairs in an old way. We put aside our electric tools and surfacing machines, and we kicked the habit of using mill-sawn, kiln-dried wood. We retreated from the cabinetmaker's craft, with its jointing and smoothing planes and sandpaper. Instead, we adopted the tools of the country joiner, who rives the wood and shaves it into sticks and panels.

The joiner's craft has been practiced for centuries in peasant communities, where everyone, for at least part of the year, produces food, shelter, clothing, utensils and furniture. Originally a homely craft, it evolved into a specialized profession, which in parts of this country is being revived as part of the modern-day homesteader's diversified livelihood. The country joiner does not employ a sawmill, but goes directly to the local tree and, treating wood like the bundle of fibers that it is, pries it apart with wedges, gluts and froes. He shapes this riven wood with drawknives and spokeshaves, retaining the

From *Fine Woodworking* magazine (March 1982) 33:50-56

continuity of the fibers that a rip saw would sever. Riven wood is stronger than sawn wood, easy to work while green, and more resistant to the deterioration of age and weather. Its grain and figure can be felt, not just seen as in planed and sanded wood. Its texture is rich and varied. And when you rive and shave wood, there is no dusty air to breathe. Green woodworking relies upon simple tools, cheap materials and direct processes. The result can be as useful, beautiful and inspiring to make as the chair pictured here.

Our classroom was an old tobacco barn on Drew and Louise Langsner's 100-acre homestead in Marshall, N.C. To get there, you drive along increasingly rural roads, till the last half-mile or so of the Langsners' driveway, which is best walked. "When you come to Country Workshops," remarked Langsner as his truck bounced us up to within reach of the farm, "you come to the country." Each summer, the Langsners sponsor as many as five week-long workshops in country crafts, alternating their workshop responsibilities with their farm chores. We helped a little with those chores, ate three bountiful meals a day of farm produce, and slept in our own tents. We worked long days and into the night, not exploring our individual bents, but practicing craft in the age-old sense. We did not design, for instance, but copied a traditional design. And though we initialed the parts we made, we didn't take the identification too seriously—on the first day we shaved more than a hundred rungs and threw them into a communal pile. In this way we concentrated on acquiring skills and minimized prideful fussing, making extra parts when we were finished with our own, and sharing them readily.

The workshop reflected the character of its teacher, Dave Sawyer, a 45-year-old New Englander who now lives in East Calais, Vt. Sawyer has an M.I.T. degree in mechanical engineering, but he retired from that career at age 28. "If I'd lived a hundred years ago," he said one evening in the barn, while tenoning rungs at the pole lathe to help some of us catch up, "I'd have done fine in mechanical engineering, because then people built what they thought up." The rhythmic slap of the lathe punctuated his words. "But thinking's pretty far from doing nowadays in that field." So Sawyer tried restoring old cars, he spent a half year in Bolivia in the Peace Corps Craft Program, and he worked for a while with the Amish. His turning point was the summer he spent working in the shop of Daniel O'Hagan, another sometime teacher at Country Workshops. O'Hagan's example encouraged Sawyer to do direct, simple woodwork. In 1969 he put together his own shop, and he has been making furniture and utensils from green wood ever since.

The ladderback chair we made is little changed from the first one Sawyer made ten years ago. He took the measurements from the first comfortable ladderback he'd found, a factory-made chair from the 1920s that he saw in an antique shop. After some minor changes in the way he made the first six, Sawyer had his product and his procedures down. I asked him, while he was showing us how to shape the back slats, if he was ever tempted to vary the design, to make a fancy chair with carved slats, for instance. "No," he said, "I don't believe in art. I never carved anything in my life, and I don't believe I ever will." Why, I asked? "Because I have no imagination," he said. "I never got into that individual expression bit, and I never made anything original. I work on the Volkswagen theory. You stay with something that works, and you make little improvements as you see them. I tried making an arty

Sawyer produces as many as 50 ladderback chairs a year without using jigs. "In my power-tool phase," he said, "I made some very fancy jigs. But it turned out to be mindless.... And I'd be looking for them and fiddling with them, and they'd end up in the fire." So now Sawyer just clamps the posts to the bench, shims to "close enough" and guides his brace and bit with a T-bevel and his eye.

Top, Sawyer marks a bolt end for splitting with a froe. Finished rungs are ⅞ in. in diameter; he lays out squares only ⅛ in. oversize. He controls the work by splitting relatively equal portions (figure 2, page 28) and splitting slowly. If the split begins to run out, he exerts pressure against the heavier side (figure 3, page 28). Above, a student splits rung blanks in a small brake—two boards mounted like scissor blades to hold the work. During the first day we shaved over a hundred rungs, trying various styles of shaving horses and drawknives. The two horses, top right, are roughed out from thick slabs; the stone holds them steady. Right, Sawyer loads the rungs into an oil-drum kiln.

chair once. I prefer being productive." I remembered that Drew Langsner had warned me on the way to the farm: "You're going to meet a lot of reactionaries here, people who figure rough woodworking is just fine."

Sawyer's ladderback *is* fine. It is just as strong-lined and as comfortably proportioned as you'd expect a chair to be that has been unchanged through ten years and hundreds of copies. Its high back is well balanced by the thickening of the back posts below the seat. Sawyer steambends at the thickest part of the legs to increase the chair's stability and to angle the back comfortably. Other ladderback chairs—such as John D. Alexander, Jr.'s, version—bend above the seat at the thinnest part of the back posts. Sawyer's chair is stouter than Alexander's elegant rendition. Sawyer's is a professional chairmaker's pre-industrial product, and he makes 20 to 30 of them a year, sometimes as many as 50. It takes him 12 hours from

tree to finished chair, and he gets $115 for each. When he needs more money, he makes wooden hayforks for $17 apiece (all 1982 prices). He once made 200 hayforks in two months.

So we learned how to make chairs in batches. For a week we became a green-wood chair shop. Our industry was interspersed with demonstrations and learned, talky meets; the ten of us went home knowing not only how to bust a chair from a tree, but also how to do it efficiently within a daily work rhythm. We began by making rungs because they are easiest to make, and because they want to be drier than the posts into which they are mortised. After assembly, the tenon absorbs moisture from the post and swells while the mortise shrinks, locking the joint firmly. It took us a day to split and shave the rungs, but by the end of that day, the best among us could shave a rung almost as fast as Sawyer, in under 3 minutes. While the rungs dried in a jury-rigged kiln—a

The chair parts are bent without steel straps. First we boiled the 1½-in. to 1-in. diameter posts in water for a couple of hours (the boiler rests between cement blocks in the background of the photo top left). Then we coaxed the bend into shape on the shaving horse. A pad under the horse's head prevents the stock from being marred. The posts are muscled in pairs onto drying forms, above, and held in place with leather thongs while they set overnight. The slats, left, were also boiled, but only for a half hour or so, then bent on the horse and over the knee until they fit on their own drying form. Plans for the forms are given at right.

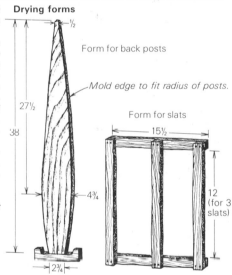

Drying forms

½

Form for back posts

Mold edge to fit radius of posts.

Form for slats

27½

38

15½

4¾

12 (for 3 slats)

2¾

70-gal. oil drum perched over a smoldering campfire—we split and shaved the posts. By the third day we were dumping the back posts into a smaller drum full of boiling water to prepare them for bending. We flexed the hot posts on a shaving horse, then strapped them to simple forms and laid them in the kiln to set their curve while we split and shaved slats, which went through the same process. All the parts made, we bored the mortises for the front and back rungs and chopped the mortises for the slats. The evening of the fourth day we turned tenons on the ends of the rungs.

We assembled our batch of chairs on the workshop's last day, banging them together with a lead-filled rawhide mallet wielded over a hefty stump. It was heady stuff. First we pounded the front rungs into the front posts, then the back rungs and slats into the back posts. In these sub-assemblies, we bored the mortises for the side rungs, nicking the front

and back rungs so the side rungs would interlock with them, like Lincoln logs. Tension was high as each of us brought our sticks to the assembly stump, sticks that represented a week's shaping and scraping. Driving oversize tenons into slender posts means real fear in that moment when the mallet is poised between blows. Yet chair after chair popped into being. I asked Sawyer why he preferred this daring finale to a project so painstakingly prepared—why not use clamps? It was easier and faster this way, he said, but also the experience should be intense. "If you can get a chair together without splitting, it's not going to split afterwards," he said. "Assembly is the worst time. It's like being born. If you can survive that, chances are you'll last another fifty years."

* * *

For most of us, the workshop was over that fifth night. Whether or not we stayed on for Sawyer's optional seat-

Assembly is tense. Under that lead-filled mallet a week's work might end up a pile of broken sticks. Everyone went home with a chair.

weaving demonstration the next morning, each of us went home with a chair, and that alone was worth the workshop's tuition. But the real value was in what we'd learned, and the chair was there to remind us of that. I left with an appreciation for green woodworking that continues to grow. It was not the first time I'd sat on a shaving horse, but it was the first I'd done enough work on one to get sore. You learn a lot this way, subtle understandings along with plain, common sense. Surrounded by others to watch and new tools to try, the revelations come, and the horse gets comfortable. Here is some of what I learned.

Measuring—There's nothing novel about cutting a number of parts to size and checking one against another. It's faster, easier and more accurate than measuring each individually. But many of us feel we need drawings covered with dimensions to be able to build anything. We didn't need a drawing to build Sawyer's chair, and there weren't many numbers to worry about either. All we needed to know was recorded on the two sides of a flat stick. It didn't get wrinkled and messy in the shop, and it was always handy to place on the wood to

lay out tapers, bores, mortises or whatever. Figure 1, on the facing page, represents Sawyer's chair stick, and it's all the blueprint you need to make his chair.

Getting the most out of the wood—We split enough wood for ten chairs from a single white oak veneer-quality log 18 in. in diameter and 6 ft. long. We could get a back post and a front post, four short rungs, three long rungs or various other combinations out of the length. With wedges we split the log into quarters, then we read the grain to make best use of the wood. We crosscut the quarters into bolts, pieces the length of the various parts. Then a froe, that long-bladed, long-handled, clumsy-looking tool, dimensioned the blanks

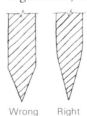

Wrong   Right

faster, neater and more efficiently than a saw could. We were splitting blanks for rungs ⅛ in. oversize, blanks for posts ¼ in. oversize, and rarely having to reject a piece. The secrets of the froe are as follows: First, it doesn't need a sharp edge, but the bevel must be properly shaped. The bevel on a new froe is usually

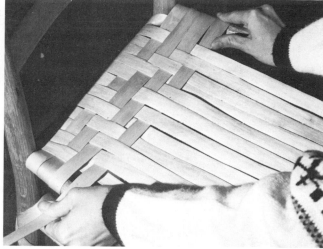

Scribing a back leg for final trimming.

To weave the seat, first wrap the warp in one continuous strip from front to back, splicing your material underneath. Bark and splints shrink as they dry, so leave the warp overnight, then push it tightly together to fit another round or two of warp. The weft can create any number of patterns, here a diamond-shaped herringbone. The triangular spaces at the sides of the seat will be filled with short lengths woven into the weft.

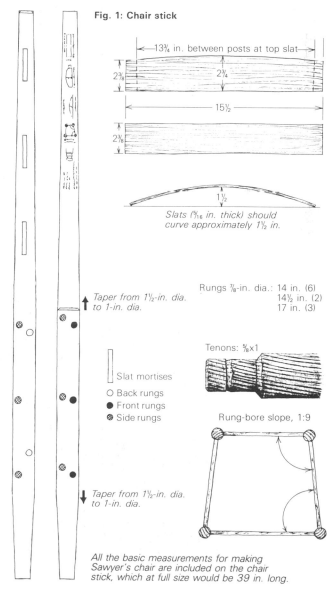

Fig. 1: Chair stick

13¾ in. between posts at top slat

2⅜   2¾

15½

2⅜

1½

Slats (⁵⁄₁₆ in. thick) should
curve approximately 1½ in.

↑ Taper from 1½-in. dia.
to 1-in. dia.

Rungs ⅞-in. dia.: 14 in. (6)
14½ in. (2)
17 in. (3)

Tenons: ⅝x1

▯ Slat mortises
○ Back rungs
● Front rungs
◉ Side rungs

Rung-bore slope, 1:9

↓ Taper from 1½-in. dia.
to 1-in. dia.

All the basic measurements for making
Sawyer's chair are included on the chair
stick, which at full size would be 39 in. long.

too blunt and too angular. It should be no more than 30°, and it should blend smoothly into the sides of the tool to form a single, convex surface. A facet, as in a chisel or plane-iron bevel, tends to stick in the wood and does not rock smoothly during levering.

Second, the froe must be properly placed on the bolt. When you have to make a number of splits in one bolt, don't start at one end and work across, but start in the middle and then again in the middle of each of the halves, and so on (figure 2, next page). With equal portions on either side of the split it's easier to control its direction. The handle of a good froe is about 16 in. long, the blade about 10 in. Make sure the whole edge is in full contact with the wood before you strike— you're liable to shift the froe if it is slightly angled off the surface. Once you start a split (give it a good rap) you have to follow through, so make sure you begin in the right place.

Now, put down your mallet. One or two blows are all that's needed—the rest is levering not severing. You need a rigid, fork-like arrangement of boards or logs, called a brake, to hold the bolt while you bear on it. If the wood begins to split unevenly, place the heavy side of the split down, and use your

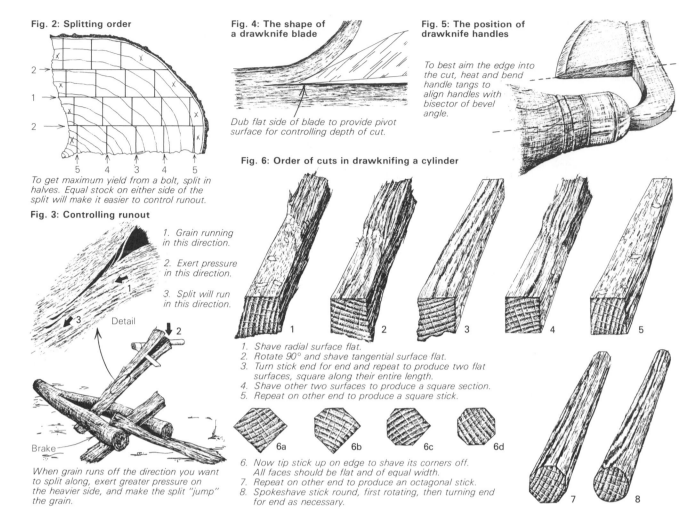

Fig. 2: Splitting order

To get maximum yield from a bolt, split in halves. Equal stock on either side of the split will make it easier to control runout.

Fig. 3: Controlling runout

1. Grain running in this direction.
2. Exert pressure in this direction.
3. Split will run in this direction.

Detail

Brake

When grain runs off the direction you want to split along, exert greater pressure on the heavier side, and make the split "jump" the grain.

Fig. 4: The shape of a drawknife blade

Dub flat side of blade to provide pivot surface for controlling depth of cut.

Fig. 5: The position of drawknife handles

To best aim the edge into the cut, heat and bend handle tangs to align handles with bisector of bevel angle.

Fig. 6: Order of cuts in drawknifing a cylinder

1. Shave radial surface flat.
2. Rotate 90° and shave tangential surface flat.
3. Turn stick end for end and repeat to produce two flat surfaces, square along their entire length.
4. Shave other two surfaces to produce a square section.
5. Repeat on other end to produce a square stick.

6a   6b   6c   6d

6. Now tip stick up on edge to shave its corners off. All faces should be flat and of equal width.
7. Repeat on other end to produce an octagonal stick.
8. Spokeshave stick round, first rotating, then turning end for end as necessary.

hand to bend the heavy side away from the split. Go slowly. You need time to see which way the split is going and to direct it. If you have split firewood only, where you strike a single blow with a maul and pick up the odd pieces, you will be surprised at the control you have with a froe. Sure, wood splits along the grain. But by bending the wood away from the split, you can cause the plane of failure to jump the grain (see figure 3, above).

Shaving wood—If I never work another piece of green wood, I will still use my new drawknife and the shaving horse I recently built. These tools are surprisingly handy for all kinds of work. The shaving horse quickly clamps stock of various shapes and sizes so you can shave it, plane it, scrape it, or (heaven forbid) sand it. It doesn't take long to coordinate hand and foot: clamp down, take a stroke, release pressure, move the stock, and clamp down again. You can't do this sort of thing as fast with a bench vise. Your whole body works on the shaving horse, not just your hands and arms. The harder you pull with your knife, the more you push with your leg, and the tighter your stock is clamped. And all the while you're on your butt, building a chair while you sit.

I tried a number of different shaving horses and I like the dumbhead horse best (photos, pages 22, lower right, and 25, top). I tried different drawknives, too, and it seems most can be made to work well, if properly sharpened. The angle of the bevel should be relatively small, between 28° and 32°. I

dub the edge on the flat side, the sort of thing that you'd never do to a plane iron. A plane iron is positioned in relation to the surface of the work by the sole of the plane. Only the edge of the blade touches the work and dubbing the back dulls that edge. The drawknife, having no sole, is guided by the back of the blade sliding on the wood (figure 4). You can regulate depth of cut—from ½-in. thick slabs to paper-thin shavings—simply by tilting the handles. To best aim the edge and control the cut, the handles should be parallel to a line that bisects the bevel angle (figure 5). You will have to heat the upper portion of the tangs and rebend the handles of most drawknives to establish this relationship. Some drawknives work better bevel-side down, as this surface provides something to rock the blade on. I find that dubbing the flat face produces a fine pivot surface for sensitive work.

Sawyer showed us how to hold the knife diagonally to the stroke, and to slide it sideways, slicing as we pulled it. He liked long, consistently thick shavings from long, even pulls. As we worked, he would wince at the crackling sound of badly cut wood. Good shavings whisper off the knife. □

Rick Mastelli is video producer/director for The Taunton Press. For details on classes, write Country Workshops, 90 Mill Creek Road, Marshall, NC 28753. John D. Alexander, Jr., explains how to make his post-and-rung tree in Make a Chair from a Tree: An Introduction to Working Green Wood (The Taunton Press, paperback, 128 pp.).

Repairing Wobbly and Broken Chairs
Two shops relate their methods

In a Q&A section (see page 57), David J. Wood inquired as to methods of disassembling a maple rocking chair that had been repaired with epoxy. George Frank pointed out quite correctly that a "sharp" blow is not really possible with a rubber mallet, and suggested instead the use of a steel hammer. We feel this will result in unacceptable damage to the surface. We have found that the following procedure works well for the five or so chairs a week that we rebuild in our shop.

If the joints are tight, drill the smallest possible hole directly into the bottom of the mortise and inject white vinegar. This will dissolve most glues and loosen others. While vinegar has no effect on epoxy, experience shows that joints repaired with epoxy are rarely cleaned out properly during the repair. The epoxy then is holding the old glue together rather than the wood. Dissolving the old glue effectively loosens the joint.

Knock the chair apart with a Computhane dead-blow hammer. These leave almost no mars and with even less rebound than a steel hammer deliver the better part of the force to the work. Stubborn joints sometimes require fixing one piece, say the rung, in a vise while the leg is knocked off with alternating blows to each side of the joint. This concentrates the energy on breaking the joint rather than moving the piece around the workbench.

If this doesn't do it, leave the joint intact and fix the rest of the chair. We glue with cascamite after a careful cleaning of the joints. Its strength, long open and closed working time, good gap-filling qualities and low pressure requirements for a good set make it unbeatable for most chair repairs. Cascamite glue injected by syringe through a small hole drilled into the joint will strengthen the loose tenon that cannot be removed.

We do not use fox, or blind, wedges to spread tenons because we've seen them split seats and legs rather than be driven down into the tenon during regluing. A more consistent problem is that it is all but impossible to remove a fox-wedged (or, for that matter, a pinned) tenon if it gets loose again, and experience shows that tenons get loose in time whether wedged or not. Seasonal changes in humidity cause the tenon to expand, its confined fibers to be crushed, and the tenon to shrink smaller than it was before expansion. We often see amateur repairs with nails, screws or epoxy—all ineffective and problematic in themselves. The old-timers were right to assume they'd have to disassemble their chairs periodically and reglue them.

—*Jane Clarke and George Danziger*

When I am called upon to repair a chair leg, stretcher or arm support that has broken in the middle or toward one end, I use a scarf joint that leaves most of the original intact. However, many times a break will shear exactly at the joint line and perpendicular to the grain direction, especially on a chair stretcher (figure 1). In these cases I use a repair method that is easier than the scarf joint and nearly as

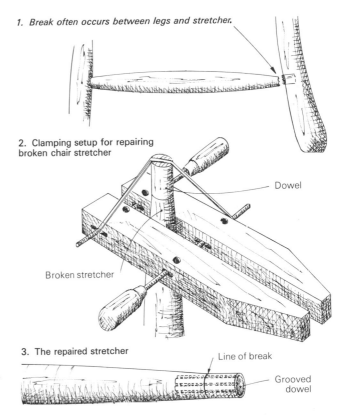

1. Break often occurs between legs and stretcher.

2. Clamping setup for repairing broken chair stretcher

Dowel

Broken stretcher

3. The repaired stretcher

Line of break

Grooved dowel

strong. Also, if you are dealing with a chair in original paint or finish, little or no finish touchup is required.

First, file or saw the broken end perfectly square. Find a dowel the same diameter as the broken joint and cut off a piece the same length as the broken end, usually ¾ in. to 1 in. Butt-glue one end of this dowel to the broken member as follows: Take a small handscrew clamp and tighten the section between the threaded rods onto the broken member about an inch down from the top. Glue the end of the dowel to the end of the broken member, securing it by stretching a heavy rubber band between the threaded-rod ends of the clamp and up and over the end of the dowel (figure 2).

When the piece has dried, carefully drill through the dowel and into the old part of the broken piece with a drill ⅛ in. to ³⁄₁₆ in. smaller than the dowel diameter. Glue a new section of smaller dowel into this hole (figure 3). Cut grooves into the sides of this dowel to allow air and excess glue to escape because the broken member's diameter is quite small and easy to split. The second dowel gives the joint all of its strength. Though it is ⅛ in. to ³⁄₁₆ in. less in diameter than the original joint, in my experience it proves to be a sound repair.

—*Robert C. Kinghorn*

Clarke and Danziger's shop, The House Doctor, is in Leverett, Mass.; Robert Kinghorn repairs furniture in Excelsior, Minn.

The Dowel Joint

Why round tenons fall out of round holes, and the elastomer compromise

by R. Bruce Hoadley

Dowel joints must surely be among the oldest methods of joining wood. What could be more basic than a cylindrical tenon fitting a drilled-round mortise, locked forever with good glue? The image of perfection.

But not quite. For our experience suggests that if anything is as old as dowel joints, it is loose dowel joints. We have become resigned to loose and wobbly chairs, and to our mothers warning us not to tilt back at table. Accepting this has always seemed unreasonable, so some years ago I set out to study the traditional dowel joint, to find out why such joints fail and especially to discover how to make a joint that would not fail. After many experiments I arrived at the troubling conclusion that no matter how well the joint is made, the conflicting dimensional behavior of the mortise and the tenon in response to humidity variations in our everyday environment can cause self-induced loosening. The very nature of wood ensures that it eventually can come loose. However, some recent research encourages me to believe that soon we will have a dowel joint that is successful, virtually indestructible. In this article I will explore the self-destructive effect of moisture variation on the traditional dowel joint, and I will suggest some remedies and some lines for further exploration.

A plain round tenon in its simplest form, such as an unshouldered rung inserted into a chair leg, responds to external loading differently from a shouldered tenon, a dowel in a rail/stile frame joint, or a grooved, serrated or precompressed tenon. This article makes no attempt to address such special cases, but focuses on the individual dowel or tenon insertion.

Obviously, the species of wood and the dimensions of a successful joint will accommodate the loads it must sustain. In a typical chair (figure 1), analysis can determine the dimensions and proportions of the joint so that axial stresses along the mating surfaces are safely within the strength properties of the wood. Adding glue provides shear resistance to whatever minor withdrawal load might be imposed. And the commonly used dimensions, which have evolved by experience and tradition, are more than adequate to resist loads imposed by use—or even moderate abuse. Chair rungs are rarely so small in diameter that they fail simply because of excess bending stress and break off at the joint. When they do break here, it is usually because the other end has fallen out of its socket, and someone then steps on the rung. Likewise, as long as the joint remains tight, its bearing areas are usually large enough to distribute the racking loads.

But two common shortcomings lead to problems. First, the mortise may be too shallow in proportion to its diameter. In a Windsor chair, for example, the thickness of the seat limits the mortise to a shallow hole compared with the rather large tenon diameter at the top of the leg. Second, the mating surfaces may be of poor quality. Poor turning or shaping of tenons is not nearly as common as badly bored holes. If the spurs of the auger aren't in top condition, the surface of the

hole is liable to be lined with damaged cells, which can neither support the bearing loads nor develop a successful glue bond. Proper fit is also critical. With water-based emulsion glues (white or yellow), highest withdrawal resistance develops when the dowel diameter is several thousandths of an inch less than the mortise diameter. If the tenon is oversized, the joint will be scraped dry upon assembly; if undersized, the glue line will be excessively thick.

Moisture variation is to blame — If a joint is properly designed and well made, it will carry any reasonable load at the time of assembly. The mystery is why an apparently successful joint loosens due to nothing more than humidity change. The humidity variation in typical indoor situations is wide. In Northern states, humidity in the 80% to 90% range may prevail through August and September, only to plummet to 15% to 20% relative humidity in the subzero days of January and February. This may cause the average equilibrium moisture content of wood to cycle from as low as 4% in winter to as high as 15% in the summer. Even greater extremes occur in such areas as basement rooms, with condensation dampness in summer and a nearby furnace causing excess dryness in winter. Furniture assembled in Scottsdale, Arizona, later moved to New Orleans, and ultimately back to Scottsdale, would go through a similarly drastic moisture cycle. An unfinished wooden ladder, stored flat on the ground and covered with a tarp in summer, then returned to a heated shop for winter storage, would suffer likewise. As a result of moisture cycling, the dimension of wood perpendicular to its

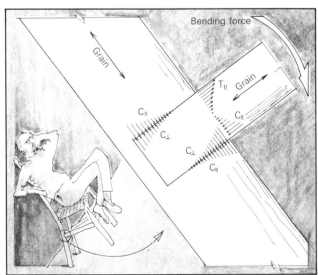

Fig. 1: Tilting back in a chair racks the joints. The rung tends to bend, causing axial stresses (tension, $T_{\parallel}$ and compression, $C_{\parallel}$). In turn the rung tenon bears against the mortise walls, compressing the rung perpendicular to the grain ($C_{\perp}$) and the mortise parallel to the grain ($C_{\parallel}$).

From *Fine Woodworking* magazine (March 1980) 21:68-72

Fig. 2: *Paired discs of American beech, left, dramatize the effect of cyclic moisture variation. The top two are as originally turned at 7% moisture content—the wood tightly fits its steel sleeve. The central pair has been moistened to the fiber saturation point (about 30% MC). The lower two were moistened to fiber saturation, then dried to their initial 7% MC. Compression set makes the restrained disc smaller than it started out, whereas the unrestrained disc has returned to about its original size. Right, the handle was tight when this hammer head was sectioned by hacksaw. Then it was stored in a damp place and later redried—the hickory shows severe compression shrinkage, and moisture variation, not the pounding of use, is to blame. This is why soaking a tool in water to tighten a loose handle is a temporary solution at best.*

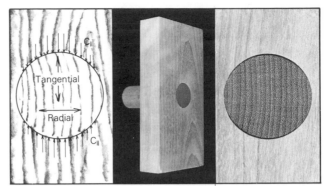

Fig. 3: *Increased moisture swells the mortise across the grain by about the same amount as the tenon swells radially. But the mortise doesn't change in height (parallel to the grain). Thus, like the steel sleeve, the end-grain surfaces of the mortise restrain the tangential swelling of the tenon (diagram, left). When the unglued birch joint shown in the photographs was cycled from wet to dry, compression set made the redried tenon smaller tangentially than it originally was, yet still a snug fit radially. Since most woods move more tangentially (in the plane of the annual rings) than radially (perpendicular to the rings), the orientation shown here is not optimum. Turning the tenon 90° in the mortise would be better.*

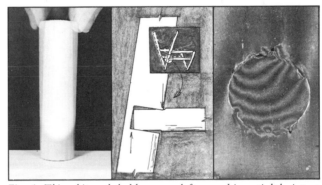

Fig. 4: *This white ash ladder rung, left, was driven tightly into a western hemlock rail, then put through a severe moisture cycle. The double exposure shows how loose the joint has become. The diagram shows that once looseness develops in a joint, racking results in concentrated load that may further crush the wood: The worse it is, the worse it gets. Right, a birch dowel in ponderosa pine was coated with moire strain-analysis material and photographed through a grill of undistorted lines. The light-dark patterns show that compression damage extends well into the end grain of the mortise.*

grain direction can change by up to 4% of its original dimension. This amounts to a change of 1/32 in. across a 1-in. diameter tenon.

First, consider a wooden dowel confined in a metal socket, such as a hammer handle tightly fitting into its steel head. For our experiments, we simplified this to a dowel of wood fit snugly into a stainless-steel sleeve, then cycled from low to high and back to low moisture content. An unconfined dowel would simply swell and reshrink to approximately its original diameter. However, the restrained dowel crushes itself, and upon redrying to its original moisture content, assumes a smaller-than-original size. Confining a piece of wood to prevent it from swelling by 4% is essentially the same as allowing the piece of wood to swell and then squeezing it back to its original dimension. The trouble is that in confining wood perpendicular to the grain, the limit of elastic behavior (that is, its ability to spring back) is less than 1%. Any additional squeeze will cause permanent deformation, or "set," as in figure 2. In addition, the wood surfaces, already somewhat damaged by machining, do not behave elastically, and seem simply to crush. The result is a concentrated surface layer of crushed and mangled cells.

The wood-to-wood mortise-and-tenon joint is a special situation in that the restraint is unidirectional. The diameter of the mortise does not change parallel to the grain, but its diameter perpendicular to the grain varies right along with the diameter of the tenon. It becomes ovoid during moisture cycling (figure 3). After a dry-wet-dry cycle, compression set is greatest against the end-grain surface of the mortise, while the tenon remains snug at the side-grain surfaces of the mortise. The tenon will therefore be looser in a plane parallel to the grain direction of the mortise.

Such looseness in the side rungs of a post-and-rung chair will allow the chair to rock forward and back. As soon as this

looseness begins, the joint-surface load is no longer distributed evenly, but is concentrated at specific points. The concentrated loads may now exceed the strength of the wood at these points, further crushing the surfaces. So the joint gets looser—the worse it is, the worse it gets (figure 4). With woods of equal density, most of the damage will turn up as crushed tenon because of the lower strength of wood in compression perpendicular to the grain. However, where the mortise is in a lower-density wood than the tenon, such as a hard maple leg tenoned into a white-pine seat, the crushing may be worse on the end-grain walls of the mortise. This bad situation is compounded if the end grain was damaged when the mortise was bored, especially in fragile woods like pine.

Now consider glue. If a good glue bond develops between the tenon and the end grain of the mortise, the shrinking of the compression-set tenon during the drying cycle can be significantly retarded. This is apparent when we make matched samples with and without glue. The unglued joint will open with even the slightest cycle. Glued joints resist moderate moisture variation without failure. With exposure to more

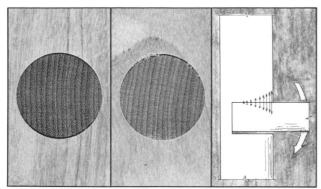

Fig. 5: Dowel joints without glue (left) and with glue, after severe moisture cycling. Once one side of the joint has opened, the other glue line is no match for racking stresses and usually fails in tension. If the mortise was badly drilled, a layer of wood may pull away with the glue.

severe cycles, the joint eventually fails, at first along only one of the end-grain surfaces. The remaining glue bond is now no match for even moderate racking, for the critical stress has become the tensile loading of the glue line (figure 5). When a joint loosens, we assume that "the glue has let go." Close examination may show, however, that a layer of wood tissue has been pulled from the inside of the mortise. This is common where a high-density tenon is glued into a lower-density mortise—the maple leg in the pine seat.

One more point bears elaboration: the behavior of wood in tension perpendicular to the grain. As we have seen, if wood is compressed perpendicular to the grain to well beyond its elastic limit (that is, by several percent of its original dimension), the cell structure is permanently crushed but it remains intact. However, in tension perpendicular to the grain, the strain limit is 1% or 2% of the original dimension, whereupon the wood pulls apart. Therefore if the moisture cycle develops between 1% and 2% compression shrinkage, a glued tenon may be pulled apart during the drying cycle, no matter how perfectly the joint was machined and glued. The tenon actually splits near the glue line. So one way or another, the joint will fail if the moisture cycle is severe.

What to do? — I really didn't appreciate how destructive moisture cycling could be until I ran some experiments. I had arrived at a standard test assembly consisting of a 4-in. by 1-in. dowel inserted into a 1-in.-dia. hole, 1⅛ in. deep, in a 3-in. by 5-in. by 1¼-in. block. In one series, I made 20 similar maple-tenon-in-pine-block joints, using wood that had been conditioned to 6% moisture content. I used a PVA adhesive (white glue). Ten of the joints were stored in sealed plastic bags; the other ten were conditioned up to 18% moisture

content and down to original weight, over a period of several months. The cycled joints weren't wobbly, although visible fracture of the squeezed-out glue along one side of the joints suggested that compression set had developed. Then, by racking the joints with hand pressure, there was an audible snap and the joints became wobbly. When pulled apart in a testing machine, the average withdrawal load of the uncycled specimens was 1,550 lb., while the cycled specimens averaged only 42 lb. This was a terrible predicament, for under commonly encountered moisture variations, even well-made joints were destroying themselves. I didn't want to believe it, but further experiments confirmed this cold, hard truth. To minimize the problem, I arrived at a list of five checkpoints for making joints with the best chance of survival:

1. Proportions. Avoid shallow mortises. I try to make the mortise 1½ times as deep as it is wide. However, if the mortise depth approaches twice its diameter, a new set of problems make the situation worse again.

2. Original moisture content. The wood (especially the tenon) should be slightly drier, not wetter, than its eventual average equilibrium moisture content. Better a little compression than tension at the joint interface.

3. Mortise surface quality. Carefully bore the mortise. Sharpen the bit, especially the spurs, with extreme care to produce the cleanest possible surfaces. Using a drill press or boring guide will improve the hole.

4. Grain/growth-ring orientation. If possible, bore the mortise radially into the female member; orient the tenon with its growth rings perpendicular to the grain direction in the mortise (figure 6). This minimizes the stress by putting radial, rather than tangential, dimensional change in opposition to long-grain structure.

5. Finish the product. Completed work should be given a coat of finish selected to provide maximum protection against short-term, but potentially disastrous, extremes of humidity. Lacquer, varnish or paint is best. And remember to finish all over, especially end-grain surfaces.

All of the above conditions cannot always be optimum, and there will be situations where severe moisture variation cannot be avoided. What other solutions might be possible? For unidirectional stress problems (the chair leg and rung in figure 3), I tried providing stress relief by making a saw-kerf slot in the tenon, thinking that compression would be relieved during the swelling cycle. This helped, but it had the disadvantage of shearing the glue line adjacent to the kerf as each half swelled. Finally I split the tenon—a plane of failure that would relieve stress during the drying phase of the cycle. As compression shrinkage took place, the split could open rather than the glue line failing. In our initial tests with circu-

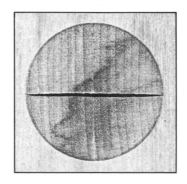

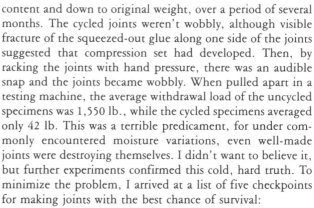

Fig. 6: The optimum condition (left): tangential movement coincides in both mortise and tenon, while the lesser radial dimensional change in the tenon opposes the stable long grain of the mortise. At right, tangential movement varies the depth of the mortise and may 'walk' the tenon out, while compression will cause the greater change in tenon height.

Fig. 7: Birch tenon was split both radially and tangentially before assembly. After moderate moisture cycling, compression shrinkage has developed entirely in one direction, opening the radial split, while the tangential split remains tight. The entire glue line remains intact. This may be what actually happens when tenons are wedged.

lar plugs in flat boards, the presplit tenon opened as predicted, and the glue line remained intact. In matched specimens without splits, the glue line failed. Analysis confirmed that in the compression-shrinkage phase the wood could actually distort itself by enough to relieve the strain. When I made regular, full-depth joints, splitting the tenon to the full depth of insertion, the joint stayed together under moderate moisture cycling (figure 7). I suspect that this mechanism is the real reason why wedged tenons work. Although the wedge is intended to supply lateral pressure to the glue surfaces and perhaps also to splay the tenon for a dovetail-style mechanical lock, it may actually do no more than provide a stress-release slot and thereby help the glue line survive.

Under moisture extremes, a new problem emerges: The mortise depth changes, and the glue line shears. After repeated cycling the tenon remains glued around the bottom of the hole, but shear and compression set develop near the outside junction, and racking eventually completes the break (figure 8). An especially tight fit, good gluing and finishing, and close control of moisture content at assembly can help prevent the mortise from changing depth relative to the tenon. The price is liable to be an unsightly bulge or a check on the back side of the chair leg. So the simple split has promise, but it is not the best solution.

Silicone adhesives — It has always intrigued me to see a heavy motor set into a base with rubber-sleeve motor mounts. Why not set tenons into some kind of rubber sleeves inside the mortise? The rubber might yield enough during the swelling and shrinking phase of the cycle for the glue joint to survive. First, I bonded rubber tubing 1/16 in. thick around a 1-in.-diameter dowel and glued it into the mortise. A tedious procedure, but I was encouraged when the joint survived severe moisture cycles without failure. Next I experimented with General Electric's RTV (room temperature vulcanizing) silicone elastomers. A translucent formulation, RTV-108 (in hardware stores the product name is Clear Glue and Seal) worked well. To keep the tenon centered and parallel to the mortise while the silicone cured, I glued thin splines onto it at 90° positions (figure 9). Later we figured out how to machine a four-spline tenon with its base diameter undersized by the thickness of the glue line. Hand-carving a dowel to leave four or six thin ribs also works. If the modified portion of the tenon is slightly shorter than the depth of the mortise, the elastomer sleeve can be fully hidden in the joint. Before gluing, slide the tenon into the mortise to be sure the ribs fit snugly. Then wipe a dab of silicone adhesive into all mating surfaces. Next, quickly squeeze a dab into the bottom of the mortise and firmly push the tenon home, allowing the silicone adhesive to flow back up along it. Within an hour it will skin over firmly and you'll soon discover the point at which the squeeze-out solidifies enough to be neatly peeled off. The joint cures within 24 hours but does not reach full strength for a week or more.

I have experimented with various dowel sizes, adhesive layer thicknesses and wood species, and compared the results with conventional assembly glues. Predictably, with fairly thick elastomer layers (0.060-in. layer in 1-in.-diameter mortise) the joints are able to withstand severe moisture cycles (6%-24%-6% MC) without losing withdrawal strength. The same cycle destroys a standard PVA (white glue) joint. For example, in oak joints with white glue, it took an average of

1,100 lb. to pull apart uncycled joints. But after a 6%-24%-6% moisture cycle the average withdrawal resistance was only 41 lb. (most joints were loose enough to be wiggled apart by hand). With RTV-108 (silicone), the original joint strength averages 264 lb.; after cycling, 262 lb. Even though the white-glued joint was stronger in withdrawal to begin with, the silicone-glued joint is strongest after cycling. The silicone joints that withstand the severest moisture cycling are not nearly as rigid as conventional glues and unmodified tenons, and the silicone-glue approach cannot be considered a direct substitute for traditionally made joints. In defense, I point out that after severe cycling, the white-glued joints were often far worse than the silicone joints. However, the rigidity of silicone joints can be improved by increasing the relative depth of the mortise and by making the adhesive layer thinner. It is best to keep the depth of the mortise at

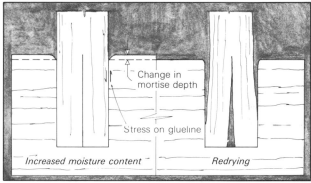

Fig. 8: In moisture extremes, typically high moisture content followed by redrying, the changing depth of the mortise and compression set near its mouth shear the glue line. The split tenon accommodates stress at the bottom of the hole, but racking will soon break it loose.

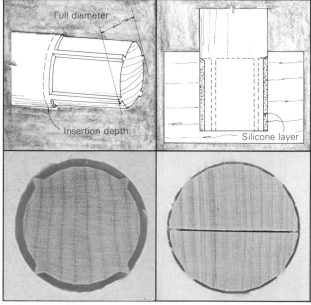

Fig. 9: The elastomer compromise. Four thin ribs are formed on the tenon, by machining, whittling or by gluing splines onto the tenon. The ribs should be 90° apart, and oriented at 45° to the grain of the mortise. The ribs keep the tenon centered and contribute to rigidity. Their depth determines the thickness of the silicone layer; their length can be short of full mortise depth, thereby concealing the modified portion of the tenon. A split in the tenon contributes to strain relief and allows the silicone layer to be quite thin. The silicone compounds with better adhesion to wood now being developed may solve the problem of wobbly chairs.

least 1½ times its diameter. With 1-in. tenons, as the glue layer is reduced to about 0.020 in., the joint stays rigid, will have reasonable withdrawal strength and will withstand fairly drastic moisture variation. Effecting this can be a problem in leg-to-seat joints for Windsor chairs, where the seat thickness limits the mortise depth. If the glue layer is too thin, compression will develop. A good point of departure for experiments with 1-in. dowels would be a silicone layer of about ⅟₃₂ in. or slightly less. This should give a good compromise between durability under moisture variation, and rigidity.

I have also tried assembling several different types of woods with silicone adhesives. One style of captain's chair, having a pine seat and arms and maple turnings, was assembled using nominal 0.020 in. silicone layers. After six years, all joints are still secure. While seated in the chair, by intentionally racking the frame, you can feel slight springiness due to its non-rigid joints. But nobody who hadn't been told about the special system of joinery has ever commented on the slight wobble. In a set of twelve thumb-back chairs, half the joints were assembled with silicone, half with white glue. The chairs were left in a library lounge for six months of student use. The only failure was in one white-glued joint.

In other items silicone joints seem to be the perfect solution—attaching the smokestack to toy tugboats for the bathtub, where alternate hot-soak and drying of unpainted wood is a most severe exposure. Bathtub toys assembled with conventional glues compression-set and fall apart easily, but silicone joints can take it. Another application is attaching laminated beech sculptor's mallets to their maple handles. Silicone not only solves the loosening problems, but the layer of elastomer seems to contribute to shock absorbancy. I have also used it to reassemble a few pieces of furniture whose

tenons were woefully undersized and loose because of compression shrinkage as well as fist-pounding reassembly many times. Success was predictable according to joint proportions: Shallow mortises didn't work out, but where the tenons were long and the mortises deep, the silicone did a perfect job of filling the gaps and solving the looseness problem, perhaps forever.

Note that all of these remarks apply to rectangular structures, which rely on joinery for rigidity. A triangulated structure, on the other hand, is inherently stable, and silicone glues might be exactly right. I hope some craftsmen may be encouraged to experiment along these lines.

Combining silicone with a stress-relief split in the tenon also looks promising. I found that the glue layer can be held to a minimum (0.010 in. to 0.015 in.), since part of the problem is handled by the opening of the split tenon. Some typical values for direct withdrawal of a maple tenon from a pine mortise, before and after moisture cycling, are: with white glue, 1,553 lb. and a mere 42 lb.; with a layer of silicone 0.010 in. thick, 830 lb. and 290 lb.; and with silicone plus a slit in the tenon, 753 lb. and a surprising 580 lb. The limiting feature of silicone adhesives has been adhesion to the wood surface. Average tensile strengths perpendicular to the surface are only about 200 PSI. Recently, however, we have tested some formulations (prior to their retail release) that have more than double this strength. I am confident that we will hear a lot more about silicone elastomers, and see them specifically incorporated into joinery work. □

Bruce Hoadley teaches wood science at the University of Massachusetts in Amherst. For more on repairing wobbly chairs, see page 29.

For more on repairing wobbly chairs, see page 29.

One Chairmaker's Answer

(EDITOR'S NOTE: The following is excerpted from *Make a Chair from a Tree: An Introduction to Working Green Wood,* by John D. Alexander, Jr., published by The Taunton Press, 1978.)

The goal is to employ the compressibility of green wood without exceeding the elastic limit of the fibers in the tenon. When the moisture balance is right, we can drive in an oversized tenon and create a tight bond between the surface of the mortise and its tenon. . . . At the time of mortising and assembly, the post should contain about 15% to 20% moisture (air-dried outdoors) and the rung about 5% dried indoors near the stove).

. . . I flatten the sides of all the tenons in my chair—slightly more so

on the tenons of the rungs near the top of the front posts. Flats not only prevent posts from splitting during drying, but after drying they act as a lock that prevents the tenon from rotating in the mortise. . . . Taper the flats a mite so they are broader and deeper toward the shoulders. This makes them slightly dovetailed when viewed from above. If all goes well, the shrinking post locks the dovetailed tenon into its mortise. Last, notch the tops and bottoms of the tenons so that when the compressed end grain of the mortise dries and straightens, a ridge of post wood will be forced into this notch. . . .

When the chair is assembled, the wood rays in the tenon should be oriented vertically, in the same direction as the long axis of the post. This orientation aligns the direction of maximum rung movement (the tangential plane) with the direction of maximum pressure from post shrinkage. . . . Looking from the top of the post, bore the mortises so that the plane of the wood rays bisects the angle between the front and side rungs. This allows each tenon to be compressed equally as the wet wood shrinks. . . . Bore the bottoms of the side mortises about ³⁄₃₂ in. lower than the tangent lines laid out earlier from the tops of the front and rear rung mortises. This locks the rungs together inside the post. . . I use glue. I use every technique I can that might help the chair hold together. —J.D.A.

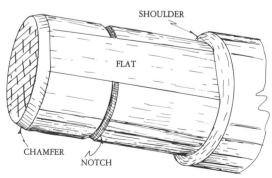

SHOULDER

FLAT

CHAMFER

NOTCH

Interlocking tenons secure the joint; tapered flats and notches also help.

Two Easy Pieces
A frame chair and a sofa

by Simon Watts

This chair and sofa are two variations on one simple theme: a wood frame spanned by tensioned canvas that supports loose cushions. The canvas is kept taut by nylon lacing running through brass grommets. Both pieces are light, easy to make and economical.

I designed the chair as a practice project for apprentices in their first six weeks of training. It teaches the mortise and tenon as well as bridle joints, and it can be made from a drawing with minimum supervision. Since little material is involved, a poorly cut joint could be made over again without either the student or myself feeling badly about the waste.

Later I used the same basic design for a small sofa and then for a larger one. The former succeeded but the latter was a failure. Although amply strong to support three adults, it *looked* weak because the end frames were too far apart. The only structural difference between the sofa and the chair is in the thickness of stock—1⅜ in. instead of 1¼ in.—this is as much for the sake of proportion as for strength.

Sofas are bulky and awkward to move so I also made a knockdown version by substituting loose wedges for the glued mortise-and-tenon joints. This detail is shown at *B* in the drawing and can be used for either piece.

This design can be made in any straight-grained hardwood. Before deciding on the wood, consider how it will look against both the canvas and the fabric chosen for the cushion covers. I like a black canvas because it doesn't show dirt, goes with any wood (except walnut) and looks good with brass grommets and white lacing.

Construction — Starting with 6/4 stock, cut out the pieces for the end frames and rails. You will need two pieces 24 in. long, four pieces 22 in., six pieces 32 in., and three pieces for the long rails: 35 in. for the chair and 59 in. for the sofa. If you are making the knockdown version, be sure to add 3 in. extra to two of the long rails to make room for the mortises and wedges. Plane all these pieces down to 1⅜ in. if making the sofa, 1¼ in. for the chair.

The next step is to join up the end frames by bridle joints at each corner. Bridle joints are best cut on the table saw; a carbide blade helps ensure accuracy and smoothness. If I were making this chair by hand, I would use a different joint, a mitered dovetail, because I don't like to do things by hand that are better done by machine and vice-versa. I'll describe how to make the bridle joint first, then the mitered dovetail.

After cutting the pieces to exact length, set a marking gauge to the width of the stock plus 1/16 in. Mark out one of the pairs to be joined on all four surfaces of each piece. If you are using a table saw, there is no need to mark more than one pair because saw and fence settings will take care of the rest. Usual practice is to make the tenon two-fifths of the thickness of the stock—about ½ in. for 5/4 stock.

Holding the stock vertically, saw the tenons first. For this operation I screw a wooden fence 8 in. high to the standard metal one. This gives more support and greater accuracy. The saw should be set a bare ⅛ in. lower than the gauge marks. Then, with a miter gauge accurately set at 90°, saw the shoulders. If you set the blade down so the waste is not quite sawn through, it will not come whistling back in your face. The remaining wood is easily cleaned up with a chisel or a shoulder rabbet plane. If you don't have a good enough blade for finish cuts, mark all the shoulders with a knife, saw 1/16 in. on the waste side and then chisel to the line. The shoulder must be left square, not undercut, because it shows.

Next saw the mortises, vertically, in the same way. They should fit the tenons snugly without any forcing. Remove the waste by drilling a single hole (halfway from each side) or with a coping saw. With a chisel, clean up the end grain to the gauge mark on the inside of the mortise.

The mitered dovetail, the handmade alternative, is a one-pin affair that does the job of a bridle joint, only more elegantly. Begin by marking all four surfaces of each pair to be joined (dotted lines in the drawing at *A*). Mark out the miter lines on each side of both pieces with a knife, but do not saw them yet. Next, mark out the space for the tail on the horizontal piece *(a)* as shown. This can be sawn either on a table saw, with the blade angled, or by hand using a tenon saw. Cut out the waste with a coping saw and chisel to the line *y-y*

Chair in cherry with black canvas sling and woolen cushions.

From *Fine Woodworking* magazine (May 1980) 22:51-54

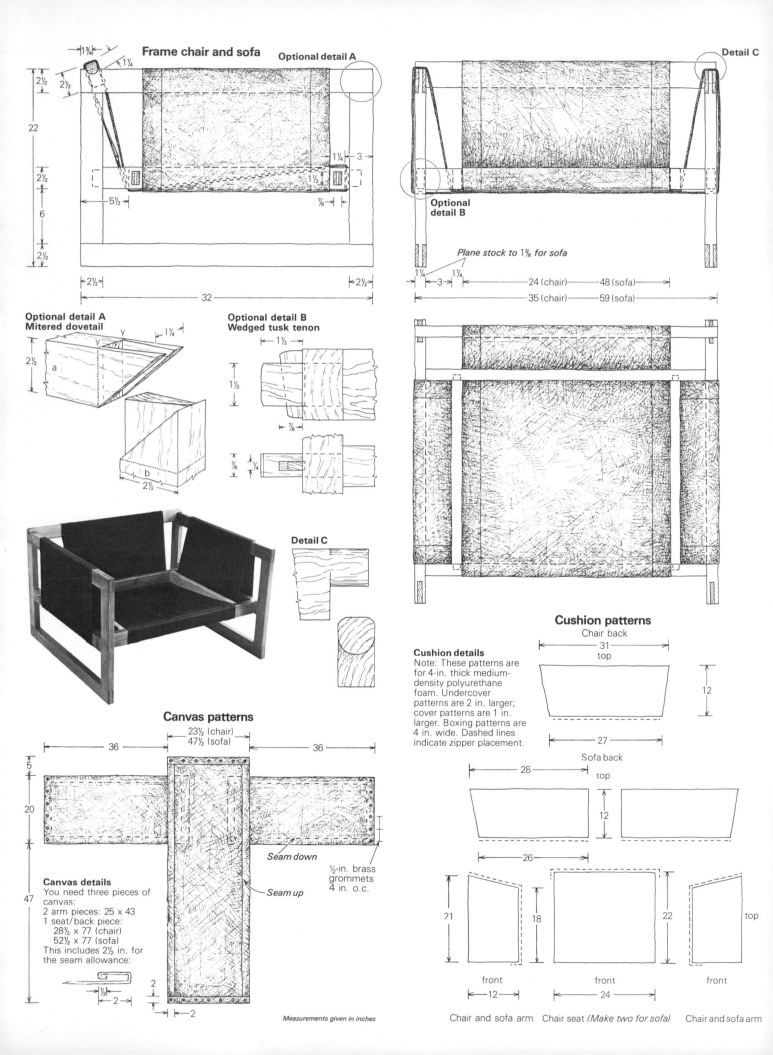

Frame chair and sofa

Optional detail A

Detail C

Plane stock to 1⅜ for sofa

Optional detail B

1¼ · 3 · 1¼ · 24 (chair) · 48 (sofa)
35 (chair) · 59 (sofa)

Measurements given in inches

Optional detail A
Mitered dovetail

Optional detail B
Wedged tusk tenon

Detail C

Canvas patterns

23½ (chair)
47½ (sofa)

36 · 36

Seam down

Seam up

½-in. brass grommets 4 in. o.c.

Canvas details
You need three pieces of canvas:
2 arm pieces: 25 x 43
1 seat/back piece:
  28½ x 77 (chair)
  52½ x 77 (sofa)
This includes 2½ in. for the seam allowance:

Cushion details
Note: These patterns are for 4-in. thick medium-density polyurethane foam. Undercover patterns are 2 in. larger; cover patterns are 1 in. larger. Boxing patterns are 4 in. wide. Dashed lines indicate zipper placement.

Cushion patterns

Chair back
31
top
12
27

Sofa back
28
top
12
26

21 · 18 · 22 · top

front · front · front
12 · 24

Chair and sofa arm · Chair seat (Make two for sofa) · Chair and sofa arm working from both sides. Lay piece *a* firmly on the end of *b* and mark the pin with a scribe or thin-bladed knife. Mark out the other limits of the pin and saw the cheeks. Remember to stop the sawcut when close to the miter line.

The last step is to saw the miters on both pieces and trial-fit the joint. You should saw the miters a little to the waste side of the line, push the joint together and then run a fine saw into the joint, on both sides, until the miter closes.

With the joints in the side members cut, the middle rail is next mortised into the two verticals and then all five frame pieces can be assembled and glued up. When gluing a bridle joint, be sure to put clamping pressure (protecting the work with pads) on the sides of the joint until the glue has set. When gluing a mitered dovetail, put glue on the miters as well as on the pin and tail. Clamp lightly across the cheeks of the tail. Check with a square. After the glue has set (but before it is bone hard) flush off the surfaces with a sharp plane.

Next, cut the through mortises for the two long rails. Mark accurately on both sides with a knife, drill out the waste, then chisel to the knife mark. The semicircular cutouts are best done by clamping the top edges of the two frames together and drilling a single 1¼-in. hole. Remember to use a backing piece to prevent splintering.

The edges of the frames and rails must be rounded over. If they are left sharp, the canvas will eventually wear through on the corners. I use a router with a carbide rounding-over bit fitted with a ball-bearing pilot. It can also be done by hand, with a wood file and sandpaper. All the edges are treated in the same way except where two horizontal rails meet. Here they are left square.

Next, the four pieces of the underframe are cut and joined. The short pieces are stub-tenoned into the long rails because a through mortise would weaken the structure. This assembly is then attached to the end frames using either a glued-and-wedged mortise-and-tenon joint or, for the knockdown alternative, a through mortise and loose wedge. In both cases the wedge is vertical, at right angles to the grain.

When making a tapered mortise for a wedged mortise-and-tenon joint, it is best to make the wedges first. Lay a wedge on the outside of the tenon and mark the slope with a pencil. Then, with a mortise gauge and a knife, mark the two mortise openings top and bottom. Most of the waste can be drilled out (working from both ends) and the remainder cleaned out with a chisel. I always leave the wedges 1 in. overlong so when they are tapped home they can be marked, then removed for trimming. The top of the wedge should project slightly more than the bottom. In time they invariably get driven lower.

The top rail, at the back of the chair, is not fastened but is held in place by the tension of the canvas. It is rounded on the upper side and fits loosely into the half-rounds in each frame. Its two ends are best sawn out square and then shaped with a rasp or wood file.

Canvas — The canvas is wrapped around the completed frame and laced across the back and under the seat. You will need 45 ft. of ¼-in. lacing, double for the sofa, which must be of nylon or the equivalent. Don't use clothesline or sash cord. I use

Back and underside.

an 18-oz. treated chair duck, which is a rather heavy material for a domestic sewing machine, and you may want to have the canvas made by a tent and awning manufacturer, a sailmaker or an upholsterer. The 2-in. seams are sewn with the edge turned under ½ in. They must be made exactly as in the drawings so only the smooth side of the seam shows. The brass eyelets, or grommets, are easy to put in yourself. You need about three dozen ½-in. grommets (five dozen for the sofa) and a ½-in. punch-and-die-set.

Cushions — To make the cushions you need a piece of medium-density polyurethane foam 4 in. thick, 1-in. Dacron wrapping, medium-weight unbleached muslin, a 26-in. zipper for each cushion, and fabric for the outside covers.

First make a full-size pattern of each different shape of cushion in heavy, brown wrapping paper. Transfer the patterns to the foam using a soft pencil or blue chalk. If you don't have a band saw, the easiest way to cut polyurethane is with a fine panel saw or hacksaw. An electric carving knife will work, too. Support the foam on the edge of a piece of plywood, saw with light strokes along the lines, and keep the plane of the saw vertical.

The Dacron batting gives the cushions some extra bulk and makes them less hard—both on the seat and on the eye. They are padded a little more on one side than on the other as follows: Using the same patterns, cut out with scissors one piece of batting for each cushion. Lay this on the side of the foam, which, when in place, will be *toward* a person sitting in the chair (away from the canvas). Next wrap each cushion, including the ends, once around with the batting. You may want to keep this in place with a spray glue (foam or fabric adhesive) while making the muslin undercovers. To cover the ends of the foam, either cut the batting over-wide and fold it over the ends, like wrapping a parcel, or cut separate pieces of batting and spray-glue them in place.

Undercovers — Muslin undercovers are essential. Without them it is practically impossible to remove and replace the outer, or slip, covers, for cleaning. Inner and outer covers are made in the same way: two panels joined by a strip (called *boxing*) that runs around the edge of the cushion.

Lay the original patterns on a piece of newspaper and then, with a felt pen, draw a line around them. Draw another line ½ in. outside the patterns and a third one ½ in. outside that. Cut around the outside line. Using these new patterns, cut out two pieces of muslin for each cushion. Next, cut the boxings, strips 4 in. wide and a little longer than the perimeter of the cushion. They don't have to be one piece.

If you are an old hand with a sewing machine, machine-stitch the covers directly, sewing ½ in. in from the edge of the material (on the middle line of your pattern). This is best done by putting a piece of tape as a guide on your sewing machine, ½ in. from the needle. Sew the boxing to one panel all the way around and then, starting from one corner, sew the other panel, leaving one long edge unsewn. If you are a novice, pin or hand-stitch (baste) the covers before machining. Turn the covers right side out and insert the wrapped foam. Turn the loose edges inside and blind-hemstitch by hand.

Fabric — As in choosing a wood, certain criteria apply when picking fabric for the outer covers. Leaving aside matters of color and pattern, you must choose a fabric that is strong enough. It must not stretch in use—which means a tight weave—or shrink when washed, or wear too quickly. Think of the climate, too. Wool is fine in Vermont, but it would be a poor choice for the heat and humidity of a Washington summer, where linen or heavy cotton would be preferable. Remember that light colors need cleaning more often, blues fade in bright sunlight, and some synthetics not only can melt but are flammable. The chair will require 5 yd. of 30-in. to 36-in. material, the sofa 8 yd. If you use 48-in. or 54-in. material, the chair will require 4 yd. of material, the sofa 6 yd. The undercovers will require roughly the same amount of muslin. Make sure the material is preshrunk. If it is not, you must wash it once to shrink it. Ironing makes the sewing easier.

Outer covers — Taking the same newspaper patterns that were used for the muslin covers, cut ½ in. off the perimeter (to the middle line) all the way around. Then pin the patterns to the fabric and cut out the panels as before, together with enough 4-in. strips for the boxing. The innermost line on the pattern is now the one to sew on.

The alert reader will notice that the muslin-covered cushions are ½ in. bigger than the outer covers. Like putting a sausage in its skin, this helps keep the outer covers tight and free from wrinkles. Wrinkles in the muslin will not show through—the muslin is too thin.

The inner and outer covers are made exactly the same way, the only complication being the zipper. This must be put where it won't show, and the best placement is indicated on the drawing. To install the zipper, take a piece of boxing 1 in. longer than the zipper and fold it in half lengthwise, making a crease. If it won't stay creased, iron it. Lay the zipper down on the crease so that the zipper teeth are just level with the folded edge of the boxing. Pin or tack it in place and then stitch it using the zipper foot of your sewing machine. Now take another piece of 4-in. boxing, crease it lengthwise, and stitch it to the other side of the zipper. You should now have a 4-in. strip of boxing, double thickness, with a zipper running neatly up the middle.

When sewing this piece of boxing to the side panels, remember to face the zipper *in*. Then, when the cover is turned right side out, it will face the right way. A professional upholsterer covers the two ends of the zipper by overlapping the adjacent boxing. Or you can simply join it with a neat seam.

It is a good policy to sew the seams twice, once along a line ½ in. from the edge and again as near to the edge as you can manage. This prevents the material from unraveling at the seam if it is roughly laundered.

This chair and sofa have never been made in quantity but the design could easily be adapted for production by machine. This is because there is no hand-shaping, boards do not have to be selected for color and grain, and most of the joints can be cut by machine. The design could be further simplified by using only one thickness of stock (1⅜ in.), which would cut the number of separate parts in half. Bridle joints lend themselves to machine production but I would replace the mortise-and-tenon joints with stub mortises using allen-head machine screws and *T*-nuts. The whole piece could then be shipped knocked down and easily reassembled. The canvases could be made in quantity and enclosed with plenty of lacing and suitable instructions in several languages.

Perhaps someone would like to take this up? ☐

Hidden Beds

Two ways to get more sleeping space

by David Landen

Beds for which there is little space or which are used only occasionally pose interesting problems for a furnituremaker. They should not only be comfortable to sleep on and take up a minimum of space when not in use, but also should work reasonably well as another piece of furniture. Of the two pieces discussed in this article, the couch works better as another piece of furniture while the settle, with its full-sized mattress already made up, is the most useful as a bed.

Neither one is a particularly original design (couches with sliding seats probably originated in Denmark or Sweden, and settles have been around for a long time), but each had to be worked out to fit a client's specifications. The couch was made of red oak and the settle of cherry. Almost any strong hardwood will work for the couch and the settle could be made from almost anything, including plywood for the carcase. Cherry was used because of the client's preference and because eight-foot sections of clear stock in reasonable widths are still available.

The Couch. Overall dimensions are not critical. It must be long enough for someone to lie on, and the seat deep and high enough to be comfortable. The depth of the seat determines to some extent the width of the slide-out bed. In this couch, the extended width is something over 40 inches, which is wide enough for two people to sleep on occasionally. Aligning the slats in the back of the couch with the stationary slats in the seat would have made it possible to extend the sliding slats through the back and thus gain several inches of bed width. But this wasn't done because it would have kept the couch out too far from the wall or would have made it unsightly when positioned with the back exposed.

Construction of the couch is relatively straightforward once the basic dimensions are determined and a layout sheet drawn up. I used 8/4 stock for the frame. The two end pieces and the back are joined with open mortise and tenon joints. The end cross pieces and the slats are mortised into the frame. A dado about 1/2-inch deep cut into the inside of the top piece of the end frame at the appropriate angle for the slant of the back and a rabbet the same depth and corresponding angle at the bottom end of the vertical piece on the back hold the back and ends together. The front rail rests on two legs glued to the end pieces. A third leg is added in the center.

Slats milled from 4/4 stock, with a rabbet cut on each side, cut square on the front end and beveled to match the angle of the back on the back end, are spaced evenly and screwed and glued to the top side of the front rail and to a cleat fastened to the bottom piece of the back. The sliding part of the seat consists of three legs supporting a front rail into which has been cut a series of dadoes to hold the sliding slats which are

From *Fine Woodworking* magazine (Fall 1976) 4:24-27

Author used mostly 8/4 stock for the couch because it was readily available. Drawing below gives general dimensions and an idea of how it was put together. Owners use a foam-rubber mattress for sleeping rather than the cushions shown.

first fastened with screws to allow for adjusting the fit, and later marked and glued. These slats can be left a little short of the edge of the front rail and a facing strip attached later to cover the end grain and the gap left by the rabbets.

Because the large number of pieces compounds any tendency to bind, about 1/4-inch of play per slat was initially allowed, and the rough spots later cleaned up. I briefly considered tongue and groove slats for the sliding mechanism. They are probably esthetically superior, but less likely to

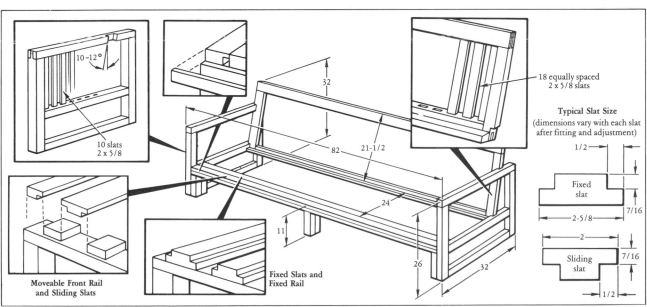

10-12°

10 slats
2 x 5/8

Moveable Front Rail
and Sliding Slats

Fixed Slats and
Fixed Rail

32

82   21-1/2

24

11

26   32

18 equally spaced
2 x 5/8 slats

Typical Slat Size
(dimensions vary with each slat
after fitting and adjustment)

1/2

Fixed
slat

2-5/8   7/16

2

Sliding
slat   7/16

1/2

maintain a flat surface for the seat, difficult to fit and nearly impossible to keep working smoothly.

The Settle. Dimensions are determined from the size of the mattress and the room into which the piece has to fit. The mattress should be measured for length, width, thickness, and the amount of compression that results when one sits on the edge. After some allowance has been made for bedding, these measurements are used to lay out the box that holds the mattress. The sides of the box are cut from 6/4 stock and dovetailed together. Dovetails are somewhat awkward to cut on long pieces, but, if done accurately, they prevent winding and make assembly much easier.

To support the mattress, strips about 1-1/4 x 1 inch were glued to the inside of the box on all four sides. A center strip, with 1/2-inch rabbets on each side and 1/2-inch thicker than the side strips are wide (so the top of the strip will be flush with the plywood bottom set into the rabbets), was set into dadoes cut into the strips around the inside edge. The strips supporting the plywood bottom should all stop about an inch short of the bottom of the box in the same plane so a support for the center arm can be added later and so the foot can support the entire bottom of the bed, not just the two sides.

Because they form the back of the settle when the bed is raised, the two pieces of plywood are placed good face down in the box. They should be selected for color and figure match with the wood in the settle and the plywood for the back of the carcase. One-half inch plywood is probably the thinnest one can use for the bottom. Three-quarter inch would be more secure, but it makes the bed rather heavy to raise and lower, particularly if the mattress is anything other than a light foam rubber.

Once the box is complete, the layout for the rest of the piece can be drawn up. The width of the bed plus an inch or so clearance becomes the inside dimension of the carcase.

General dimensions and some details of settle are shown in drawing opposite. Those wishing to make their own should first design

Both the height and the depth of the carcase are determined by the location of the pivot point. Perhaps the easiest method for working out this detail is to make a cardboard cutout the same size and shape as the side of the bed with the mattress in place and to use a pin as an easily movable pivot. Assuming one centers the pivot in the side of the bed, trial and error shows that as the pivot moves toward the foot of the bed, the carcase becomes deeper and shorter, and that, if the bottom of the bed rests on the seat, the distance the center of the pivot is above the seat has to equal the distance the pivot is behind the seat. The seating height, plus one-half the width of the bed side, plus the distance from the pivot point center to the top corner of the bed or the top corner of the mattress, whichever is greater, becomes the minimum inside height of the carcase. The seating depth, plus one-half the width of the bed side plus the distance from the pivot center to the top corner of the head of the bed or the top corner of the mattress becomes the minimum inside depth of the carcase interior. The overall dimension of the carcase should be checked against the dimensions of the room into which the settle is to go to make sure it will fit through the doorway and can be tipped upright once inside.

When the layout has been drawn up from these dimensions, the carcase sides are glued up from 4/4 stock, the profile cut, and the top and sides dovetailed. Again, the dovetails are hard to cut, but well worth the trouble saved during assembly. The seat, which gets put together at this time, is simply a box with a hinged lid. The front and back of the box are set into slots cut in the carcase sides and reinforced with glue blocks and screws, and the bottom is set into rabbets cut in the front and back of the box and is supported on each end by cleats attached to the carcase with screws in slotted holes. The front of the box should be set back about 1/2- to 3/4-inch from the front edge of the carcase to

around the mattress they get and the room it will be in. In photos, removable legs can barely be seen stored under the closed settle.

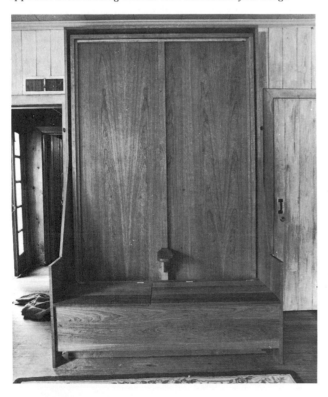

allow for overhang of the hinged seat lid. Attached to the top of the back piece of the box is a piece of 8/4 stock with a rabbet the thickness of the seat lid cut in the top front. This piece will support the seat when the hinges begin to sag, which they will inevitably do.

After the carcase has been assembled and the seat fixed in place, rabbets can be cut to receive the carcase back. In this case, three pieces of 1/2-inch plywood were used, each being separated by a strip similar to the one used down the center of the bottom of the bed. Three pieces help break up the space and also yield better cuts from 4 x 8 sheets. The dividing strips are fastened into the rabbet at the top of the carcase and into a rabbet cut in a cross piece installed near the bottom of the back of the carcase.

Once the carcase has been squared up with the back, it should be carefully leveled in every direction, using shims, clamps, props, or whatever is necessary, because pieces this size tend to shift alignment whenever they are moved or rest on an uneven surface, even though every effort is made to avoid winding and lopsidedness during assembly. After leveling, the seat lid can be mounted on the hinges. Remember to keep them far enough away from the sides of the carcase to avoid being hit by the descending bed. The seat is cut into two pieces three or four inches off center so that the box can be gotten into without removing the center arm rest.

While the carcase is still level and the seat lids are in place, the bed can be tried in the open position to check for alignment of the pivot points. If these have been carefully laid out on both the carcase and the bed, 1/16-inch holes drilled through the carcase and partway into the bed should line up when a piece of stiff wire is stuck through the carcase hole. With the bed resting squarely on the seat, there shouldn't be much trouble in readjusting the pivot point one way or another to allow the bed to close squarely. Once the alignment is as close as possible, holes about 2 inches in diameter can be drilled straight through the carcase and through the sides of the bed. Pins about 8 inches long were turned with a slight taper so they could be driven tightly into the inside of the bed frame and still turn freely in the same sized hole in the carcase. The pivot pins can be fastened with wedges or some other device, but whatever is used should permit easy

disassembly since the carcase is heavy to move around even without the bed. With the bed raised and clamped in the closed position, two more holes drilled through the carcase and partway into the bed frame about five feet above the floor and fitted with turned pins will hold the bed in place when it is not being used.

The center arm rest is mounted onto the center strip of the bottom of the bed. A slot dovetail was cut into a piece of stock the same width as the center strip and the same thickness as the distance between the strip and the bottom of the bed frame (it rests on the seat and helps support the bottom of the bed). A corresponding pin on the edge of a board supporting the arm fits into the dovetail slot snugly and permits the arm to rest squarely on the slotted piece and tightly against the center strip. The pinned piece can be removed easily to let the bed come down.

The legs to support the foot of the bed are joined together with a crosspiece using open mortise and tenon joints. The leg assembly is a separate, detached piece, trimmed for a friction fit inside the bed frame against the strips holding the plywood bottom. The cross piece at the top supports the plywood bottom in the center where it is the weakest, and it does this especially well if the legs are positioned 12 to 16 inches from the end of the bed when it is let down. The legs are stored under the seat when not in use.

The seats in both the settle and the couch are completely horizontal rather than sloped slightly toward the back. In the couch, cushions help alleviate this comfort problem somewhat. But in the settle, the problem is compounded by the back not being slanted either. Cushions on the seat or on the back might help. The deeper than usual seat helps some as does the tendency to sit in the corners.

The variations possible with either of these designs are almost unlimited. With the couch, any sort of end piece and back design is possible, and the slats for the seat could be replaced with two pieces of plywood, or possibly three to make the seat slide out to full double-bed size. With the settle, changes in the profile of the sides, edge treatment, facing strips and so on can change its appearance considerably. One could even eliminate the carcase and mount the bed in a hole cut in a wall. □

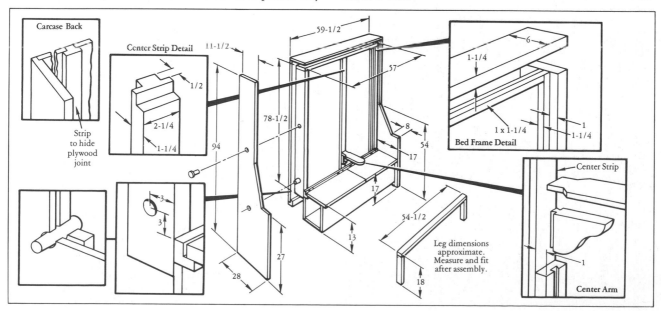

Chippendale Sofa
Templates for the basic frame,
and some design options

by Norman L. Vandal

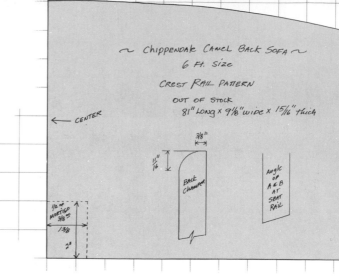

Any professional woodworker has to keep an eye on the market. Over the years I've earned a living making things that simply weren't available anywhere else, everything from period architectural components to period planes for restorers who wanted to stick their own moldings.

Many of my furniture customers come to me because of the double jeopardy of buying antiques: originals are not only very high in price, they may also be in very poor condition. In January 1983, for instance, a Philadelphia camelback sofa sold at Christie's, New York, for the record price of $264,000, even though it had some serious problems—amputated leg bottoms had been pieced in, the rear legs had been cut off and refastened, and the stretchers had been replaced. Keeping all this in mind, I thought it a good idea to add a camelback sofa to my designs.

I wanted to stay faithful to the lines and solid joinery of the originals, so I studied Chippendale sofas in museums and period-furniture books. Surprisingly, my best source turned out to be copies of *The Magazine Antiques.* Dealers like to sell furniture stripped of its upholstery to ensure buyers that it's original, and many of the ads showed the entire frame and the joinery. I saw that period cabinetmakers varied the shape of the legs, front seat rail and crest rail without changing the shape of the basic frame much. I figured that I could do the same for my customers, and build a good frame to sell for a little over a thousand dollars, which compares favorably in price with factory "reproductions," and, in my opinion, greatly surpasses them in quality.

Templates and variations—Joinery details are shown on the facing page. Sofas are not as difficult to make as they may look. Unlike upholstered chair seats, which are always trapezoidal, sofa seats are rectangular. Thus a measured drawing of the frame's end view shows many parts in true dimension. With these parts as a starting point, I worked out a reliable set of templates, shown throughout this article, for the angled parts. The templates take care of the tricky problems, ensuring that everything will go together and stand square.

When building a sofa, you first make the end frames, which include the legs, end rails and side stretchers. Then you connect these with the seat rails, center and frame stretchers, and back frame, and finally you add the arms. In period sofas, there are variations in the arm roll and its supports, and I selected the system I felt worked best. The templates given here are for a New England style sofa with Marlborough legs, which can be blocked or left plain. Straight-leg sofas were the most numerous, exemplifying the Chinese influence in the Chippendale style. Yet the molded leg and the cabriole leg shown on p. 47 work just as well. For the Philadelphia look, as shown at left, the variations are simple: Marlborough legs, peaks on each side of the crest, and a serpentine front seat rail. You'll also find templates for the crest rail, vertical arm supports, and upholsterers' bar (the upright member underneath the arm at the back—it gives the upholsterer a surface around which to pull and tack the material).

Scale up the templates to full size, either by following the grid lines or by photo-enlarging them. I made the templates from heavy cardboard so I could cut them out and trace the parts directly from them. As you can see in the drawings, on my templates I've carefully laid out mortise and tenon dimensions and other useful information.

You don't need templates for the front and rear seat rails—just mark them out

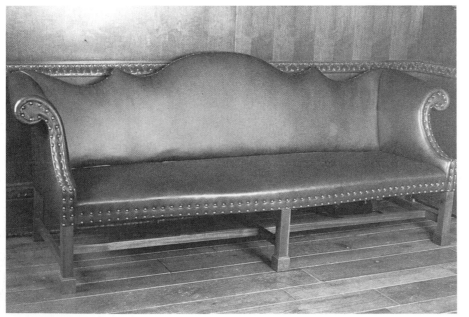

Adapting the basic templates yields this Philadelphia-style sofa with serpentine front.

From *Fine Woodworking* magazine (November 1984) 49:60-65

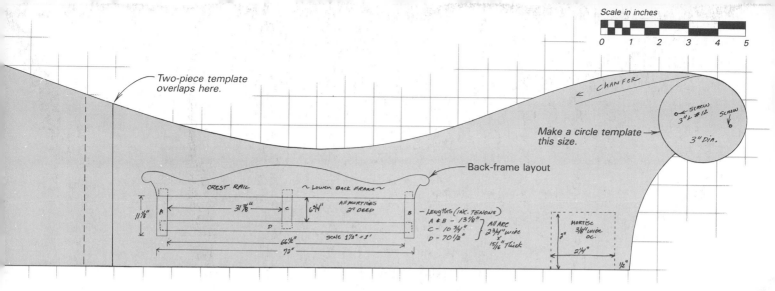

Two-piece template overlaps here.

CHAMFER

Make a circle template this size.

3" DIA.

SCREW 3"L #12

SCREW

Back-frame layout

CREST RAIL

LOWER BACK FRAME

11⅛"

A

31⅞"

C

6¾"

D

ALL MORTISES 2" DEEP

B

— Lengths (inc. tenons)
A & B – 13⅛"
C – 10¾"
D – 70½"

All ARC 2¾" wide × 15/16" Thick

66½"

72"

SCALE 1½" = 1'

MORTISE 3/8" wide oc.

2"

2¼"

½"

directly on the stock. (If you plan a serpentine front seat rail, of course, you'll have to work out a full-scale top-view template for the curve.) The center legs, front and back, fall exactly in the middle of the rails. As shown in the photo on p. 45, the front seat rail is one piece; the rear seat rail is two pieces, each tenoned into the back center leg, which needs to be full length to support the center of the back. In addition to the low stretcher between the center legs, an upper stretcher prevents the frame itself from spreading. This frame stretcher (which will be hidden by the upholstery) is tenoned off-center into the seat rails, so as not to weaken the legs. Locate it toward the bottom of the rails, where it will not interfere with the setting of upholstery springs. Original sofas didn't have springs, just webbing, but your upholsterer may suggest that the modern method is better. For more on upholstery and whether to agree with your upholsterer or not, see p. 46.

The tenons on the side stretchers have only one shoulder, at the outside. I make the center stretcher the same way, and offset the mortises in the center legs so the stretcher will be centered.

Materials—Most of the frame will be hidden by upholstery, and period cabinetmakers knew this full well. Legs, which showed, were top-grade wood. Mahogany predominated in Philadelphia; cherry was peculiar to Connecticut. Walnut was used in high-style pieces from all areas, and you'll find that the finest sofas, with formal Marlborough legs or ball-and-claw feet, are always mahogany or walnut. But secondary woods are another matter. I've seen seat frames made of maple and oak, and even chestnut in some New England examples. The back frames are usually of a softer wood, sometimes pine, although yellow-poplar or basswood holds the

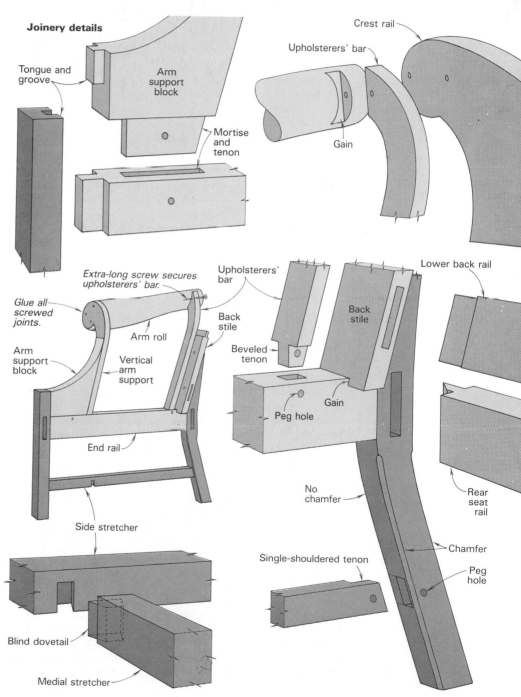

Joinery details

Tongue and groove

Arm support block

Mortise and tenon

Crest rail

Upholsterers' bar

Gain

Extra-long screw secures upholsterers' bar.

Glue all screwed joints.

Arm support block

Arm roll

Vertical arm support

End rail

Side stretcher

Blind dovetail

Medial stretcher

Upholsterers' bar

Back stile

Beveled tenon

Peg hole

Gain

Lower back rail

Back stile

No chamfer

Rear seat rail

Chamfer

Peg hole

Single-shouldered tenon

Drawing: Karen Pease

Chairs and Beds   **43**

tacking better. If you can find it, soft maple is an excellent wood for the frame. Whatever you use, test some scraps, and avoid any wood you can't easily drive a tack into, or one that won't hold it well.

Arm rolls are always a soft wood, and pine or poplar is suitable. The vertical arm supports should be hardwood, but avoid woods such as oak or ash because they may split when the upholstery is tacked on. Curly maple would be my first choice here (somebody once suggested plywood, but it doesn't hold upholstery tacks well).

Construction—Many of my construction notes are shown on the templates, but here are some additional hints.

The tablesaw jigs shown in the photos below will help when cutting the back legs to shape. They ensure that the legs will match each other exactly and that the straight sections will be true.

Begin construction with the end frames. Before test-assembling them, cut all the joints shown on the end-rail and leg tem-

plates, and shape the legs and side stretchers. Then permanently assemble the end frames. The arm rolls, their support blocks and the vertical uprights will all be added later. Secure the tenons with pegs.

Trial-assemble the end frames to the front and rear seat rails and the center parts. Do any fitting of the joints now, making sure that the tenon shoulders are square and the mortises true. This will ensure that the frame assembles squarely when you're gluing up. Muster all your speed and dexterity and glue up the frame. I don't install the medial stretcher yet, but measure it off the frame and slip it up into the other stretchers from below as one of the last steps in construction (it has dovetails at each

Stock sizes and joinery details are shown on most templates. Sizes for straight pieces are listed in table at lower left corner of page.

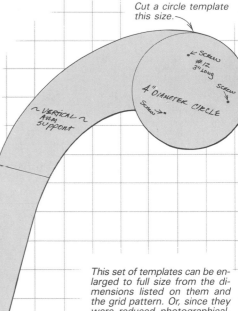

Cut a circle template this size.

This set of templates can be enlarged to full size from the dimensions listed on them and the grid pattern. Or, since they were reduced photographically, they can be enlarged the same way by a stat camera. Make them of heavy cardboard, add joinery details, and trace them directly on the stock.

Other dimensions:

Rear seat rails:
stock, 35⁷⁄₁₆ x 3 x 1¾; 33⅜, shoulder-to-shoulder; tenons, ⅞ long at center leg (butt), 1³⁄₁₆ long at end legs (mitered).

Front seat rail:
stock, 71⅛ x 3 x 1¾; 68½, shoulder-to-shoulder; tenons, 1³⁄₁₆ long (mitered); center-leg mortise, 1¾ long, ⅝ wide (through, centered).

Center and side stretchers:
stock, 24¹³⁄₁₆ x 1¼ x ¹⁵⁄₁₆; 22¹³⁄₁₆, from shoulder to long point of rear shoulder.

Medial stretcher:
stock, 72 x 1¼ x ¹⁵⁄₁₆; scribe to fit.

Frame stretcher:
stock, 24 x 1¾ x 1½; scribe to fit during trial assembly.

Leg template also shows top of leg and mortises.

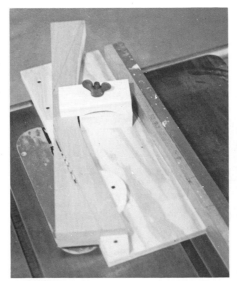
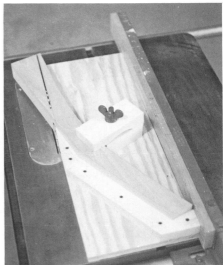

Tablesaw jigs position each rear leg exactly the same, ensuring that the frame will stand square.

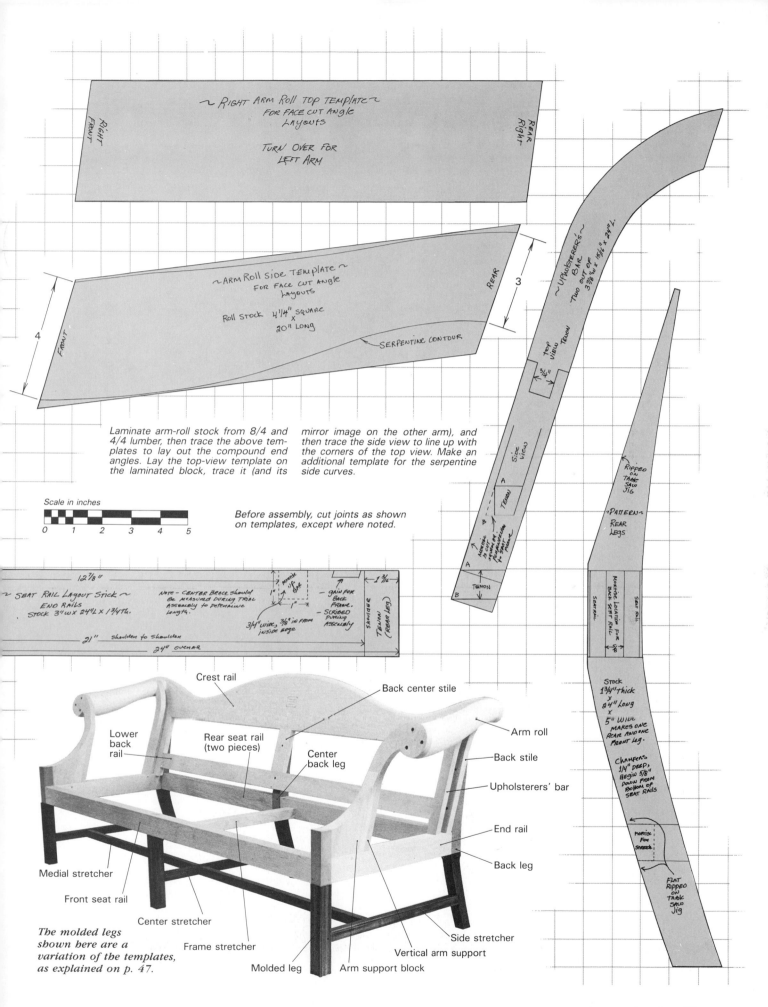

Right Arm Roll Top Template ~
FOR FACE CUT ANGLE
Layouts

TURN OVER FOR
LEFT ARM

RIGHT FRONT

REAR RIGHT

~ Arm Roll Side Template ~
FOR FACE CUT ANGLE
Layouts

Roll Stock 4¼" SQUARE
X
20" LONG

FRONT

REAR

SERPENTINE CONTOUR

~ UPHOLSTERERS BAR ~
Two out of 15/16" x 24" L.
3⅞"W x 15/16" x 24" L.

TOP VIEW TENON

¾"

Side View

TENON

MORTISE IS CUT SQUARE BY EXTRAPOLATION TO SURFACE

A
B

TENON

RIPPED ON TABLE SAW JIG

~ PATTERN ~
REAR LEGS

MORTISE LOCATION FOR BACK SEAT RAIL

SEAT RAIL

SEAT RAIL

Stock 1¾" thick x 8¼" Long x 5" WIDE MAKES ONE REAR AND ONE FRONT LEG

CHAMFERS ¼" DEEP, BEGIN 5/8" DOWN FROM BOTTOM OF SEAT RAILS

MORTISE FOR STRETCHER

FLAT RIPPED ON TABLE SAW JIG

Laminate arm-roll stock from 8/4 and 4/4 lumber, then trace the above templates to lay out the compound end angles. Lay the top-view template on the laminated block, trace it (and its mirror image on the other arm), and then trace the side view to line up with the corners of the top view. Make an additional template for the serpentine side curves.

Before assembly, cut joints as shown on templates, except where noted.

Scale in inches
0 1 2 3 4 5

~ SEAT RAIL LAYOUT STICK ~
END RAILS
STOCK 3"W x 24"L x 1¾"Th.

12⅞"

21" Shoulder to Shoulder
24" OVERALL

NOTE - CENTER BRACE SHOULD BE MEASURED DURING TRIAL ASSEMBLY TO DETERMINE Length.

¾" WIDE, 3/8" IN FROM INSIDE EDGE

MORTISE UP 1 BAR

GAIN FOR BACK FRAME

SCRIBED DURING ASSEMBLY

SHOULDER
TENON (REAR LEG)

Crest rail

Back center stile

Lower back rail

Rear seat rail (two pieces)

Center back leg

Arm roll

Back stile

Upholsterers' bar

End rail

Back leg

Medial stretcher

Front seat rail

Center stretcher

Frame stretcher

The molded legs shown here are a variation of the templates, as explained on p. 47.

Molded leg

Arm support block

Vertical arm support

Side stretcher

Chairs and Beds   45

end and a lap joint in the middle). Next make the back frame—the specifics are shown on the crest-rail template. I prefer a single board for the crest rail, as on the originals, but you could glue it up. Size the materials, cut the joints, test-assemble, then glue the frame together. Peg the joints and cut the crest profile with a saber saw.

Glue the back frame to the leg uprights, and, when dry, fasten it securely with #10 or #12 wood screws, driven through the softer wood into the hardwood legs. (Period cabinetmakers usually used clinched nails, and for this reason the legs on many of the original frames have split.)

With this much of the frame assembled, you can go on to the front arm supports, which consist of a curved vertical upright and a support block. I first cut the support block's straight edges, either with the tablesaw leg jig or with the saw's miter gauge. The block's joints into the leg post and the end rail are critical: a tongue-and-groove at the front leg allows you to slide the block down until its tenon fits in the end-rail mortise. If these joints are not precise, the arm will soon fail. I cut the tenon and the tongue on the table-saw with the rip fence as a guide, sawing them in length and thickness to fit. Then I bandsaw the block's top curve.

Bandsaw the curved uprights and bevel the bottom edges so they set flat on the end rails. Glue and screw the uprights to the blocks, then fasten the assembled units to the frame with glue and pegs.

For the arm rolls, I always use clear pine, laminated from two pieces of 8/4 stock and one piece of 4/4. Period cabinetmakers used solid pine blocks, but nowadays these are hard to get. The arms meet their supports at compound angles,

Getting a frame upholstered

by Bob McCarthy

First, the bad news: a good upholstery job can cost as much as $1500, and you may have trouble finding a shop that will do it right. Now the good news: if the job is done right—and I'll tell you how to be sure that it is—it will easily last 15 years.

The period sofa: Upholstery and woodworking have both changed a lot since 1780. A true reproduction sofa frame would not have screws, modern glues or upholsterers' bars. There wouldn't be a machine mark anywhere, nor any trace of sandpaper. And a period upholstery job would have no springs or cushion, and would be stuffed with Spanish moss or horsehair. To most people, such a sofa would be very uncomfortable.

Yet modern upholstery methods can re-create the period look—taut, crisp lines—and provide comfort at the same time. As you read on, keep the following basics in mind: A Chippendale camelback sofa should be padded very tightly and never overstuffed. The back should not be padded too thickly or it will push the occupant forward. The seat should slope slightly from front to rear to hold a cushion, if used, in place. Do not allow staples anywhere; someday your sofa will be reupholstered, and staples are difficult to remove without breaking them, which leaves razor-sharp studs sticking up.

Finding the right shop: Many shops specialize in reupholstering and are not qualified to tackle a bare frame, but any large city probably has a shop that can do your job right. Ask a nearby museum for recommendations, check with interior decorators, and keep looking.

Request a list of references from the shop, then take the time to go and look at some of their work. A good shop will co-operate with you in making your sofa what it should be—they will allow you to specify materials and methods, and will put the agreement in writing.

Springs: Springs weren't used in upholstery until the mid 19th century, but they lend support critical to appearance and comfort. Well-tied springs should last for years; webbing alone simply will not, which is why I recommend springs even though they aren't authentic. For the seat, I would insist on coil springs, hand-sewn to the webbing and hand-tied together. For the back, I'd ask for Marshall spring units (light, muslin-covered springs).

Padding: Instead of horsehair, cotton batting commonly is used today. Period materials are hard to acquire, will increase your costs, and won't show anyway. Make certain that muslin is used to hold all padding in place.

Seats: If you want a traditional fabric, you should specify a tight seat, which means one with no cushion. This will look best, and avoids the problem of a cushion that won't stay put, but of course it wears faster. If you want a contemporary fabric, then a single thin cushion wouldn't look bad. The cushion's box (the distance between the edge pipings) should be no more than 3 in. Cover the cushion on both sides so it can be flipped over. Zippers on the back prevent you from flipping it four ways, but are hard to talk upholsterers out of. Use down filling if you can afford it.

Fabric: A 6-ft. camelback sofa with a cushion requires 10 yards of 52-in. wide fabric. A material without a pattern can be "railroaded," that is, run horizontally, thus saving some material.

Documentation for period fabrics can be found in old advertisements and, sometimes, from remnants uncovered during reupholstery. Period fabrics are readily available, and I've listed a few of the best suppliers here. If you have a business letterhead, try to get wholesale prices. Still, be prepared to spend $20 to $50 a yard. It's poor economy to save on fabric or its support, as these are the most obvious features of a piece. Damasks were popular on period sofas (a damask is a woven-pattern material, usually with floral motifs, whose design is accentuated by alternating glossy and dull surfaces). Period damasks were wool or silk. Many fine reproduction damasks are available today, in wool, silk or synthetic blends. Another good fabric choice would be wool moreen, a heavy fabric of a solid color embellished with a subtle embossed design. If you're fortunate, you may even find a decorator with some leftover fabric (designers often buy excess material as insurance against running short of a particular dye lot). I've bought such bolt-ends for a quarter of their normal price.

Have the upholsterer pad the rolls slightly to accentuate crisp curves. Ideas for piping, decorative brass tacking and other traditional variations can be seen in antiques books and museums.

If all attempts at locating a qualified local upholsterer fail, do not despair. Learning upholstery is not all that difficult. There are many books on the subject in libraries and bookstores. Few tools are required—mostly patience.

Sources: For traditional fabrics, try Colonial Williamsburg, Box CH, Williamsburg, Va. 23187; Historic Charleston Reproductions, 105 Broad St., Charleston, S.C. 29401; Brunschwig & Fils, Inc., 410 East 62nd St., New York, N.Y. 10021; Cowtan & Tout (chintzes), D&D Building, 979 Third Ave., New York, N.Y. 10022; and Stroheim & Romann, 155 East 56th St., New York, N.Y. 10022. For contemporary fabrics, contact Gretchen Bellinger Inc., 330 East 59th St., New York, N.Y. 10022; and Hasi Hester, 138 South Robertson Blvd., Los Angeles, Calif. 90048. □

Bob McCarthy upholsters period pieces and teaches adult-education courses on the subject. He lives in Columbia, S.C.

both front and back. It's best to cut these angles before shaping the arms. Trace the angles from the side-view and top-view templates on the blanks, taking care that the left and right arms will be mirror images, then cut the angles. You could set up a bandsaw for these cuts, but I find a fine-toothed handsaw easier.

Test-fit the blanks, truing up their ends with a low-angle block plane if necessary. With the blanks in place, trace the circles of the crest rail and the arm supports on their ends as far as you can reach with a pencil. Then remove the blanks and use the two circle templates to complete the end shapes. Bandsaw as much waste as possible, then carve the rolls to shape. I use a drawknife, spokeshave, carving tools and planes.

Preparing for upholstery—On period frames, fabric was tacked directly on the part of the frame it was covering. Most modern upholsterers prefer to pull their material through narrow openings in the frame and tack it down on the back side. On our sofa, the lower back rail is higher than the seat rail, and provides such an opening there. The upholsterers' bar shown on p. 43 provides another opening at the junction of the sides and back frame. Although these bars aren't authentic, they add strength, and a frame with bars *is* easier to upholster.

The bar fits into a gain in the arm, also shown on p. 43. Fair the edges of the bar to the shape of the arm and ease them so as not to strain the fabric. Then relieve all the other sharp milled edges of the frame with a file so the fabric will lie over them smoothly.

The top edge of the crest rail should be rounded toward the front of the sofa. I scribe a line ¾ in. down the face, then round over the edge to this line with a drawknife and spokeshave. Don't bring the top back edge to a sharp point.

After finishing the legs, I seal the entire frame with a coating of two parts boiled linseed oil and one part turpentine. This helps keep dimensional stability, and it also improves the frame's appearance. One of my customers, upon receiving his completed frame, liked the look of it so much that he put off the upholstery job for six months. People like that make the extra touches worthwhile. □

Norm Vandal makes period furniture in the winter and period architectural components in the summer in Roxbury, Vt. Photos on pp. 44-45 by the author.

Variations on a theme

The Chippendale sofa frame I've designed is a foundation that can accept many stylistic variations. For instance, I made the classic Philadelphia-style sofa shown in the photo on p. 42 with Marlborough legs, a serpentine seat rail, and peaks on each side of the crest. The sofa frame shown in the photo on p. 45 is a simpler New England design with molded legs.

Some of these modifications can be accomplished with very few changes in the basic templates. A serpentine front rail, for example, requires a curved template and affects the length of the two stretchers in the center. That's all—everything else can remain the same. Some variations call for more work. If you'd like to change the slope and splay of the arm roll, obviously you'll have to change the template for the vertical arm support as well as the length of the arm-roll templates and their end angles. The arm support block would probably be affected as well.

In the leg designs shown below, I'm recommending that you choose 1⅞-in. stock for the front molded leg. This allows you to reduce the size of the leg post above the carving to 1¾ in., the same size as the post on the Marlborough leg. On my sofas, I do it a little differently, because I like to keep the front and back legs the same overall width. I start with 1¾-in. stock, reduce the post to 1⅝ in., then vary

the end-rail length, front-seat-rail shoulder distance and stretchers to accommodate the smaller post. If you'd like to try this yourself, you'll need to work out gains, chamfers and other minor changes at the front corners so the parts fit neatly. The arm-roll length also shortens by ⅛ in., but this takes care of itself during truing-up.

All the following variations are found on original period pieces.
Legs: Straight, square; straight, molded; tapered, square; blocked-foot Marlborough, plain or carved; ball-and-claw cabriole (no stretchers). Some pieces have eight legs, but six-legged sofas are more common.
Seat rails: Straight; serpentine curved; exposed and ornamented. A 6-ft. length is common; other lengths are options.
Crest rail: Single-hump; peaked to each side of hump; varied in curve.
Arm rolls: Straight, tapered, cylindrical; serpentine; varied in slope and/or flare.
Stretchers: Plain; beaded-edged; relief-carved or with open fretwork.

You'll note that I show no stretchers between the back legs, yet you might see them on many period sofas. Rear stretchers take great abuse from climbing children if the piece is placed near the center of the room. Also, they make it difficult to clean under the sofa. They're not needed structurally, and I prefer to leave them out, but the choice is up to you. —N.V.

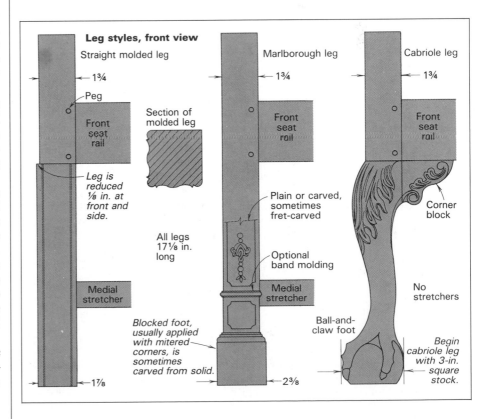

Leg styles, front view

Straight molded leg — 1¾ — Peg — Front seat rail — Leg is reduced ⅛ in. at front and side. — Section of molded leg — All legs 17⅛ in. long — Medial stretcher — 1⅞ — Blocked foot, usually applied with mitered corners, is sometimes carved from solid.

Marlborough leg — 1¾ — Front seat rail — Plain or carved, sometimes fret-carved — Optional band molding — Medial stretcher — 2⅜

Cabriole leg — 1¾ — Front seat rail — Corner block — No stretchers — Ball-and-claw foot — Begin cabriole leg with 3-in. square stock.

Two-Board Chairs
Plans and methods from a Swiss woodworker

by Drew Langsner

The craftsmen of southern Germany, Austria and Switzerland have long been known for their fine sense of design and their excellent craftsmanship. From woodcarving to the magnificent log-and-timber-frame farmhouses, examples of their skill can be found throughout the Alps. This is also the region of the famous fairy-tale chair with the cut-out scrollwork back, painted or chipcarved with hearts, flowers, initials and dates. The chair is called a *Bretstuhl* (board chair) in Germany, or a *Stabelle* in the Swiss-German dialect, Berne Deutch. In English it is sometimes known as a two-board chair or fiddleback. It ranks with the Windsor and the ladderback post-and-rung chair as a great example of folk furniture.

The construction is almost identical in chairs made throughout the region; individuality is emphasized in the contour and carving of the chair back. Most prominently defining a two-board chair is the beautifully simple manner in which the back and seat are joined—by two through mortise-and-tenon joints secured with tusk tenons under the seat. The backboard tenons pass through mortises not only in the seat board, but in battens in the seat bottom. These battens, which receive the leg tenons, are sliding dovetails, held in place by the backboard tenons. The battens are thicker than the seat board, but set back from the front of the seat to maintain

the overall appearance of lightness and simplicity. Their thickness allows the straight-tapered octagonal legs to be mounted free of stretchers.

These chairs can be knocked down for storage or shipping. The backboard comes loose by removing the two tusk tenons. The sliding-dovetail battens and legs can then be driven out of the tapered housings in the seat bottom, and the disassembled package measures 18 in. by 20 in. by 8 in.

My introduction to the two-board chair was in Switzerland, where I've twice had the pleasure of working with Rudolf Kohler, a cooper who also makes a fair number of these chairs each year. In the fall of 1980, Kohler and I took a break from coopering to build a chair together. Kohler gets the credit for the more difficult work, as he wanted to be certain that the *Stabelle* going to America would be a good one. The chair dimensions given in this article are in inches, and vary slightly from Kohler's metric measurements. Exact equivalents would be awkward, and they are not necessary. As chairmaker John Alexander says, "Chairmaking is an approximate craft." There can be considerable variation from one chair to another, even in a matching set.

Kohler's two-board chair is made from ten pieces of wood: The seat, the back, four legs, two sliding-dovetail battens and two tenon tusks. In the

Alps, two-board chairs are usually made from hard maple. Ash is sometimes used for the legs and sliding dovetails.

Kohler buys his chairwood in the form of plainsawn slabs from a local mill. He never buys edged boards, as every bit of wood is used. The slabs are stickered to air-dry in a drafty loft for at least two years. The wood we used had seasoned for eight years. Several weeks before starting a chair, Kohler moves his wood to the overhead racks in his shop. No moisture-content measurements are taken, but the shop is usually very dry. Most of Kohler's chair work is done during the long winter, when his shop woodstove burns every day. The warm shop acts as a kiln. Cold, dry air infil-

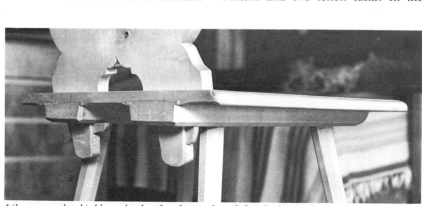

Like many other highly evolved crafts, the two-board chair looks simple, but demands considerable woodworking skill and attention to detail during construction. Its tusk-tenoned back and sliding-dovetail battens to receive the legs, above, make it a sturdy, yet light, knock-down design.

trates from outside. As the air warms inside the shop, it picks up moisture from the wood and then leaks out, letting in more cold, dry air. The relative humidity in the shop remains low.

Although the *Bretstuhl* design has been around for generations, the introduction of power tools has affected the actual construction methods. The most prominent machine in Kohler's tiny shop is a massive combination planer/jointer/shaper. Kohler also uses a bandsaw, a sabersaw and a router where a turning saw (a bowsaw with a narrow blade whose orientation can be varied) and planes were traditionally used. Leg tenons are turned on the lathe.

As is usual, the first step is milling the rough lumber. The planer is large enough to handle the 16¼-in. wide seat blanks and the backboards, both dressed to ⅞ in. The sliding-dovetail battens are planed to 1⅜ in. Kohler used to make these battens only ⅞ in. thick. In those older chairs the leg tenons were mortised through both the sliding-dovetail battens and the seat board. The tenon ends were then

wedged from above. Kohler says that the thicker battens, which house stopped mortises, allow the seat board to move freely with moisture variation. Also, the end grain of the tenons is encased, making them less responsive to changes in humidity. After dressing both faces of the sliding-dovetail stock, Kohler joints one side. Using a bandsaw he rips the second side so that the width tapers from 3⅜ in. to 2⅞ in., then joints this resawn side to a finished width tapering from 3¼ in. to 2¾ in.

Dressing the leg blanks begins with planing all four sides to a 1⅜-in. square. To make the taper Kohler runs the legs through his planer on a wooden tray with a tapered bottom board that inversely matches the taper of the leg. The final dimensions taper from 1¼ in. to 1 in. square. Kohler turns the leg tenons 1⁹⁄₁₆ in. long with a diameter of ¹⁵⁄₁₆ in. He chamfers the end and the tenon shoulder at 45° for ³⁄₁₆ in. To size the diameter Kohler uses a test hole bored in a ¾-in. hardwood board. He likes a very snug (but not extremely tight) fit so the tenon squeaks when it is

twisted in the hole. The legs are finished by hand-planing to an octagonal section, with proportions judged by eye.

Outlines for the bottom and backboards are transferred from cardboard patterns. Kohler has used the same patterns for over 30 years, with just one variation—the addition of three small curls to the C cutouts on the sides of the backboard. The outlines are traced with a pencil and sawn on the bandsaw. Small details of the back are shaped with an electric sabersaw. The scrollwork is dressed with flat and half-round rasps, then sanded smooth. The front edge of the upper section of the seat back is rounded, nowadays with a router, formerly by spokeshaving and sanding. The remaining scrollwork is dressed square to the faces. Edges are then softened about ¹⁄₃₂ in. with a piece of sandpaper. The tapered mortises through the seat-back tenons are made after the sliding-dovetail battens are fitted to the seat bottom.

The tapered housings for the sliding-dovetail battens are laid out parallel to the sides of the seat bottom after the

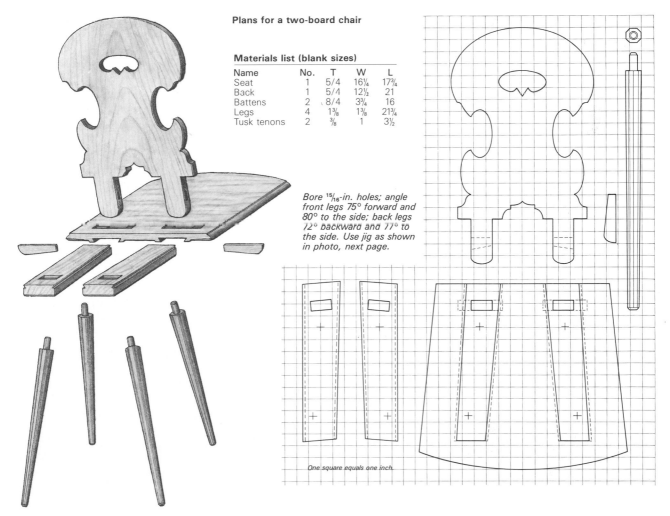

Plans for a two-board chair

Materials list (blank sizes)

Name	No.	T	W	L
Seat	1	5/4	16¼	17¾
Back	1	5/4	12½	21
Battens	2	8/4	3¾	16
Legs	4	1⅜	1⅜	21¾
Tusk tenons	2	⅜	1	3½

Bore ¹⁵⁄₁₆-in. holes; angle front legs 75° forward and 80° to the side; back legs 12° backward and 77° to the side. Use jig as shown in photo, next page.

One square equals one inch.

Kohler uses a wooden box with slots in boards across the top to jig his brace and bit to the proper angle for boring the leg mortises.

Design variations on the two-board chair include a slatted back, right, and battens running the width instead of the length of the seat, left. Note that the decorative cutout in the back serves also as a handhold. Photos: Armin Erb.

sides and back of the blank have been jointed, and the curved front dressed with a spokeshave. The outside edges of the housings should be 2½ in. from the sides. To excavate the housings, Kohler starts by chiseling out the last 2 in. before the front stop. He then uses a backsaw to cut the side kerfs at an 80° angle, 5/16 in. into the board, and cleans out the cavity using an electric router and a dovetail bit. The whole cavity could be excavated with the router and a fence, but instead Kohler uses his router freehand, and the saw kerfs are useful boundaries

The tapered sliding-dovetail battens are individually fitted to the finished housings. Kohler cuts the side angles using a router with a dovetail bit. A dovetail hand plane can also be used. The front of the dovetail tongue is cut back so that the end of the batten overlaps the chiseled stop in the housing. A simpler batten with beveled sides instead of a dovetail tongue is sometimes used on plainer chairs. This version doesn't require using a router or dovetail plane; the stock can be cut on a tilting-arbor saw or planed to shape.

Mortises through the seat board and battens are chiseled at an angle of 80°. They are cut a little wider than the tenons, to allow for expansion and contraction of the backboard, which runs cross grain to the seat board. In addition to

the through mortises, Kohler chisels a ⅛-in. deep housing for the shoulders of the backboard tenons. This conceals any gap between mortise and tenon. The backboard tenons are fitted, and the baselines for the tusk-tenon mortises are marked flush with the bottom face of the battens. The back is removed, and the tapered mortises are chiseled in the backboard tenons 1/16 in. inside the line scribed when the back was in place. Kohler makes these mortises ¼ in. wide, tapering from ⅞ in. to ⅝ in. The tenon tusks are 3½ in. long.

While the chair is apart (the sliding-dovetail battens are also removed), Kohler dresses the upper and lower edges of the seat board. He routs the upper edge with a beading bit. The lower edges of the front and sides are deeply chamfered with a plane, which adds to the visual lightness of the piece. The chamfers on the back of the seat are carefully shaped with a drawknife. All four lower edges of the sliding-dovetail battens are relieved by routing with the quarter-round bit.

Kohler bores the mortises for the leg tenons with the dovetail battens back in place. The front legs cant forward at 75° and to the sides 80°. The rear legs angle back 72° and to the sides 77°. For accuracy, Kohler uses a homemade boring jig (photo, above). The jig is a wooden box about 16 in. by 16 in. by 6 in. The

bottom of the box has a large trapezoidal opening that fits snugly over the mounted battens, and the top of the box has a central opening and four angled slots ⅝ in. in width. Kohler punches predetermined centers on the battens, the jig is fitted into place and correct angles are bored by holding the auger at the end of the slots. Kohler doesn't use a depth control, but he aims to stop just at the base of the battens.

Just before the final assembly, the separate chair parts are given a careful sanding. Fitting the legs is simply a matter of dabbing a little white glue on the tenons, then pounding the legs in place. After assembly, the legs are trimmed. On Kohler's standard chair the upper front edge of the seat is 18⅝ in. high. The seat angles downward slightly so that the upper rear edge is 18⅜ in. from the floor.

The next stage is decorating the back. Kohler is an excellent chipcarver, but that's a skill for someone else to write about. The *Stabelle* for America was finished, and we picked up where we'd left off with our coopering. □

Drew Langsner is director/instructor at Country Workshops. For details on this year's offerings of classes in woodworking, toolmaking, chairmaking, write him at Country Workshops, 90 Mill Creek Road, Marshall, NC 28753.

Three-Legged Stool with Back
Design around the construction

by Tage Frid

I hate three-legged chairs, especially those with a full seat and back, and one leg under the back. They always look ridiculous when viewed from behind and make dangerous contraptions to sit in. If the person seated in such a chair leans slightly sideways against the back, the chair will tip over. The person might get hurt, and you might get sued if you are the designer and maker of the chair.

Many students and designers mistakenly decide to make a three-legged chair just to be different. They must then construct around the design. This usually results in some awful kind of hodge-podge. There are well-designed chairs that are a result of their function or space allowance dictating three legs instead of four. For example in some valet chairs, the rear leg and back are designed primarily to support clothes hanging on top. The requirements of such chairs do not include the comforts of long-term sitting and leaning, as would a lounge or dining chair.

Three-legged chairs might also be made for a round dining table where the designer wants to fit as many seats as possible. The natural solution is to make the chairs pie-shaped, with the one leg in front. This is fine, because the person's two legs will help support the front, and the chair will be very stable.

There are sculptural three-legged chairs made of wood or metal that are so heavy it is impossible to tip them, but this of course doesn't mean they are well designed.

The designer of a seating unit should first decide precisely what function the chair or stool is to have. Then he should choose his construction technique and design around the construction. The result is usually a well-designed and functional seat. Of course the designer must have a feeling for form and dimension. The forms must be consistent so that the piece ties together and doesn't look like one base with a different top placed on it. I found proportion—the right relationship in thickness, width and sizes—the most difficult thing to learn. Most of my students have the same problem. A poorly proportioned chair can spoil an excellent design.

When I started designing my seat, I did not have in mind at all that I wanted to make a three-legged stool. But as the design progressed, I did not have any choice. I wanted a stool with a back, and a system where I could use the same seat in three different heights by changing the length of the legs. I wanted the stool to be comfortable, but of minimum size—as light but as strong as possible. The middle-size stool is more like a small chair, but I will refer to them all as stools in this article.

Here is how the whole thing started: My wife and I went to a horse show. We were sitting on a six-inch wide rail for several hours, yet we felt quite comfortable. Of course I am well upholstered, but my wife is just right. And she didn't complain either. All of a sudden I realized that when you sit on a straight wooden seat, you sit only on your two cheek bones. The rest of the seat is unnecessary. Of course, a full wooden seat allows a little freedom for moving around, unless it is carved to hold you in position.

I began experimenting to find the smallest comfortable seat I could get away with. I came up with a piece 6 in. wide and 16 in. long, with a 7/8-in. curve. This piece is very pleasant to sit on, and I could bandsaw it out of an 8/4 plank.

I wanted a back, but I wanted a minimum of wood for the seat, so I morticed and tenoned a small section to the back of the seat. This piece connects to the backrest with a through dovetail. (In production, finger joints could be used.) Now, because the piece behind the seat was small, there was only room for one leg in the back. This meant the backrest had to be narrow and low, which was fine as I only wanted to support the lower part of the spine.

The tee-shaped seat counteracts the tendency for the stool to tip over, because there is no seat area in the back to push against. The weight of the body locates on top of the two front legs. I ended up with a stable three-legged stool, with the third leg in the back. Of course, with a little extra effort this stool can be toppled more easily than a four-legged chair.

As mentioned, I wanted the chair to be comfortable and strong yet as light as possible. I needed width at the top of the backrest for support, but not at the bottom. So I removed the excess and curved the two outside lines, which resulted in a pleasant oval-type shape. At the same time, I needed the full wood thickness at the backrest bottom for a strong joint, but not at the top. I removed the excess, but in a straight line, because in the side view all tapers are straight lines. If a curved line had been used it would have looked bulky, since there was not much thickness to play with. I also replaced the corners of the seat with a rounded line which gave me more of an oval. I needed the thickness of the seat at the center for the mortise and tenon, but not at the ends, so I removed the excess there also, which added another curved line. Now from the front and top view everything was oval. I continued this form in the handle for moving the stool. I curved the ends of the seat and backrest, and eased the corners so that all the lines would flow together smoothly. I eased off the front edge of the seat for comfort, but gradually brought the line crisply around the top of the back. This type of detail gives a piece a little more of a handmade feeling. A hand router that removed the same radius all around would have given the piece a machine-made look.

The legs were turned on the lathe and angled out to give

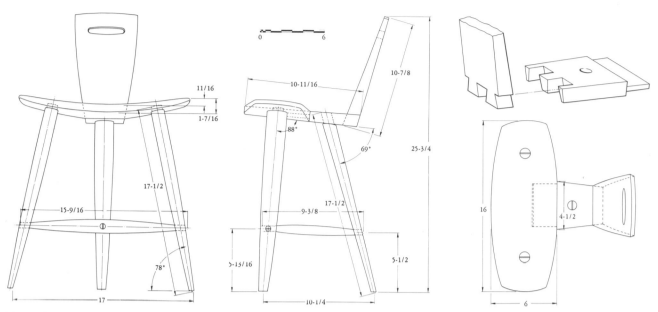

To avoid errors, Frid superimposes front, side and top elevations into one full-size drawing. In the shop, each view would be in a different color. Dimensions shown above are for middle-sized stool; detail at top right shows seat and back joinery.

the stool more stability. The ends were turned down to 3/4 in. and joined through to the top of the seat. (When wedging legs through a solid top, always place the wedge so it goes across the grain of the top to prevent splitting.) The stretcher was a simple tee, joined through the legs and wedged.

I made my prototype after making simple preliminary drawings. I always make a mock-up when I make a new chair or other seating unit to test the comfort and to see how the shapes relate in three dimensions. I assemble the prototype the easiest way possible, usually with nails. I make it out of the cheapest materials I can and don't bother to sand it.

In this case, I made my mock-up stool exactly like my preliminary drawings, and found it very comfortable, but it looked awful. I could not put my finger on what was wrong,

Seat heights shown here are about 12 in., 16 in. and 21 in.

so I set the stool aside in my shop in a place where I could not miss it when I came in. During the next few weeks several people came in and sat on it and found it very comfortable, but no one was crazy about its looks. One day I was sitting and staring at it, and I suddenly realized what was wrong. Everything on the stool was oval except for the legs and stretchers which were turned round. The piece looked like a base from one chair with a top from another. I cut off the legs and made the legs and stretchers oval, and then the stool looked like one unit. Testing the prototype a little further, I discovered that if I moved the backrest one inch back, I could sit on the stool just as comfortably backwards. I didn't start designing with the notion of making a three-legged stool, but the shape resulted naturally from the construction and from the requirements I originally assigned to the design.

Then I was ready to make the final working drawings for the stool. It is impossible to make a chair or stool without a full-scale working drawing from which to take all angles and measurements. The drawing must have a side, top and front view. (In some chairs, a back view is also necessary.) I always superimpose the three views, using a different color for each view. Having all three views on one drawing takes up less space in the shop. But more important is that by superimposing the three views, it is harder to make mistakes. If a small mistake is made in a dimension on one view, it will be transferred to the other two, and easily noticed. This ensures that the chair will go together. With three separate drawings it is much easier to make an error because dimensions have to be transferred from view to view by measuring. But when the three views are on the same drawing, all the lines can be projected from one view to another.

Three-view drawings might seem a little confusing at first, but after a short time you get used to reading them. It is possible to transfer the lines onto three separate drawings by projecting them, but this requires a big drawing table. I still prefer to make one drawing with all three views, and if later I want separate drawings I can trace them from the three-view drawing with less chance for error.   □

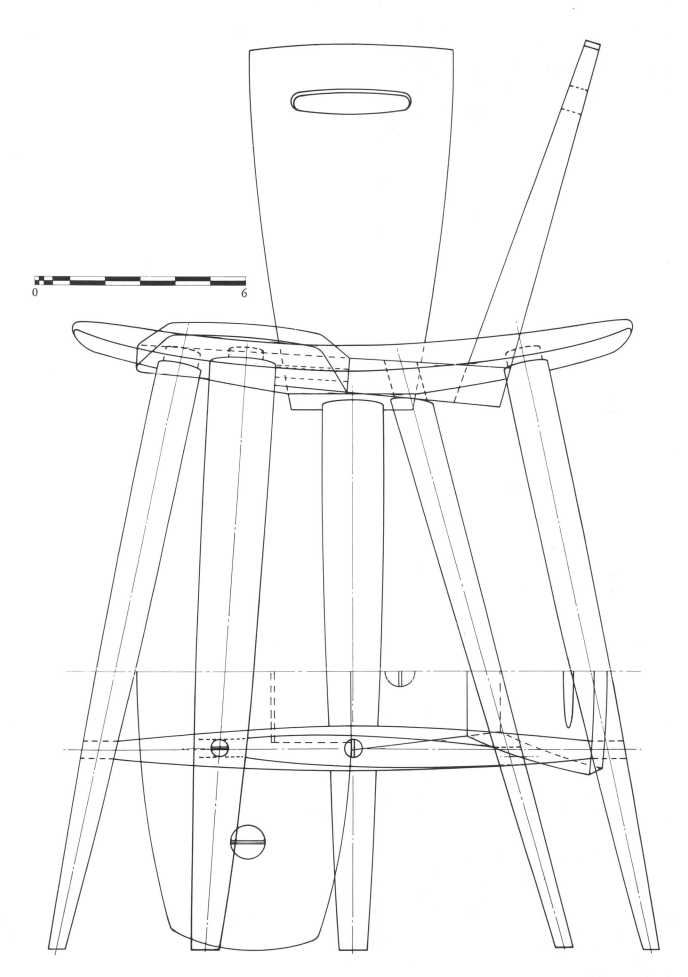

Stools: A slightly different angle

by Jim Cummins

Ron Curtis doesn't "relate" to his table-saw, a 16-in., 5-HP beauty, though he respects it. "You just can't slow it down," he says. He's an established woodworker in Bloomfield, Conn., with a one-man shop full of good equipment. Curtis has been building furniture and stools he describes as "free-form construction with sound joinery" since 1968, and these days he's able to make his living from his work.

But he's not a tablesaw type of woodworker, the kind he defines as thinking square and parallel all the time. Not that he doesn't build square himself, when that's his intention, but he usually feels a little looser than that. He'll use any jig that makes his work easier or better, but he'll eyeball everything he can.

Mostly with power sanding equipment, Curtis shapes the top of his stool seats freely. But he leaves at least the middle of the bottom flat, so it will bear against his leg-angle jig: a tapered piece of wood about 8 in. long made from a 2x4 that he clamps to the drill-press ta-ble. He drills clear through from the top at locations he works out with a compass—he'll wedge the tenons later. The jig for the stool in the photos is 17°, but he uses 15° as well.

Curtis takes leg blanks that he has pre-cut with a taper jig on the tablesaw, and makes the tenons with an adjustable hollow auger that he bought at a garage sale. With the three legs stuck in the seat, he stands the stool up on an assembly table and proceeds to his other jig: a plain board with drilled holes for the feet of the stool. With all three legs locked into the seat at the top, and two legs fixed at the bottom by the jig, he measures the height for the first rung, then eyeballs the direction for the holes.

With a Stanley ½-in. Powerbore bit, shortened so the electric drill can fit between the legs, Curtis drills from the outside until he feels the point of the bit coming through. Then he drills back through the hole from the other side, so as not to tear out chunks at the exit hole. He drills the second leg like the first. If the holes do not line up perfect-ly, he says it just puts a little tension on the rung and helps tie the stool together.

For stretchers, he makes up octagons (he likes the way they catch the light in the finished stool), gauges them by eye for length against the legs while they are still in the foot jig, and then uses the hollow auger to make long tenons. He bandsaws the rung to a taper that will meet the tenon smoothly, then removes the marks with a drum sander.

Curtis is quick to give Wharton Esherick credit for the inspiration behind his type of stool, and Sam Maloof credit for the finish: beeswax and oil over a sealer that's part polyurethane. But when it comes right down to it, Curtis's eye makes each stool. □

Instead of tilting the table, Curtis uses this angled block. He sets the seat blank on it when he drills the holes for the legs.

Ron Curtis eyeballs a mortise as his foot jig steadies the work, left. The stool has an elm top and legs, and is about to be fitted with ash rungs. Curtis prefers native woods and will go out of his way to get them, but admits, 'I usually cut up some South American stuff for the wedges.'

The stools sold for $195 (1982) at Pritam and Eames in East Hampton, N.Y.

From *Fine Woodworking* magazine (September 1982) 36:67

Pat Pollard

The Three-Legged Stool
Furniture turned on the lathe

by David W. Scott

The three-legged stool is the essence of casual furniture, good for a brief perch in the kitchen or shop or for a longer sit when the body is leaning forward and partly supported by a desk or counter. For a turner, the stool may serve as an introduction to joinery and a chance to go beyond the usual turned work.

The idea of individual turnings coming together to form a finished piece of furniture is fascinating. Building furniture and doing production lathe work in a small shop, I have long been intrigued with the structure of the three-legged stool—the variations on its simple theme seem endless. Free-form slab seats in the style of Wharton Esherick, with no two seats alike; seats that are turned and then carved; other rung configurations and legs at other angles; even different angles in the same stool—all open up new design possibilities.

I make stools between 25 in. and 28 in. high, a good size for general use. A 25-in. stool with legs angled at 78° has feet about 17 in. apart—graceful and stable in appearance and in use. I determine the placement of the rungs according to appearance, intended use of the stool, and the user's leg length. If the rungs are too low, the stool looks clumsy; if too high, it begins to look storky. Two-rung stools, like one of those in the photo at right, have the rungs' mortises all at the same height from the floor. Three-rung stools have rungs staggered in height 1 in. to 1¾ in. so as not to weaken the legs. In order to be able to choose the rung heights and lengths for each stool individually, I turn the seat first and then the legs. The legs join the underside of the seat in 1-in. diameter holes about 4 in. to 5 in. from the seat center. I mark and drill the holes in the legs for the rungs, test-assemble the legs and seat without glue, and measure the lengths of the rungs. Then I turn and finish the rungs, take care of details and glue the pieces together.

Making the seat—Usually, I turn the seat from 6/4 or 8/4 stock, 12 in. to 14 in. in diameter, mounted inboard on a Glaser center-screw chuck (an innovation of engineer Jerry Glaser) on the lathe. I bought the chuck, which lets me mount and unmount the seat blank quickly and precisely, from Turnmaster Corp., 11665 Coley River Circle, Fountain Valley, Calif. 92708. My preference is seats made all from one board, but seats glued up to get that width look fine too. First I drill the hole for the center screw on the seat-blank underside, then, using a protractor, I mark three lines radiating out from the center at 120° intervals. Then I bandsaw the rough shape, mount the blank on the lathe, and pencilmark a circle that sets the distance the legs will be from the center. This ensures that the legs will center up with the finished seat. The holes for the legs must be drilled before the seat is turned, because the top's final shape may not lie flat on the drill-press table without wobbling. I tilt the table to 78°, and drill 1-in. dia. holes in the bottom of the seat

Two graceful and perky stools: turned furniture.

blank, making sure that the holes angle out from the center. Multi-spur bits make clean holes. You can make holes only 1 in. deep or so, if you don't want the legs to come up through the top of the seat.

Legs—I turn legs from 8/4 stock. With my production stools, particularly those I make in sets, I use a router and a homemade duplicator, a long, open-ended box that fits over the lathe, similar to many homemade dowel-making jigs. The router rides on the flat top of the box, and a ½-in. dia., 2½-in. long, double-fluted straight carbide bit makes a shearing cut on the side of the spindle as it turns. The router collar rides against a template of ⅛-in. hardboard cut to the final leg shape, and mounted just above the stock. I rip the leg blanks octagonal on the tablesaw before turning, to minimize stress on the router and bit, and I take a number of end-to-end passes to work down to template size, working from the tailstock to the headstock on each pass. The final pass leaves a rough surface, which I clean up later with a gouge or skew, when I turn the details of the feet and the top tenons.

Rungs—Because most stools have rungs at different heights from the floor, the rungs will vary in length. I turn rungs from 4/4 stock. Conventionally, rungs taper to ½ in. or ⅝ in. at the ends, and this diameter enters a mortise in the leg. This is the weakest link in the stool's structure, however, since the rung is vulnerable to the concentrated weight of a careless

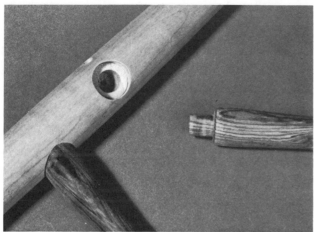

To strengthen the stool's weakest joints, Scott turns shouldered, round tenons that will be pinned in the legs.

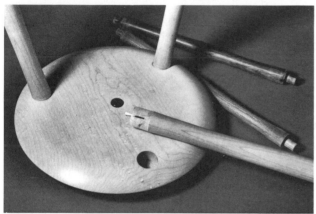

This fox-tailed wedge will lock the leg to the stool. The rosewood plug in the center of the seat fills the single hole left by the chuck's center screw.

When easing a stool together dry, Scott makes sure the joints all draw up at the same time, or the last pieces will be difficult to get into place.

person. To beef up this area without removing too much material from the leg, I turn each rung with a double-diameter end—in effect, a shouldered, round tenon. The larger diameter, ⅞ in., penetrates only ¼ in. into the leg, while the ½-in. tenon goes a full 1 in. deep. Size the rung ends carefully and check them in a sample hole; they should fit snugly.

Assembly—The legs are now ready to be drilled for the rungs. The placement of these holes will determine the height of the rungs from the floor, the angle of the rungs to the legs (the same as the angle of the leg hole in the seat), and the relationship between adjacent rungs, which should be 60°.

Adjust the drill-press table to the same angle used for boring the leg holes in the underside of the seat. Then clamp a long V-block to the drill-press table. Fix an adjustable stop-block at the lower end, at the distance one of the rungs should be from the foot of the leg. With the stop thus set for the proper hole height, drill one shouldered, round mortise in two of the legs for the lowest rung. You need to drill two holes in the same place, the larger, shallower one first and then the smaller, deeper one. Dry-assemble these two legs and one rung (the longest) with the seat to ensure that the angles are going in the right directions. Now move the stop block 1 in. farther from the drill bit to set the height of the next rung, and drill a hole in the remaining leg. Leave this stop block in place on the drill press. The next steps will determine the proper relationship of the remaining three holes to these first ones.

Dry-assemble the legs and seat with the lowest rung in its holes in the back legs. Placing your forehead against the front leg opposite the hole you have drilled in it, sight with one eye to either side of the leg directly across to the leg adjacent. This will locate the center point of that leg for the fourth hole to be drilled. This point could also be located by using a piece of dowel with a pencil lead in one end, but the eye produces an accurate result. After marking the point, drill it using the same setup as for the third hole.

Finally, drill the holes for the third rung, using the same procedures as before, with the stop blocks moved to allow for the new distance from the floor.

Dry-assemble the entire stool to get the feel of how it must go together during glue-up—you must ease all the joints together simultaneously, or you won't be able to get the last pieces into place. You will have to flex the rungs into place in any case—and a rubber mallet will help drive them home—but be sensitive to their breaking points. While the stool is still dry-assembled, wax around all the joints to protect the wood against glue squeeze-out.

The wedges that hold the legs in the seat should be perpendicular to the grain line of the seat. For further security, the rungs should be wedged too, or else cross-pinned. If you use wedges in the ends of the rungs, orient them perpendicular to the leg grain. I cross-pin the rungs into the legs using a small finishing nail set in a shallow ¼-in. dia. counterbore. I then cut ¼-in. decorative plugs with a plug cutter, turn their ends while I hold them in a drill chuck on the lathe, and leave them proud to cover the pins. To cover the screw-chuck hole in the seat bottom, I turn a rosewood plug.   □

David Scott is a full-time woodworker. He and his wife, Kathy, are also caretakers of the Museum of North Carolina Handicrafts, in Waynesville. Photos by the author.

Q & A

Knocking epoxied chair apart

I am repairing a turn-of-the-century maple rocking chair that was broken apart in a drunken brawl a few years ago, then reglued with epoxy glue. My problem is knocking the chair apart to repair and reglue. Knowing the low shock resistance of epoxy, I tried sharp blows with a rubber mallet. I tried using a small drill bit in a Dremel drill motor. Laying in to the side of the spindles as flat as possible, I drilled holes all around—no good.
—David J. Wood, Sterling, Colo.

Your approach is right, but you cannot deal a "sharp blow" with a rubber mallet. Go for broke. Use a steel hammer.
—George Frank

EDITOR'S NOTE: See page 29 for another suggested procedure.

Removing nails

When I reglue wooden chairs, sometimes the spindles and legs are locked into place with nails. I can usually cut around the heads and pull them out, but sometimes the nails are driven too deep or the wood is too hard and the nails break off at the top when I pull them.
—Maurice H. Revkin, Cranston, R.I.

If you can't pull the nail out, try driving it through with a small drift punch. If that is not possible, then drill a small hole alongside the nail about the same diameter. This will relieve the pressure on it and often make it possible to pull. If necessary, drill a hole on each side—but as close to the nail as you can get.
—Simon Watts

Dissassembling glue joints

I repair old furniture, and would like some tips on breaking glue joints.   —Henry J. Retzer, Beltsville, Md.

Heat, moisture or both will release most wood-glue joints. White glue seams often release simply with warm water. A common trick is to inject warm water directly into the seam with a hypodermic needle. A tiny hole can be drilled to allow access to hidden mortises or dovetails. It helps to wrap the seam with a damp cloth for several hours.

Heat will quicken the softening of most glues (except plastic resin glue). Sunlamps, heat lamps, hair dryers, even ordinary light bulbs work well. A household iron can be used to heat a wider area, but use a towel or some other means of protecting the wood to prevent damage to the finish.

You can also use steam, which has the advantage of carrying heat and moisture simultaneously. You can make a makeshift steam pot from an old coffeepot or teakettle, but the ideal setup is a cappuccino pot, available in gourmet or department stores. Most generate a relatively dry, high-pressure steam, and have a cutoff valve and a self-tripping safety release valve. Attach a length of reinforced heat-resistant hose to the output valve with a hose clamp and put a basketball needle valve or a hypodermic needle on the other end, to reach the bottom of deep glue joints. A slight jolt with a mallet to break the seam, followed by a gentle rocking motion during steaming, should release almost any seam quickly and easily. Scribe seams that have been lacquered or polyurethaned so that you don't fracture the finish. These methods should work for all water-soluble glues.

Try solvents for waterproof glues: acetone for cyanoacrylate; acetone or methyl-ethyl ketone for model cement; naphtha or rubber-cement thinner for contact cement; tetramethylguanidine for epoxy (heat aids release).   —Dick Boak

We've found that vibration is the only way to separate parts joined with plastic resin glues. Place one of the parts to be separated in a vise and strike the other a sharp hammer blow.

Protect the part with a soft block of wood before striking it. It usually takes two people to do this job, one to hold the parts and one to jar the joint. Reverse clamps are handy in getting joints apart—they produce a steady, controllable push that makes damage less likely.   —Allen Cochran

Repairing split chair seats

I have two plank-bottom rocking chairs whose seats have split. One was repaired with crosspieces housed in routed slots. These failed. Would applying a strip of thin plywood about 4 in. wide to the bottom of the chair create problems or would I be better off with a solid-wood strip?
—Daniel R. Williams, Maryland Heights, Mo.

I have a plank-bottom chair that failed in exactly the same way. I closed the gap with a clamp and then screwed two pieces of oak about ⅝ in. thick, 1¾ in. wide and 6 in. long at right angles to the split and about 10 in. apart. If neatly done, such repairs become part of the story of that chair.

Attaching a piece of thin plywood would certainly hold the two halves together, but the seat would probably flex when you sat on it. I would find this annoying.   —Simon Watts

Broken rocker legs

All four legs on my antique rocker have broken, been glued, and broken again. The grain runs across the legs at a 45° angle, and the breaks occur where the rung holes are drilled. I softened the old glue with white vinegar and removed it by wire-brushing and scraping down to the wood. Is further cleaning necessary? I plan to inlay splines across the breaks and shape them to match the leg. Will aliphatic glue work?   —John Ramsay, Pollock Pines, Calif.

It sounds like you've cleaned the joints sufficiently. I would use very fresh aliphatic glue. Good alignment is more important than glue-joint strength since the problem is in the construction: the grain runout in the legs. If you use epoxy, the wood may break somewhere else.

To align the parts for glue-up, use firm gluing blocks (I like ½-in. Baltic birch) on all four sides of the leg, and clamp lightly in each direction. Use plastic, waxed paper or silicone release paper under each block. I prefer silicone release paper (from Conservation Materials Ltd., Box 2884, Sparks, Nev. 89431) because it seems to allow moisture vapor through, so the glue dries more quickly. Apply light pressure to align the joint; then, using another clamp from end to end of the leg, bring the joint tight. Let the leg dry for at least 24 hours.

On each side of the leg, inlay a spline of matching wood, about ⅓ the diameter of the leg in both width and thickness,

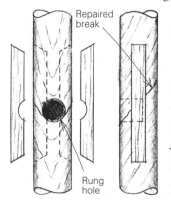

Repaired break

Rung hole

and 2 in. to 3 in. long, depending on the length of the split, with grain running parallel to the length of the leg. Either pre-cut the splines for the rung hole or re-drill the hole after the splines are in place. Lay out the mortises and carefully chisel out by hand. Unless you have a *flawless* jigging system, avoid the router. Don't glue the splines in while the rung is in place, or you may lock the rung in the leg, causing problems with wood movement and future repairs.

Leave the splines slightly proud and shave them down without disturbing the surrounding surface. Then stain and finish the splines to match the adjacent area.   —Dale Boyce

Two methods for making leather seats: In the Chariot chair, left, the leather sling (seat and backrest) is laced to the ash frame. In the elm chair, right, the seat is a cushion of leather resting on mortised slats.

Leather Seats for Wooden Chairs
Straightforward combination enhances both materials

by Stefan During

In nature, the place where two elements meet is always interesting and dynamic—if you have ever turned over a stone, you will have witnessed this. Likewise, in the world of artifact, the combination of two materials is special. In the best case, the result can be synergistic: more than the sum of the parts. Take an ax head and handle. Apart they don't look like much. Put them together (with a wooden wedge and all that) and there is meaning, beauty even.

To successfully combine two materials, you need a good understanding of both. As a woodworker this means you have to get out of your wood for a while and into the secondary material. By reading about it and trying things with it, you discover the stuff, and you become better able to combine it harmoniously with wood.

I prefer natural materials to complement my wood. In chairmaking I use leather, rope, webbing and rushes. I like a visible and uncomplicated construction that shows the way things are attached, and makes the attachment an attractive design element.

I use vegetable-tanned, as opposed to chromium-tanned, leather of some 3mm (⅛-in.) thickness. Yellow when new, it turns a rich chestnut brown in a matter of months. According to the choice of my customer, I can combine it with a light-colored wood such as ash or sycamore for maximum contrast, or with a medium-dark wood such as elm or oak for a more subtle combination. I have two types of leather-to-wood attachment. The first is what I call thong-lacing, the second is the cushion-on-slats method.

Thong-lacing—In this method, a leather slab spans a wooden frame by means of a stout leather thong. The thong passes alternately through holes in the wood and in the leather slab, like stitching. On the outside of the frame, I use a gouge to cut a shallow groove between alternate pairs of holes, so that the stitching is let into the wood surface (figure 1).

The leather slab consists of two layers of leather, sometimes with a layer of nylon fabric sandwiched between. The upper layer should be without blemish; the lower one, which is out of sight, can have some flaws. The upper layer should be cut about 15cm (6 in.) wider than the lower one, so that it can be folded around it at both sides, leaving a casing (a tunnel-like opening) running the length of the slab. Into this casing I insert a willow stick or a length of rattan. The stick distributes the tension of the thong along the entire length of the slab, and pulls the slab evenly.

To sew the leather, first fashion a piece of hardwood to the shape of a worn screwdriver, flattening and rounding the tip. Pressing firmly with this wooden marker on the good side of the upper piece, draw the lines along which you will sew. Next, bevel the leather edges that will be exposed (I use a spokeshave). Now tack the sandwich together with small nails along the lines you have drawn, backing each nail with a piece of wood at intervals of about 10cm (4 in.). This way, the whole construction is secured.

Now sew both seams, either by hand or by machine. I use thick linen thread and an old hand-operated cobblers' machine that goes through leather like butter. The machine is so

Photos: Henk van der Leeden; drawing: Lee Hov

small that it fits on a shelf when not in use, a definite advantage in my workshop. Also, it is simple and sturdy. Nothing is more frustrating than laboring over an expensive piece of leather with a machine that loops and skips for unknown reasons. Sew away, taking out the nails as you reach them. The lower layer of leather will sometimes "skate" out in spite of the nails. If this starts to happen, skip this part of the seam, to be filled in later. The more closely the nails are spaced, the less chance there is of this happening.

When the slab is sewn, punch holes in the overlapping border about 3cm (1 in.) from the sides for the thong to pass through. With a knife, cut these holes into slots, open at the sides of the slab, so that later the thong won't protrude above the surface of the slab.

For finishing the leather, I use acid-free petroleum jelly (Vaseline), worked in with the hands, especially at the edges and the stitching. Now slip in the sticks. These should be bendable if they are to follow a curved frame member, so soak them overnight or steam them if they are dry. Easiest is using them right off the tree.

The slab can now be mounted in the frame. For the slung seat of the Chariot chair (facing page), I fasten the top and bottom edges first. The top is held in a rabbet in the chair back by a thin lath and screws. The bottom is fastened similarly, but without the rabbet.

This leaves the thongs. From a piece of firm leather, preferably thicker than the leather of the slab, cut a disc about 30cm (12 in.) in diameter. By means of a fixed, vertical knife blade and a spacer block, you can cut a nice, even thong by "unrolling" the disc (figure 2). Position the spacer block to cut a thong slightly wider than the holes in the chair frame—I use 7mm (¼-in.) holes. Next, soak the thong in water for a few minutes. In a piece of scrap wood, drill a hole the same size as in the frame, and pull the wet thong through. This will round the corners of the thong, and stretch the fibers, so that less retensioning will be needed later on. I start lacing by tying a knot on the leather slab, and finish by wedging the end of the thong in a hole drilled obliquely in the underside of the frame. If after some time the thong stretches, remove the wedges and repull it tight.

The leather-and-wood structure thus made is nice to look at and very strong, and provides a comfortable seat. But it does not by itself give positive support to the lower back. In the Chariot chair this problem is solved by a small leather cushion laced with thong to the top of the slab. It is a simple envelope of leather filled with raw wool. By varying the amount of filling, I can accommodate differently built people. I leave the filling easily reachable, for later adjustments.

Cushion-on-slats—In the other kind of leather-and-wood chair I make (facing page), the seat, and sometimes the back, consists of two to four slats which hold a leather cushion. The slats support the body firmly, the cushion supports softly. Softness is more important in the seat than in the back, which I usually leave uncovered, or cover with a thinner cushion. Benches can be made in the same manner, although for larger cushions it is necessary to incorporate an inner, quilted cushion, to keep the stuffing from shifting.

In the rails that receive the slats, rout slots 2cm (¾ in.) deep and somewhat narrower than the thickness of the slats. Slat thickness is best when the slats will give a little under the weight of a body—I make mine 1.5cm (⁹⁄₁₆ in.) thick. The

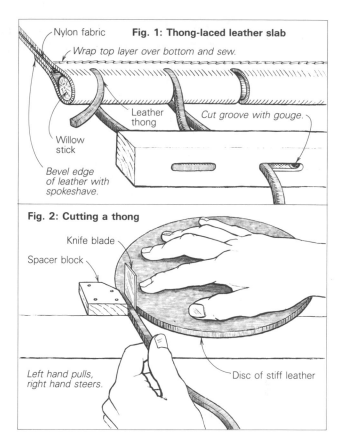

Nylon fabric | **Fig. 1: Thong-laced leather slab**
Wrap top layer over bottom and sew.
Leather thong
Willow stick
Cut groove with gouge.
Bevel edge of leather with spokeshave.

Fig. 2: Cutting a thong
Knife blade
Spacer block
Left hand pulls, right hand steers.
Disc of stiff leather

edges of the slats are rounded with a plane or a router, and the ends are beveled on the underside until they enter their slots snugly. Make sure that the wood of the slats is at least as dry as the rails are. Alternatively, you can cut proper tenons on the slats. This takes more time, but if you want the slats to go right through the rail and protrude a little on the outside, tenon shoulders are necessary.

Cushions consist of a piece of leather folded at the front and sewn along the sides and back. For filling, again I use raw wool. As my wife is a great spinner, I use the pieces that are less suitable for spinning. The lanolin in the wool oils the leather while the chair is sat in. Avoid including very lumpy pieces of wool; these should be carded first. Overfill the cushion, for the wool does compress. Of course, another kind of filling material will do the job too, but the idea of a quality material used even where you can't see it appeals to my customers, as it does to me.

Cut the leather, draw in the stitching line with the wooden "pencil" and nail together, as explained earlier. Then start sewing. When you've sewn all but the last 20cm (8 in.), without taking the leather from the sewing machine, work in the filling, stuffing the corners extra well. Then finish sewing. Leave a long end of thread at the beginning and end, and finish up with a few double stitches by hand.

Bevel the edges and work in the petroleum jelly. Now you have a cushion that can be used on both sides. For fastening it, I punch a hole near each corner, and through these I tie the cushion to the chair rails with thin leather thongs. This is all, and a very simple and straightforward combination it is. The more I use this method, the better I like it. □

Stefan During is a furnituremaker in Texel, Holland.

Modular Chairs Around a Standard Seat

With comfort settled, visual and structural design can blossom

by Kenneth Smythe

M ost chairs seem to be designed from scratch—within certain dimensions dictated by the human form, the designer refigures the basics for a comfortable sit with each chair he creates.

After about a dozen attempts, I have developed a standard seat and backrest system that is consistently comfortable while still affording me great flexibility in designing the rest of the chair. For all my chairs, the size and relationship of the seat and backrest are the same, so that when I begin a new design, I can concentrate on the visual and structural

aspects of supporting and presenting this seating.

My designs are based on a large vocabulary of modular shapes, and are supported by a goodly number of non-traditional connectors and locking devices appropriate to my material. I work with Finnish or Baltic birch plywood, but any sheet material of comparable strength would do.

My design philosophy is based on a concept that I call "integrated fragmentation," which I find provides both variety in design and economy in the use of material. The most important fragment I have designed is a multiple-hole

Plywood can be made into sturdy rails by cutting and drilling the sheets to form multiple-hole donuts, then stacking the donuts on steel rods. At each end, a disc with an embedded T-nut tightens the assembly.

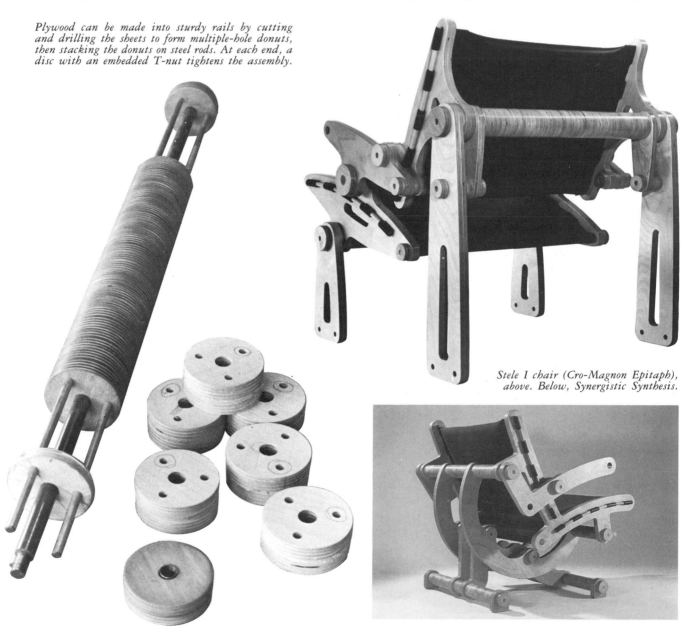

Stele I chair (Cro-Magnon Epitaph), above. Below, Synergistic Synthesis.

donut (drawing, facing page), which can be cut and drilled from almost any small scrap. This element, stacked on steel rods and sandwiched between end discs embedded with T-nuts, turns sheet stock into linear structural members.

The first step in making one of my designs is to draw the main components on Masonite, then cut the shapes out to serve as templates. I trace the templates onto plywood, rough out the parts with a saber saw, and trim them with a router and flush trimmer bit, guided by the template.

I drill the holes to receive the central $\frac{3}{8}$-in. rod, threaded at both ends, for each connection, and insert the rods to mock up the plywood parts. The parts that are connected at only one point can pivot, so I determine their angular relation to one another and drill the holes for the $\frac{1}{4}$-in. rods, three of them for each donut stack; these will reinforce the stack and fix the parts from rotating. I now cut and drill the donuts themselves, using a hole saw and the drill press with an indexing jig. For tightening the donut stack, I laminate a steel T-nut into each end disc.

Before assembly I sand all the wooden parts to 320-grit,

rinse them in mineral spirits, then apply a heavy coat of varnish, which I wipe off after 15 minutes. Two or three days later, I sand the pieces with 600-grit paper and polish them with carnauba wax. The chair frame can now be assembled.

I job out the seat and backrest to a local upholsterer, but these components don't require inordinate skill with needle and thread. Each is a canvas sandwich, 24 in. wide (the standard inside width of all my chairs), filled with a 2-in. pad of high-resiliency foam. Loops of leather along the edges of the sandwich fit through slots in the chair frame and are secured with $\frac{1}{2}$-in. maple dowels. I bend the dowels by soaking them overnight in water and drying them bent on a simple form I made.

I've designed more than a hundred chairs using this basic approach, and I title each design—my metaphoric expression. I see the chairs as a series of functional sculptures, with comfort as a given. ☐

Kenneth Smythe designs and builds furniture in Berkeley, Calif. Photos and drawings by the author.

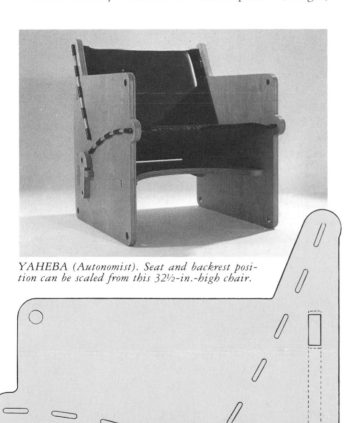

YAHEBA (Autonomist). Seat and backrest position can be scaled from this 32½-in.-high chair.

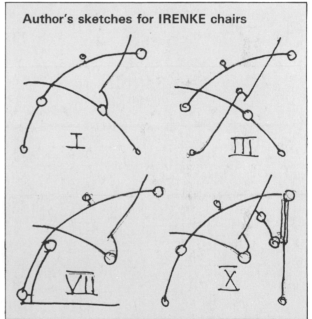

Author's sketches for IRENKE chairs

I III VII X

IRENKE, Variation I, began with the sketches shown above.

Wedges forced into kerfs bend a flat blank into a seat that is pleasing in both comfort and looks. This Windbow rocking-chair seat was formed by bending the seat halves individually, then joining the shaped pieces.

Kerf-Bent Seats

A tablesawn alternative to scooping

by Jeremy Singley

From *Fine Woodworking* magazine (January 1985) 50:30-35

Progress is often a matter of new inventions finding previously unimagined uses. When some unknown genius (from Windsor?) started building chairs with that new-fangled machine—the first practical lathe—the result was a happy event for every generation since. Although his fellow craftsmen may have branded him a heretic, it's certain that he wasn't a purist. I find that comforting, because it leads me to believe that he wouldn't have minded my using even newer inventions to improve his designs. In fact, if he had had a tablesaw and modern glues, I suspect he would have come up with innovations as interesting as my method for shaping hardwood seats.

I stumbled on the idea of bending seats by driving wedges into sawkerfs about six years ago when I found that a conventionally scooped seat felt better if its rear ridge was eliminated, so that the seat curved east to west but not north to south. This reduced the curve to two series of straight, parallel lines, and kerfing seemed an obvious possibility.

Obvious, but not easy. In the weeks of experimenting that followed, I grew wiser about wood, the laws of nature, and man's ability to endure disappointment. The first thing I learned was why woodworkers avoid wedge-bending. When you kerf wood across its grain, you cut away its strength, and it usually breaks. When you kerf wood along its grain, you exacerbate its weakness, and it usually splits. I finally resolved the dilemma when I found that wedges glued into kerfs cut at a slight bias to the grain strengthen the wood, not weaken it. The resulting bend, wider at the seat's front than at its back, turned out to be perfect for comfort.

After a lot of fooling around, I settled on a kerf angle of 77°, with the cuts spaced on 1-in. centers as shown in figure 1A. I found that eight kerfs, four in each direction, create a scoop deep enough to please both the bottom and the eye. I also discovered that I could make a center ridge by kerfing two half-blanks (figure 1B) and then joining the halves together.

Eventually these revelations evolved into a production system that's well suited to the small shop. The required jigs and fixtures can be made in a day or two, and no exotic tools or machines are needed. The single-blank method, because it is simple and cheap, became my preference for dining chairs. The double-blank method, whose effect is sinfully elegant, though costly, found its way into my top-of-the-line Windbow rocker, shown on the facing page. This rocker style, which sells for about $2,000, uses 18 wedges. If you use more than 12 on a single-bent seat, though, the scoop will be too deep to be comfortable.

I begin with the same edge-glued seat blank you'd normally hack at to carve out a conventional Windsor seat. I use 1⅜-in. stock for most of my single-bent dining chairs and 1½-in. for my double-bent Windbow rocker. All woods seem to wedge-bend equally well. Uniformly dense woods like maple and rosewood, which are too hard to be compressed slightly, don't make good wedges, however. I usually make the seat and the wedges from the same wood, but for maple seats I use oak or ash wedges.

When I'm making seats, I edge-glue two sets of blanks and have them surfaced to the same thickness at a local mill shop. One set is for the seats; the second, glued up from the wood with the straightest grain, is for wedge stock. I glue the wedge stock into blanks about 21 in. long and at least 14 in. wide to minimize waste—it's risky to run narrow wedge stock through the tablesaw, so the outside inch or so of every board gets thrown away. I make the seat blanks wide enough to fit the pattern for the particular chair I intend to build.

I work on the seat blanks as soon as I get them back from the

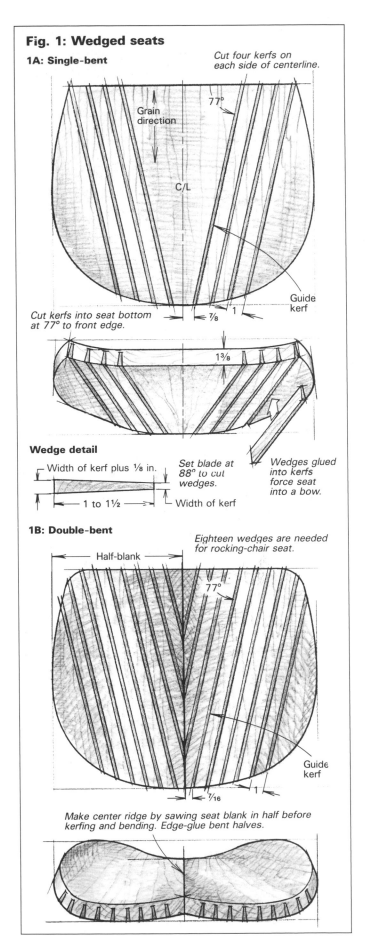

Fig. 1: Wedged seats

1A: Single-bent

Cut four kerfs on each side of centerline.

Grain direction

77°

C/L

Cut kerfs into seat bottom at 77° to front edge.

⅞ 1

1⅜

Guide kerf

Wedge detail

Width of kerf plus ⅛ in.

1 to 1½

Width of kerf

Set blade at 88° to cut wedges.

Wedges glued into kerfs force seat into a bow.

1B: Double-bent

Eighteen wedges are needed for rocking-chair seat.

Half-blank

77°

Guide kerf

⁷⁄₁₆ 1

Make center ridge by sawing seat blank in half before kerfing and bending. Edge-glue bent halves.

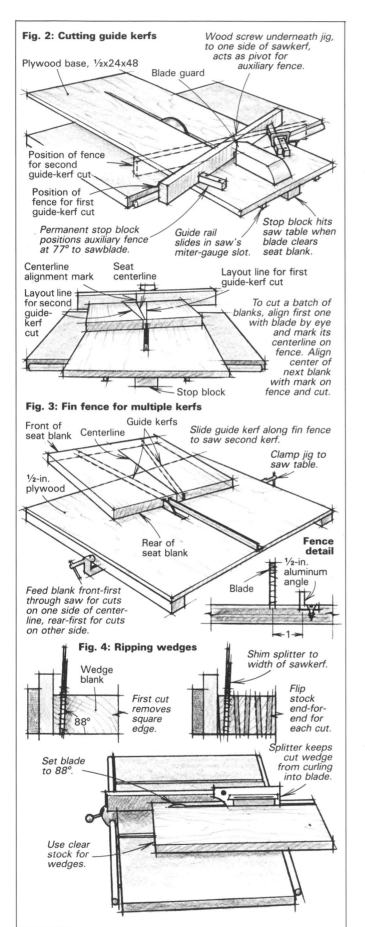

Fig. 2: Cutting guide kerfs

Plywood base, ½x24x48

Blade guard

Wood screw underneath jig, to one side of sawkerf, acts as pivot for auxiliary fence.

Position of fence for second guide-kerf cut

Position of fence for first guide-kerf cut

Permanent stop block positions auxiliary fence at 77° to sawblade.

Guide rail slides in saw's miter-gauge slot.

Stop block hits saw table when blade clears seat blank.

Centerline alignment mark

Seat centerline

Layout line for first guide-kerf cut

Layout line for second guide-kerf cut

To cut a batch of blanks, align first one with blade by eye and mark its centerline on fence. Align center of next blank with mark on fence and cut.

Stop block

Fig. 3: Fin fence for multiple kerfs

Front of seat blank

Centerline

Guide kerfs

Slide guide kerf along fin fence to saw second kerf.

Clamp jig to saw table.

½-in. plywood

Rear of seat blank

Feed blank front-first through saw for cuts on one side of center-line, rear-first for cuts on other side.

Fence detail

½-in. aluminum angle

Blade

1

Fig. 4: Ripping wedges

Wedge blank

88°

First cut removes square edge.

Shim splitter to width of sawkerf.

Flip stock end-for-end for each cut.

Splitter keeps cut wedge from curling into blade.

Set blade to 88°.

Use clear stock for wedges.

mill shop, before they can warp. The edges of these glued-up blanks are usually rough and irregular, so I first cut their fronts square and straight: I place my paper pattern on each seat blank, mark the center of the front edge, and use the front of the pattern as a straightedge to draw a line on the blank. I extend this line across the full width of the blank, bandsaw just shy of the line freehand, then nibble to it with a jointer. To prevent the jointer from sniping off the trailing end of the blank, I chamfer that corner slightly before running the blank over the jointer.

For a single-bent seat, I place a framing square perpendicular to the front of the blank and draw a line down the blank from the center point I previously marked. Then I align the centerline of the seat pattern and the blank's centerline, and transfer the position marks for the guide kerfs. I don't worry about the seat outline just yet—it will be traced onto the blank after bending. For most designs, the position marks should be ⅞ in. on either side of the centerline at the back of the seat. Using a homemade bevel gauge set at 77°, I lay out the two guide kerfs (figure 1), and to make it easier to see the lines when setting up the saw, I extend these lines down the back edge of the blank. I mount the blank on the carriage shown in figure 2 and rotate the blank until the sawblade is centered on the guide-kerf line. Then I push the carriage and blank through the saw, which I set to cut to within ⁵⁄₃₂ in. of the blank's top surface. To obtain a good gluing surface, I use a sharp carbide blade with at least 40 teeth for cutting both the kerfs and the wedges.

After I've cut the first guide kerf on one side, left or right, of all the blanks, I switch the carriage fence over to the opposite angle and repeat the procedure. Then I change to the fin fence shown in figure 3. The guide kerf drops over the fin fence—a piece of aluminum angle stock let into a plywood saw base—and guides the blank while the next kerf is cut an inch from the previous one, then that kerf lines up the next, and so on. The trick is to always bear to the left side of the fence, keep the blank firmly aligned, and push it through at a slow, even rate. The blank is fed tail-first into the blade to cut the kerfs on one side of the centerline, and front-first to cut those on the other side. This step usually isn't any trouble, but I have been known to lose count and cut one too many kerfs. It's also important to handle the blanks carefully—they're stiff enough to require gentle persuasion when the wedges are inserted, but if you snap them, they may break. Once all the blanks are kerfed, I usually cut the bottom front chamfers on a tablesaw or a bandsaw, using a fine-cut blade to keep from tearing out the walls of the kerfs. I don't cut the back seat chamfers until later.

Because setting up to cut wedges is so tedious, I always cut plenty of extras once I have the saw adjusted. The wedges won't be accurate unless the blanks are dead flat, so I hand-plane off any irregularities left by the surfacer. Before trying to cut the wedges, I shim the tablesaw's splitter, which on my Rockwell is part of the blade guard, with veneer and paper until it is exactly the width of a sawkerf (figure 4). I also replace the saw's metal throatplate with a plywood one that fits tightly against the blade, to eliminate the danger of the wedge hanging up on the throatplate slot. For ease of adjustment, I then crank the blade to maximum height and set the splitter behind and parallel to it.

I tilt the blade to 88°, lower it so it just protrudes from the wedge stock, and adjust the fence by trial and error. I initially set the fence so that the wedge point will equal the width of the sawkerf in the seat. I joint one edge of the blank and saw the first wedge, which, being tapered on only one side, is dis-

When inserting wedges, it helps to have an assistant (above). One person holds the blank with the glued kerf over the edge of the bench and pushes down on the overhanging section to fold the kerf open. The helper inserts the glue-covered wedge and forces its ends down while the first person forces the middle section down. The blank is then upended in a vise (right) and C-clamped just enough to squeeze out excess glue and to seat the wedges. When all the wedges are secure, the blank is placed on the floor and bar-clamped across its width (see next page).

carded. Then I flip the stock end-for-end and feed it far enough to cut a trial kerf about ⅛ in. long. I measure the width of this wedge tip with calipers and fine-tune the fence accordingly.

The setup tolerance for cutting workable wedges is a hundredth of an inch, more or less. Back in the old days, when I owned a used Sears saw that in a former life must have been a corn chopper, I achieved this accuracy by attrition: every third wedge or so went into the recycling box. My Rockwell does much better, but even so I'm never short of paint-stirring sticks.

Feeding the wedge stock past the blade is, unfortunately, not a science or even an art—the subtleties that can't be taught come with practice, however. So with a level head and a winning outlook, ease the stock forward at a steady rate, applying firm pressure downward and light pressure into the saw's fence. About halfway through I transfer to very light but steady pressure toward the splitter, which acts as a fence as the end of the blank approaches the sawteeth. As the blade completes the cut, I finish up with a clean follow-through to prevent the back sawteeth from scarring the blank, and lift the wedge clear of the blade with a push stick in the same motion. Do it right, and the wedge will be as smooth as a seamless stocking. Do it wrong, and you've won another paint stirrer for your collection.

Before going any further, I make sure that the wedge fits the kerfed seat blank. Gently folding the blank open over the edge of the workbench with the fingertips of one hand, I ease the wedge into the open kerf with my other hand. Once I'm assured that everything fits, I continue cutting wedges, flipping the stock end-for-end between each pass. After about ten passes, sometimes the sawn edge of the stock no longer rests against the fence without rocking, so I joint it again. I also discard any wedges that end up with glue joints down their spines.

The actual bending operation is the fun part—unless something goes wrong. Then it's a nightmare, but if you have your clamps and materials ready before you begin, your bending par-

ties should be pleasant. The wedging process is the same for both single- and double-bent seats, but the methods of clamping—as I'll explain—differ slightly. I begin by laying the blank kerf-side-up on the bench, then inserting glue-covered wedges. Yellow glue is best for wedging, and to get it on the kerf walls, I squeeze it in the kerf from the glue bottle and spread it with a flat stick, getting both sides good and gushy.

While I'm painting up the first kerf, my assistant, Jane Miller, spreads glue down both sides of a wedge with a 3-in. paint roller. Then I position the blank so that the glued kerf is directly over the edge of the workbench. Holding the center of the blank down against the bench with the fingertips of my right hand, I grasp the overhanging portion with my left hand and gently fold the blank open. Jane then inserts the wedge and pushes the ends of the piece home with her thumbs, grasping the underside of the blank with her fingertips for leverage. At the same moment, I force down the middle part of the wedge with my thumbs. As the wedge settles in, the seat makes a quiet cracking sound to tell us everything is all right. If everything isn't right (sometimes an improperly cut wedge turns up in the pile), we throw the wedge away and try another. Don't risk disaster by hammering the wedge in.

When all the wedges are in, I upend the blank in a vise and clamp the wedges home at one end of the seat while Jane does the same at the other end, using 4-in. C-clamps set in as far as their throats will allow. We snug up the clamps just enough to squeeze out the excess glue and to seat the wedges. Excess pressure may crack the seat. (If it does, a little back-and-forth action on the clamp screw will work glue into the crack, so it will be glued shut when the clamp is backed off and the pressure released slightly.)

With the C-clamps in place, I lay the single-bent blank bottom-up on the floor and apply the clamp dogs that I developed to counter the bar clamps' tendency to open rather than close the kerfs (figure 5). The dogs put the clamping pressure high enough over the seat bend to close the kerfs. In areas where the bend will be great, I sometimes have to notch the waste slightly so the dogs will fit. Once the bar clamps are tight, I remove the C-clamps.

When the glue is dry and the bar clamps are removed, I mount the blank bottom-up between the dogs on my bench. I hog off the projecting wedges with a large fishtail gouge, followed by a short plane with its iron ground slightly convex. The last 1/32 in. or so of wedges, along with the glue beads, is removed with a smooth plane. I also plane any flat areas on the seat bottom, then belt-sand with 120-grit. After sanding the bottom, I flip the seat over and spokeshave away the flats that appear between the bends on the blank's top surface. To smooth contours, I tape a foam-rubber cushion, covered with a paper pad, on the platen of a belt sander and "bag sand" the surfaces to a sweet curve with 120-grit.

Once the top and bottom of the bent blank are cleaned up, I trace the seat-pattern outline onto the blank and cut it out on a bandsaw fitted with a plywood table extension. The curved blank is unstable on the bandsaw table, so to steady it I usually wedge my fist between the edge of the seat bottom and the table, in front of or behind (and well away from) the blade. Otherwise the drag of the blade would slam the seat down onto

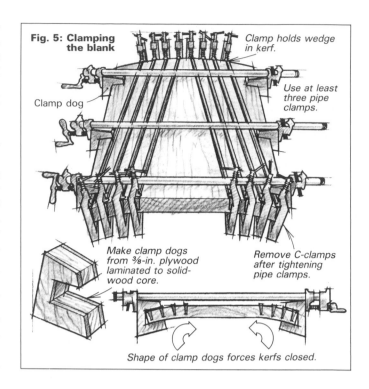

Fig. 5: Clamping the blank

Clamp holds wedge in kerf.

Clamp dog

Use at least three pipe clamps.

Make clamp dogs from 3/8-in. plywood laminated to solid-wood core.

Remove C-clamps after tightening pipe clamps.

Shape of clamp dogs forces kerfs closed.

With a large gouge, Singley chops off projecting wedges (left) before hand-planing the seat bottom. Steadying it with his fist, he then bandsaws the seat to shape (above). Steel-strap clamping fixtures (below) and tabs along the back edge allow a double-bent blank's unwieldy shapes to be glued with pipe and C-clamps.

the table, with unfortunate consequences for saw, seat and self-composure. Sometimes, if things aren't going well, I clamp a wooden block between the seat bottom and the saw table, stopping to move the block from in front of to behind the blade at about the midpoint of the cut.

If you want to try making double-bent seats, you begin with the same-size seat blanks as for single-bent ones, but this time saw each blank up the middle. Mark each set, so you can match up the pairs later. Next joint the sawn edge on each half and cut the front edges square on the tablesaw. Here the centerline will be the jointed edge. The guide kerf is the first full-length kerf nearest the centerline (figure 1B), and should be $\frac{7}{16}$ in. from it at the back. Use the carriage to cut a guide kerf in each half-blank. Then with the fin fence, add three or more kerfs to *both* sides of each guide kerf. Run the blank front-first over the blade for the kerfs on one side of the guide kerf, tail-first for the opposite side. Regardless of the blank's orientation, however, always run the wall of the guide kerf against the left side of the fence.

Bend each seat half individually, using the method described for single-bent seats—you won't need clamping dogs for these small halves, though. After bending, clean off the wedge splines, then belt-sand each half's bottom to a smooth, continuous curve before gluing the two parts together. The jointed edges twist when the blank is bent, so they must be trued up again. Set the blank on an extended bandsaw table and use a try square to position the rear of the twisted edge so it's vertical to the table. Clamp a steady block under the blank to hold it in position, resaw the edge square, then run the edge freehand over the jointer (do this back-edge-first, or the wedges will tear out).

The seat halves must make an airtight fit, so you may have to touch up the edge with a hand plane. When I'm satisfied with the joint, I stand one half-seat, joint up, in the vise and hold the mating half against it. The two chamfers never match exactly, so I use a knife to trace the outline of the shallower one onto the edge of the overlapping fatter one, then I spokeshave the fat chamfer to the traced line. When both halves are matched, I use the homemade clamping brackets shown in the bottom photo on the facing page to glue up.

After the seat has been cut out and edge-sanded, all that remains is to make it into a chair. I explained how I do this on pages 6 through 11. How you do it is up to your creativity, but be forewarned: whether double- or single-bent, the seat can be hard to handle, because it doesn't have any flat surfaces.

The biggest problem is that the underside of a bent seat curves upward and shows its underbelly for all the world to see. Instead of trying to hide my seat bottoms as traditional chairmakers do, I make them part of the design. Sometimes I round the bottom edges into an upward sweep, giving the seat a bowl-like effect. Other times I try for an undulating clamshell edge, with both the bottom and top saddled up to a thin line. I rough out much of this shaping work for the front edge on a tablesaw or a bandsaw before bending the seat, then finish with plane, spokeshave or sander shortly before assembling the chair. I also shape the back chamfers at this stage.

Designing chairs with bent seats is a challenge. Even though I've been doing it for years, the technique still excites me—there are so many things yet to try. In my wildest dreams I see chairs that wrap clear around the sitter, chairs that reach for the sky, chairs that ebb and flow, chairs tied in a bow. There are more possibilities than one person can explore in a lifetime. □

Jeremy Singley is a full-time woodworker in E. Middlebury, Vt.

A simply elegant chair

After I had developed a machine method to produce shaped hardwood chair seats, a customer asked me if I could design a chair that could be built in a day. Coincidentally, I had already been asking myself the same question, and decided to try to come up with a simple yet comfortably elegant chair.

I eventually settled on the flowing A-shaped form shown in the photo below. It's strong yet light, and with only six parts to keep clean, it's easy to care for. It's also the simplest chair I can think of—there are no turned or bent parts, no complex joints.

Begin by making full-size patterns for the seat and other shaped parts shown in the drawing on the next page. Edge-glue $1\frac{1}{2}$-in. thick clear cherry to make a seat blank and kerf-bend it as already described.

Bandsaw the legs from $1\frac{1}{4}$-in. thick boards and taper their ends. I do this freehand on my jointer, but a taper jig on the tablesaw would also work. To cut the top leg notches, use the pattern to set up a tablesaw jig to hold each pair of legs while you cut a $\frac{1}{8}$-in. wide, $2\frac{5}{16}$-in. deep notch in each one. I find it easiest to cut all the left-side pieces first, then all the right-side pieces.

The back rail is a three-step operation. First bandsaw the rail's front profile from $1\frac{7}{8}$-in. thick stock, then cut the tenons. Screw a board as long as the rail to your miter gauge to steady the concave top edge of the face-down blank while you cut the tenon shoulders. Make another pass with the rail upright against a high fence to cut each cheek.

After cutting the tenons, trace the elevation-view curve on the top edge of the back, and bandsaw the contour. To hold the back vertical, make a cradle, or tape on the scrap that was sawn from the blank's bottom. Set the blade at 90° for the front curve and at 82° for the back curve. This produces a slight belly for shaping the bottom edge, as shown in the cross section on page 68. Don't worry that the sawblade runs off the stock at the bottom

Screws and glue replace complex joinery in simple chair.

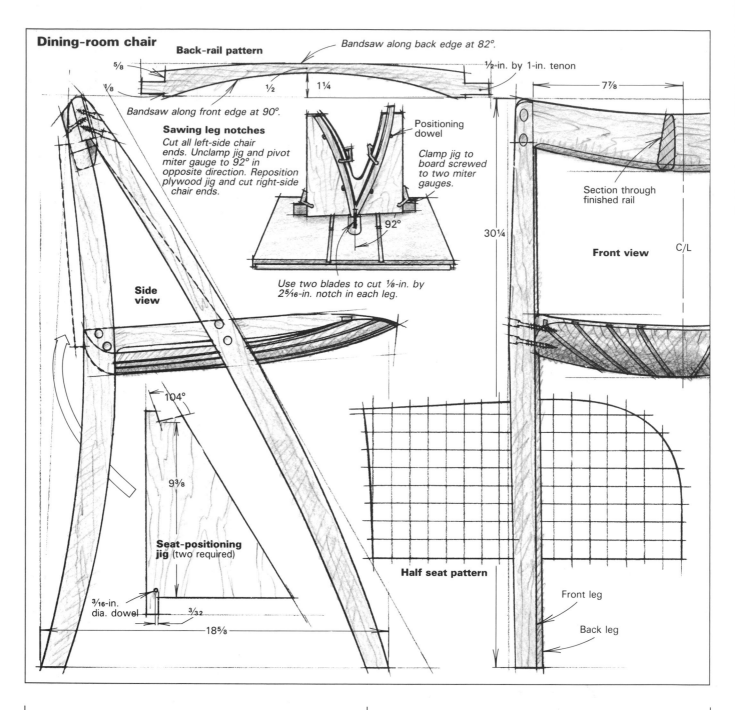

Dining-room chair

Back-rail pattern

Bandsaw along back edge at 82°.

5/8

1/8

1/2

1¼

½-in. by 1-in. tenon

7⅞

Bandsaw along front edge at 90°.

Sawing leg notches
Cut all left-side chair ends. Unclamp jig and pivot miter gauge to 92° in opposite direction. Reposition plywood jig and cut right-side chair ends.

Positioning dowel

Clamp jig to board screwed to two miter gauges.

92°

Section through finished rail

Use two blades to cut ⅛-in. by 2⁵⁄₁₆-in. notch in each leg.

Side view

30¼

Front view

C/L

104°

9⅜

Seat-positioning jig (two required)

Half seat pattern

³⁄₁₆-in. dia. dowel

³⁄₃₂

18⅝

Front leg

Back leg

edge—you can blend the curve when you sand the pieces.

Next rout the legs and back with a ½-in. piloted quarter-round bit, and finish-sand the flat surfaces of the legs. Shaping is matter of personal preference—I shape all the edges of the front legs, but stop the quarter-rounds on the back legs about 4 in. from the bottom of the seat. Center-bore the legs ⅜ in. deep with a ½-in. Forstner bit.

To assemble the frames, glue and screw the front leg to the back's tenon with a countersunk #8x1-in. wood screw in the top hole, and a #8x1¼-in. screw in the bottom hole. Angle the screws up and toward the center of the back to pull the shoulders tight. Then glue and screw on the back legs in the same way with #8x1½-in. screws.

Once the two frames are joined to the back, spokeshave and sand the back to match the contour of the leg tops, blend in all quarter-rounds, and finish-sand the back. Clamp the two spacers to the legs to align the seat. If

necessary, rejoint the seat edges for a good fit, realign the seat in the frame and drill the legs for the bottom screws. I use shanked #10x2-in. screws here to pull the joint tight, then add #8x1¾-in. shankless drywall screws (which are threaded along their entire length) on the top to hold the joint tight against shrinkage. Drill for the top screws with a ⅛-in. twist bit (no shank hole). When you're satisfied with the way the seat fits, remove it from the frame, glue the joints and reassemble. If you prefinish the chair parts, except in areas where the legs meet the seat, excess glue will be easier to remove. Although I've found that this glue-and-screw joint is very strong, you might prefer to notch the legs to fit over the seat for additional strength.

Finally, plug the screw holes with wooden plugs or dowels, then sand. I apply two coats of gel polyurethane for protection, then a coat of polymerized tung oil to give the cherry a richer tone. —*J.S.*

Taos Furniture

Southwestern style embodies Stickley's Craftsman spirit

by James Rannefeld

Nothing is ever created in a vacuum. Every masterpiece has its precursors and its pretenders, every tradition its exemplars and its exotics.

The history of furniture design makes a strong case for this argument. Although benchmarked by the Sheratons, Thonets, Wegners and Eshericks, furnituremaking has always been an evolutionary process of copying, modifying and synthesizing. It is, however, occasionally punctuated by masterful designs destined to become classics.

Taos-style furniture is popular in the desert Southwest. ("Taos Furniture" is a trademark of LifeStyle de Santa Fe, Inc.) Despite the hundreds of thousands of dollars' worth of Taos-style furniture made and sold in this area, it remains basically a handcrafted industry. Hundreds of woodworkers, including myself, make their own versions of this basic design. The style, classic in its simplicity and durability, is almost certainly derived from the Craftsman settees shown in a 1910 catalog, *The Work of L. and J.G. Stickley,* reissued

as *Stickley Craftsman Furniture Catalogues* (Dover, 1979).

Gustav Stickley, repulsed by Victorian excesses, advocated honest furniture with simple lines, preferably of stalwart, native American hardwoods. His characteristic dowel-pinned through mortise and tenon became another important detail of the original Taos daybed and its derivatives.

Jim Hill, who in 1970 began the furniture company now known as LifeStyle de Santa Fe, is generally credited with introducing the Taos style in his showroom, via a daybed made by his brother. But the Hispanic tradition has a way of working its magic on immigrants, and so it was with Craftsman furniture. The prevalent wood in the Southwest is Ponderosa pine, not the oak Stickley championed. The use of pine made it necessary to beef up the dimensions of the old Craftsman style, giving it proportions more reminiscent of Spanish Colonial furniture. And, in fact, the new Taos style was almost immediately absorbed into that 300-year-old tradition as if it had been handed down for generations. Another obvi-

The Taos-style couch, which originated in Santa Fe about fifteen years ago, is a melding of Stickley precepts with the Spanish Colonial tradition. The convertible-bed variation (detail) has two mattresses and unfolds into a queen-size bed (see fig. 2, next page).

Drawings: Robert Hannan

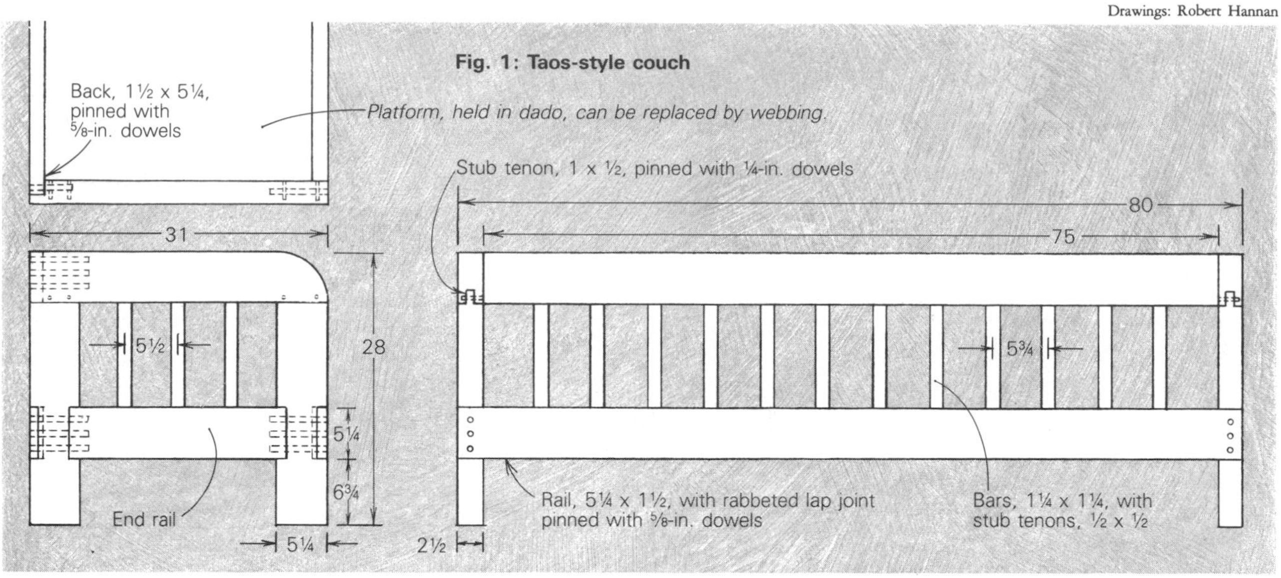

Fig. 1: Taos-style couch
Back, 1½ x 5¼, pinned with ⅝-in. dowels
Platform, held in dado, can be replaced by webbing.
Stub tenon, 1 x ½, pinned with ¼-in. dowels
80
75
31
28
5½
5¾
5¼
6¾
End rail
5¼
2½
Rail, 5¼ x 1½, with rabbeted lap joint pinned with ⅝-in. dowels
Bars, 1¼ x 1¼, with stub tenons, ½ x ½

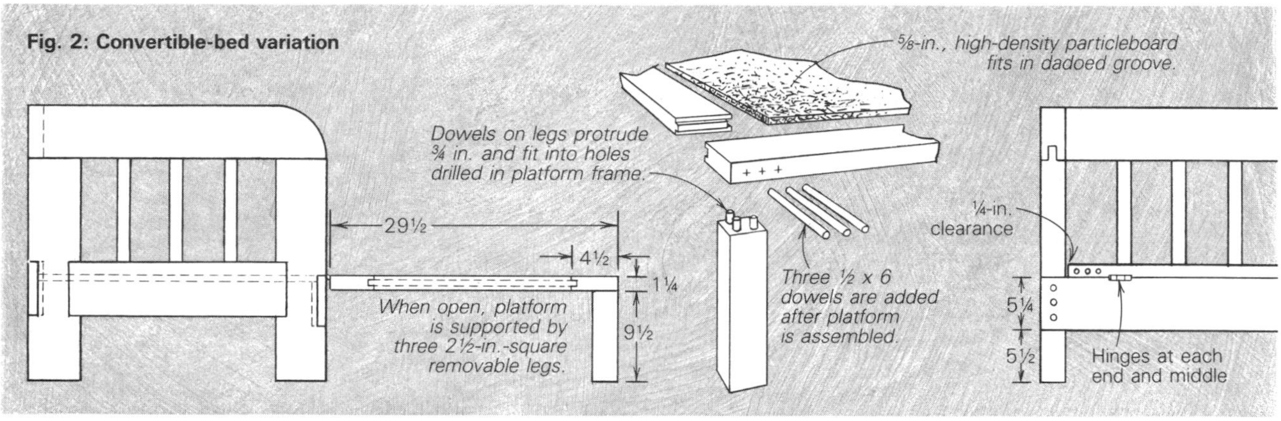

Fig. 2: Convertible-bed variation
⅝-in., high-density particleboard fits in dadoed groove.
Dowels on legs protrude ¾ in. and fit into holes drilled in platform frame.
29½
4½
1¼
9½
When open, platform is supported by three 2½-in.-square removable legs.
Three ½ x 6 dowels are added after platform is assembled.
¼-in. clearance
5¼
5½
Hinges at each end and middle

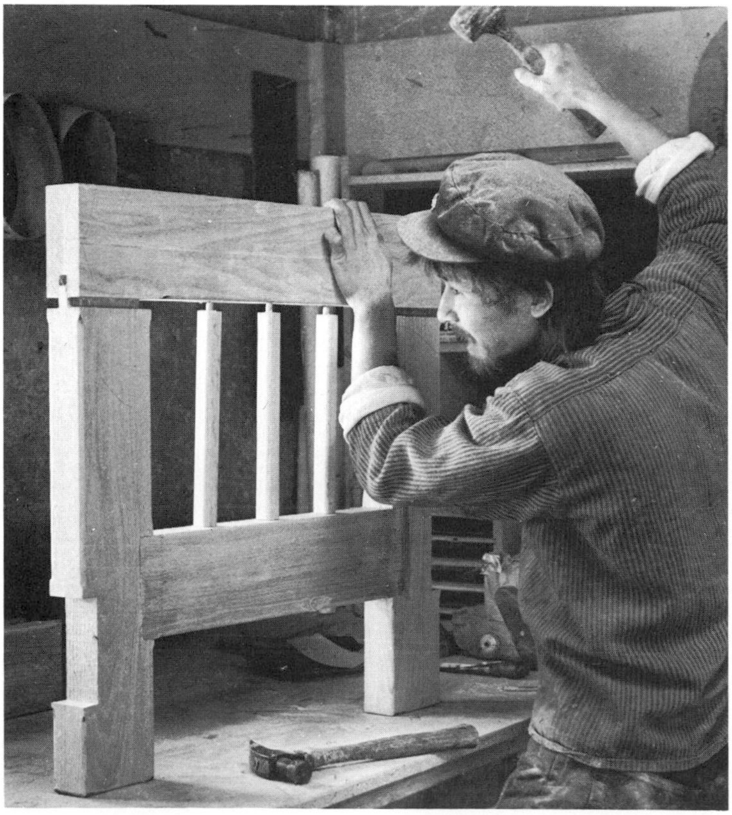

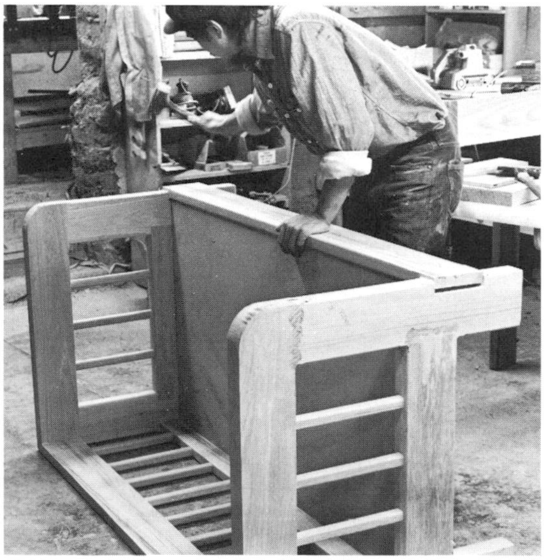

The straightforward Taos-style frame, sized to fit standard mattresses, is built up in sections. At left, Keath Sanderson, one of Rannefeld's employees, assembles a convertible-bed end, which will be clamped until the glue has cured. He will assemble the back similarly. Next, the ends, front rail and back rail will be dadoed to accept the high-density particleboard mattress platform. With this slid into the groove, as in the short convertible bed shown above, the front rail can be tapped into place, then pinned with dowels. A second particleboard panel and frame will be hinged atop the first to form an extension, as shown in figure 2.

From *Fine Woodworking* magazine (May 1983) 40:79-81

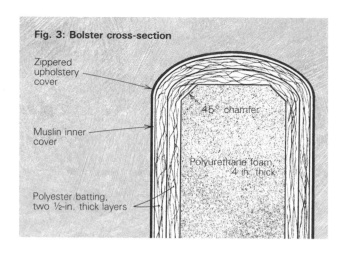

Fig. 3: Bolster cross-section

Zippered
upholstery
cover

Muslin inner
cover

45° chamfer

Polyurethane foam,
4 in. thick

Polyester batting,
two ½-in. thick layers

This pinned bridle joint, a hallmark of early Taos furniture, has been all but abandoned because of problems with wood movement. A pinned stub tenon is more in favor now.

Jim Hill's Taos Furniture Company pioneered the basic couch design around 1970. Since 1976 the firm has been under the direction of owner Bob Powell, making a full line of variations as well as Spanish Colonial reproductions. Eight employees emphasize hand work and adaptability rather than assembly-line tooling, allowing increased diversity without cutting production.

ous change was in the slats that form the backs and sides of Stickley designs. Now they became bars, sometimes carved into traditional spirals, or replaced with *latillas,* small cedar or aspen branches either left natural or peeled.

It took only a few years for this style to be regarded as the indigenous furniture of northern New Mexico, with buyers coming in from all over the United States and abroad to get it. Today's offerings usually include the daybed (designed for a twin-bed mattress), the couch (for a 30-in. cot mattress), the love seat, the occasional chair, and, more recently, the convertible bed, which unfolds to make a queen-size bed. The basic design is so straightforward and universal that it invites variation. The prototype for the style is the couch. Simple dimensional variations produce the other pieces in the group, as well as bedroom furniture and other accessories.

I generally use oak for this design, laminated from 1¼-in. stock, but more often the pieces are constructed from 3-in. Ponderosa pine cut locally and milled to 2½ in. Since material of this dimension is rarely available commercially kiln dried, most of us here use air-dried wood, which gets down to 8% to 12% moisture content in our arid Southwestern climate.

The original Taos furniture featured an open mortise-and-tenon joint (a bridle joint), pinned with dowels, at the front arm/leg joints. Although part of the beauty of this design is that wood movement isn't a serious structural problem, bridle joints do creep when the members shrink in width, causing an unsightly detail that's unfriendly to the touch. Consequently, in our shop we now use a stub tenon pinned with small dowels for insurance. The bars are likewise tenoned into the arms, although some makers dowel here. The end rails are let into the legs, and the ends are assembled as a unit.

The platform can be made from a variety of materials. I have chosen an industrial-grade hardboard to illustrate the process here, but the original pieces used 1-in. pine boards. You might use knotty-pine veneered plywood, or—for more comfort—a frame webbed with ropes or with latex strapping.

After the ends, front rail and rear rail have been dadoed to accept the platform, they are lap-joined, with a rabbeted shoulder that eases alignment when clamping up. After assembly, all the joints are pinned with dowels.

Pine is frustrating to finish with an orbital sander, so conventional wisdom here is either to leave the piece belt-sanded (100-grit) for a rustic look, or to give it a fine scraper finish.

Traditionally, Taos furniture has been stained with a tar-and-kerosene concoction, probably to mimic more expensive

walnut furniture brought in from elsewhere. Several local craftsmen have begun using aged or distressed finishes, and some just leave the wood its natural color, Scandinavian style. In any case, I recommend a mixture of Danish oil and polyurethane varnish (about 3:1), a heavy sealer coat brushed on, then two coats applied with fine steel wool and rubbed dry. This mixture has the best qualities of both products, without the drawbacks. It applies, repairs and looks like an oil finish, yet resists liquids and wear like polyurethane.

The upholstery for Taos furniture is as straightforward as the wood-frame construction. The lower cushion is usually a single (cot-size) mattress, with three 15-in. high back bolsters for comfort. These consist of a core of 4-in., medium-density polyurethane foam (chamfer the corners for a softer contour) wrapped twice with polyester batting. I would recommend an inner cover of muslin, and a zippered upholstery cover, so it can be easily removed for cleaning.

Whether contemporary or rustic, traditional or exotic, no matter how the craftsman adapts this basic design, the spirit of Craftsman furniture lives on. Direct construction, durable joinery, simple elegance and unpretentiousness remain the common denominators of the Taos style today. □

James Rannefeld designs and builds furniture at Media Seven Design Group, in Taos, N.M. Photos by the author.

A Single Bed
Basic design develops joinery skills

by Kenneth Rower

This bed, built for my son, was made to fit a mattress 7 in. by 39 in. by 75 in. It can be viewed as a particular design or as a general method of making a bed out of heavy stock and one wide board. There is much room for variation without changing the construction. While the piece shown is for those who like rectangles, certainly the tops of the posts and the headboard could be shaped to taste, and the legs could be tapered or turned from square stock. A theoretical adaptation for stacking twin beds is shown in the drawing on the facing page.

Rails and posts are the same thickness, but the rails are set back about ½ in., thus emphasizing the separateness of the posts, and yielding integral ledger strips on the insides of the rails, needing only to be rabbeted to carry the platform. The shoulders at the ends of the long rails are unequal, the inner being housed ¼ in. in the posts to assist the bolted stub tenons. The short rails bear no load, are not rabbeted and do not have a housed shoulder.

The platform is of pine boards laid the short way and fitted loosely edge to edge. Other materials could equally well be used, for greater or lesser flexibility, and the rabbets could be altered to accommodate a different arrangement, for example a grid of boards running both ways.

In cutting out the rails and posts, consider which surfaces will be seen to relate, and arrange grains accordingly. For example, the front surfaces of the head posts will be seen with the front surfaces of the foot posts. The most convenient stock to work with, especially for the posts, is the rift cut (see inset in drawing), since all faces of a piece show about the same linear pattern. Plain or quartersawn stock, which shows bolder patterns that differ markedly on adjacent faces, can nevertheless be thoughtfully organized.

There are several kinds of mortise-and-tenon joints to be cut. To make the very long tenons at the headboard, true up one face and one edge of the stock. Square the ends exactly to the overall length including tenons. Gauge the tenon cheeks from the trued face and gauge the shoulders from the squared ends. Saw or plane grooves across the grain just on the waste sides of the shoulder lines, cutting to the depth of the cheek lines. Remove the waste and finish up with a rabbet plane. Then saw away part of the tenon to yield a long haunch. Make the other half of the joint by chopping the blind mor-

Child's bed, here in red oak, can be varied in size and adapted for bunk beds by lengthening the footposts and shaping them, along with the headposts, to interlock with the feet of a top bed, as shown in the drawing on the facing page. This clean, sturdy design incorporates various mortise-and-tenon joints (as in the detail, right), housed, wedged and drawbolted for strength. Photos: Richard Starr.

From *Fine Woodworking* magazine (May 1981) 28:68-70

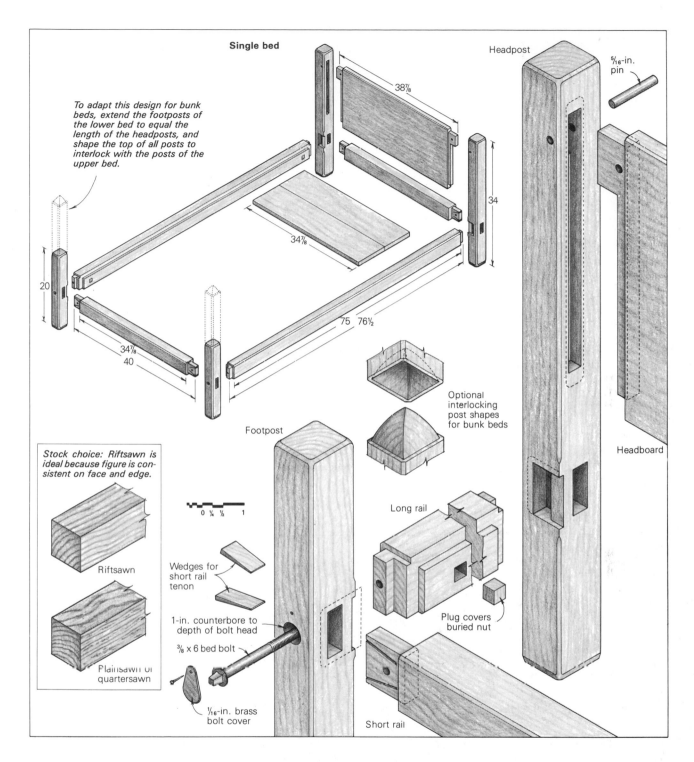

Single bed

To adapt this design for bunk beds, extend the footposts of the lower bed to equal the length of the headposts, and shape the top of all posts to interlock with the posts of the upper bed.

38⅞

Headpost

5/16-in. pin

34

20

75 76½

34⅞

34⅞

40

Footpost

Optional interlocking post shapes for bunk beds

Headboard

Stock choice: Riftsawn is ideal because figure is consistent on face and edge.

Riftsawn

Plainsawn or quartersawn

0 ¼ ½ 1

Wedges for short rail tenon

1-in. counterbore to depth of bolt head

⅜ x 6 bed bolt

1/16-in. brass bolt cover

Long rail

Plug covers buried nut

Short rail

tise first, then chopping or routing the groove. While the mortise should be as tight as possible, the groove should be a good deal longer than the haunch to allow for expansion of the headboard, and the shoulder below the haunch should be long enough to allow for contraction.

I taper the mortises for the outside-wedged tenons about ⅔ of their depth; I leave the rest straight to grip the base of the tenon. The slanted saw kerfs for wedges resist splitting. For a plainer appearance, blind tenons could be used.

Notice that in laying out mortises, the gauge should bear on the inner faces of the posts, which have been previously trued and squared to one another. Thus, post sections may vary somewhat without significantly affecting the joinery.

The order in which the parts are made does not matter, but it may be easier to bore for the bolts while the posts are free and before they are mortised for the short rails. First, working plumb, counterbore and bore the holes in the posts. Then clamp the posts to the long rails and use the holes to guide the bit into the end grain of the rails. If necessary, take away the post to finish the hole. Then, leaving the bit in the hole, draw a line on the inner face of the rail to show the actual path the bit has taken. Remove the bit and bore the crossing hole to house the square nut. As there is some danger of boring too deeply, it is prudent to stop a little short, square up the hole with a chisel, try the nut, then deepen as required. When all is well, and with the joint bolted up, shim around the nut to keep it from shifting, and dry-fit a plug. It remains to complete the bolt holes through the short-rail tenons. Clamp up the end frames, mark the tenons from each side, then remove. Bore the holes a little oversize, lest eventual shrinkage pinch a bolt.

Matching the shoulder-to-shoulder lengths of the head-board and the headrail requires care. When testing the assembly, remember that because of moisture loss through freshly cut surfaces, post faces can deform after being mortised, and in order not to be misled, check these surfaces for truth before trying the matched pieces in place. The shoulder-to-shoulder length of the footrail, meanwhile, may differ a trifle without harm.

Before final assembly of the end frames, shape all arrises with a chamfer or radius, including those underneath. Children do crawl under beds, and planed oak can cut. The chamfer is perhaps more interesting to look at and to finger, the radius friendlier and more comfortable to lean against. The corners of the post tops can be worked with a finely set block plane, or they can be sanded with paper on a block. These corners can also be left sharp, straight from the chamfering of the arrises, for a pure if rather dangerous-looking detail.

During assembly, if the tenons make good friction fits in their mortises, very little glue is desirable. Put glue only on the tenon, and then only on the first inch or so next to the shoulder. Don't put glue on the haunches of the headboard: they must be free to shrink upward toward the fixed points at the top. The lower rail will keep the bottom tight. It is not necessary to glue the wedges, and more than a drop of glue can cause them to seize before they are driven home.

Simple bolt covers can be made of ⅟₁₆-in. sheet brass, using dividers, drill, hacksaw and file, or patterned ones can be obtained, along with the bolts, from Ball and Ball (436 W. Lincoln Hwy., Exton, Pa. 19341) or from Horton Brasses (P.O. Box 120F, Nooks Hill Rd., Cromwell, Conn. 06416).

To adapt the design for stacking twin beds, make all posts the same height, and carve all the post tops and one set of bottoms to make a gravity-locking joint. One way is shown in the drawing. A master set of male and female parts should be cut first to ease the job of fitting the actual posts. When the beds are stacked, additional racking strain on the joints of the lower bed would indicate widening the rails. Some compromise may be required here between acceptable sway and visually acceptable rail width. There seems no practical way to have matched bunk beds while preserving the interesting difference in height between headposts and footposts.

As for access, if the lower bed is placed head to foot with respect to the upper, steps for climbing will be found at 12 in. (footrail), 33 in. (headboard), and 48 in. (footrail). The second interval could prove too great for some children. Another approach would be to orient the beds normally and fit a two-step ladder between the lower edge of the upper footrail and the upper edge of the lower footrail, establishing 12-in. intervals for the climb. The ladder legs should be mortised in at the top end. Since mortises would be unsightly in the lower footrail when the beds were apart, the lower end of the ladder could be located by buttons fitted to the rail and shaped similarly to the post tops. ☐

Kenneth Rower makes furniture in Newbury, Vt.

Q & A

Joining squared rails to round legs
What's the best way to join chair rails to round, slightly tapered legs? My main concern is how to use a mortise-and-tenon joint and still get a precise fit where the shoulders of the rail meet the leg.
—Fredrick Lehman, Cedar Rapids, Iowa

The easiest way to make a tight mortise-and-tenon joint in a turned chair leg is to cut the cheeks of the tenon in the regular way and then to cut the outer edge of the shoulders in at an angle that's a little steeper than the one made by the arc of the circumference of the leg. Usually the length of leg that's

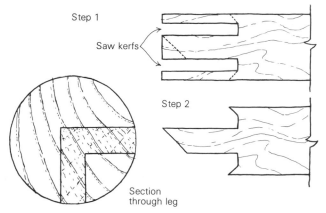

involved in the joint is left untapered; otherwise, the shoulders of the tenon must be contoured appropriately. When pulled up in a clamp, the edges of the shoulders will cut into the leg. The best glue for this joint is hide glue because it will fill the small gaps left between the shoulder and the leg.
—Tage Frid

Upholstered-chair joinery
I'm planning to make a fully upholstered wing chair. It would be difficult to make the frame with mortise-and-tenon joints since most of the parts don't meet at right angles. I've considered joining the legs to the rails with butt joints and a few 4-in. #10 wood screws running up through the legs into each rail. The heads of the screws would be countersunk and hidden by the upholstery. Would this joinery be much weaker than mortise-and-tenon joints?
—Steve Berg, Dundee, Ohio

Wood screws driven up through the legs would penetrate into the end grain of the rails, and since screws don't hold well in end grain, they'd eventually pull out. Glue doesn't hold well on an end-grain butt joint, either.

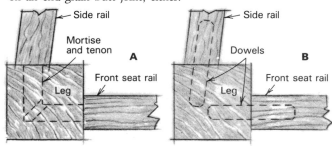

Because it's one of the strongest joints, I would use a mortise and tenon to join the rails and legs. Cutting these joints isn't as difficult as you think—only the tenons on the side rails have to be sawn at an angle. The mortises in the legs can be cut at right angles, as shown in the drawing. The front seat rail will probably be at a right angle to the legs, so the tenons on that rail should pose no problem.
—Ron Sheetz

Cabriole Legs
Graceful curves hold sway over 18th-century design

by Carol Bohdan

The cabriole leg is a decorative adaptation of a quadruped's leg from the knee down, which takes its name from the Italian *capriola*, meaning "goat's leap." It was known to the ancient Egyptians as well as to the Greeks and Romans, whose high-quality seats and beds were supported upon the legs of lions or beasts of the chase. It was from China, however, where the cabriole was known as early as the T'ang dynasty (618-907 A.D.) that it made its way West, transported by Dutch traders. Counterparts of the Chinese cabriole were seen in Portuguese, Spanish, French, Italian and English design by the last third of the 17th century. In France, the now-familiar cabriole leg with a ball and claw foot was known as early as the mid-16th century, but the Chinese cabriole came to France at a time when design was in transition from the baroque of Louis XIV (1643 to 1715) to the rococo of Louis XV (1723 to 1774), and curvilinear forms were becoming increasingly important. The French were the first to formalize the idea of the reversed cyma-curved leg, and the first to call it cabriole.

The incorporation of the cabriole leg into Western furniture was revolutionary and effected a total rethinking of design as well as construction. It made the curving line, previously an aspect of baroque design, dominant, and did not depend upon elaborate carving for its effect, but instead upon well-

The chaste and restrained approach of Chinese chairs, such as this one c. 1700, is echoed in Queen Anne designs. Photo courtesy of The Metropolitan Museum of Art.

Late 15th-century Chinese table with cabriole legs is made out of huang-hua-li wood. Photo courtesy of The William Rockhill Nelson Gallery of Art.

Queen Anne sidechair (Connecticut, c. 1725) is walnut with a damask seat. Photo courtesy of The Metropolitan Museum of Art.

Early predecessors of the cabriole date back to ancient Egypt. This carved cedar chair was found in the Valley of the Kings, in the tomb of Tutankhamun. Photo courtesy of The Metropolitan Museum of Art, Harry Burton.

Queen Anne chair construction

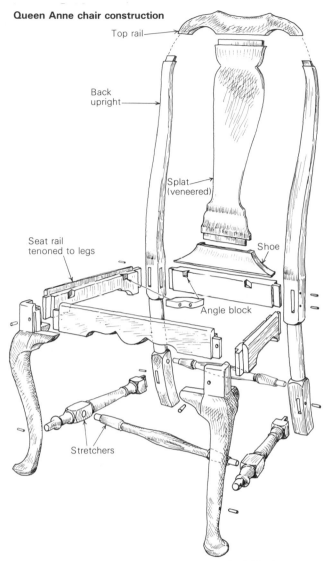

Top rail

Back upright

Splat (veneered)

Shoe

Seat rail tenoned to legs

Angle block

Stretchers

Illustration: Christopher Clapp. Adapted from *The Shorter Dictionary of English Furniture.*

Tripod legs keep furniture stable. Left, mahogany kettlestand (Newport, R.I., 1700-1785); center, mahogany basinstand (Newport, 1760-1775); right, mahogany candlestand (Charleston, S.C., 1765-1780). Photos courtesy of The Winterthur Museum.

thought-out and disciplined design. It stimulated a style of furniture in which the skirting of tables, the bonnets of tall chests and secretaries, the fronts of chests and the backs of settees, all echoed cabriole curves. This style expressed a demand for the best workmanship and a new interest in comfort, which developed in the more affluent, leisurely and relaxed atmosphere of 18th-century England. The finest expression of the cabriole is in the Queen Anne style of England and America, which closely approaches the chaste, restrained approach of the Chinese.

The advantages of the cabriole leg are simplicity, strength and stability; elegance, utility and sound construction are united in the best designs. The type of chair used almost exclusively in the first half of the 18th century, through the reigns of Queen Anne, George I and George II, has shaped hoop backs and solid center splats veneered with walnut, which had almost entirely replaced oak as the principal fine furniture wood. In early chairs, the uprights are convex and retain the vertical line of Restoration furniture. The seat rail is straight, and the narrow cabriole legs ending in simple club feet are underbraced and united by plain, turned stretchers. Later on, the bowed shape of the uprights became more pronounced, and the top rail continued down to the seat frame in one unbroken line, as in Chinese chairs. The seat rail became convex, and the legs were slightly wider. Stretchers, which interrupted the smooth line of the curve and projected awkwardly from the fetlock, became unnecessary, because lowering the chair backs lessened the strain. The seat frame became a fairly deep, visible rail, rabbeted to accept the loose seat. The legs were firmly fixed to meet the front apron or curved in a manner that gave the utmost rigidity to the chair. The knees of the cabriole widened out.

Tables and case goods of this period were similarly strong and stable. Card and dining tables without stretchers were not only more elegant, but more comfortable to use. The tripod form, made up of three cabriole legs attached to a central pillar, lent itself to furniture destined to hold delicate and breakable items on uneven floor boards. Piecrust tea tables, stands for basins, candles, urns and kettles, and double and triple-tiered dumbwaiters for the serving of food and liquor, all depended upon the tripod form and its balance of curves for support and stability.

In 1745 the artist William Hogarth published a frontispiece to his engraved works in which he drew a serpentine line and placed under it the words "The Line of Beauty." In response to requests for an explanation of this, he wrote *The Analysis of Beauty* (1753) in which he explained what constitutes beauty and grace in certain forms and lines, including the cabriole leg. Commenting on an illustrative plate show-

The cabriole curve was often extended to the entire design, as in the bonnet and doortops of this mahogany block-front desk with cabinet top (Boston, c. 1760). Photo courtesy of The Metropolitan Museum of Art.

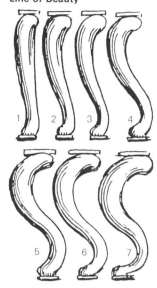

ing seven legs, the author says: "All sorts of waving-lines are ornamental, when properly applied; yet, strictly speaking, there is but one precise line, properly to be called the line of *beauty*, which in the scale of them is number 4: the lines 5, 6, 7 by their bulging too much in their curvature becoming gross and clumsy; and, on the contrary, 3, 2, 1, as they straighten, becoming mean and poor...." This observation probably had little impact in the workrooms of London cabinetmakers, because by then the cabriole leg was passing out of fashion. In his *Gentleman and Cabinet-Maker's Director* (1754), Chippendale advocated a straight leg as a refreshing change from the cabriole, which had by then dominated English design for half a century.

In the American colonies, however, the cabriole leg persisted to the end of the century, and it was here that it enjoyed its greatest popularity. Regional styles developed rapidly—Colonial craftsmen each interpreted the cabriole independently, producing a richly diversified collection of legs deviating in all directions from Hogarth's line of beauty.

There are many ways to carve a cabriole leg. Massachusetts Bay furniture (Newburyport, Salem, Boston, Roxbury) epitomizes a fine, unbroken line in the undercut leg. Connecticut legs are more angular, carved with less confidence. Pieces from this area often display the broken cabriole leg, typical of embryonic English examples. New York furniture, made for predominantly Dutch patronage, is broader and bigger than its Colonial and English counterparts, with bolder lines exemplified by an exaggerated curve at the ankle. Squared cabriole legs are typical of New Jersey furniture, as is the use of a bracelet, cuff or "wrister" carved above the ankle, sometimes seen on English pieces. In the case of New Jersey, however, this ringlet is carved on only two sides and not all around the leg in a smooth line, as in English work. Virginia-made furniture has kneeless, almost straight, rounded legs, terminating in a slanted pad foot that is typical of early English cabrioles. A certain stiffness of carving almost always characterizes English provincial legs throughout the 18th century, the secret of the perfect curve never quite mastered by the country craftsmen.

The structure of cabriole chairs, whether of the Queen Anne or Georgian period, differs from one region of America to another, just as American chairs differ from English chairs. The way in which the front cabriole legs are fastened to the seat rail is often a clue to origin. In Philadelphia chairs, the framing around the seat is one continuous piece, and does not break at the corners. The leg is pinned from the top of the inside frame. The contour of the frame does not follow the seat, but is usually a perfect square, with sufficient thickness of wood to provide extra support for the round pin that goes down into the leg. In New York and New England the legs are carried behind the seat rail up to the top, so they actually form the curved corners of the seat. They are then braced on either side with inside blocks. The construction of the English Queen Anne chair closely resembles this pattern—the leg is pushed up into the seat rail, which is tenoned into and underbraced by a large corner block.

In Philadelphia, the Queen Anne chair and Chippendale chair achieved their richest forms, with a balance of interlocking curves and a selection of tasteful ornaments, reflecting the best of English design. The fine curves of Philadelphia furniture, with its graceful legs and delicate ankles, come closest

Gate-leg breakfast table of maple and soft pine (Massachusetts, 1725-1740) has almost straight legs, pad feet. Photo courtesy of The Henry Francis du Pont Winterthur Museum.

New Jersey dressing table, walnut, c. 1720, has characteristic wrister carved above the ankle. Photo courtesy of The Henry Francis du Pont Winterthur Museum.

Curves dominate design of walnut Philadelphia corner chair (1745-1765). Note trifid foot. Photo courtesy of The Henry Francis du Pont Winterthur Museum.

Philadelphia easy chair, 1750-1790, is mahogany, black walnut, yellow poplar and pine. Photo courtesy of The Metropolitan Museum of Art.

to Hogarth's ideal. The web, trifid, claw and ball and pad foot were all used by Philadelphia craftsmen, and the hairy paw foot, reserved in America only for pieces of the highest quality, distinguishes a choice group.

New England furniture in general is characterized by delicate and light proportions. The silhouette of the New England chair is more slender than its English prototypes and tends toward greater verticality. The extreme refinement and delicacy of cabriole legs may explain the persistence of turned chair stretchers, which are found in New England into the Chippendale period after they were discontinued elsewhere.

The "easy chair," known popularly today as the "wing chair," was a much sought-after item in America. By about 1770 this fully upholstered chair, with its curved back, arms scrolling in *C* or *S* curves and cabriole legs had passed out of fashion in London, but continued to be hugely popular in America. When exposed, the frames of these chairs reveal structural differences that were dictated by regional differences in design.

The cabriole motif has never been dropped from the repertoire of Western furniture design. In the Regency period (1810-1820) the evolution of the leg came full circle, returning to the style of its early prototypes. Fantastic and often bizarre designs for chairs and tables were enlivened by naturalistic lions' legs and paws or cloven feet, developed by such designers as Thomas Hope (1769-1831), whose designs were based upon sketches of ancient furniture he saw while traveling through Egypt, Sicily, Turkey, Syria and Spain. The cabriole leg was subjected over the course of 200 years to continuous usage, evaluation and interpretation. In the 1830s it appeared in English design books as part of a revival of the style of Louis XV. It appeared in the work of John Henry Belter (1804-1863), a New York craftsman working in the rococo revival style. It was used in French and Belgian designs in the era of Art Nouveau and it was seen again in the period of Art Deco, when such designers as Emile-Jacques Ruhlmann returned to the spirit of Louis XVI classicism. But, however interesting alternate interpretations of the cabriole style may be, more often than not they lack the innocence and unaffected grace of the original. □

Carol Bohdan, of New York City, is a scholar specializing in 19th- and 20th-century furniture.

Q & A

Stenciling chairs

I need to redo the stenciling on a set of Hitchcock dining chairs. The rubbed floral design on the back slat is in good shape, but the design on the back posts needs restoration. I'd like to spray the black background and restencil, but I don't know how. Also, where can I buy stenciling supplies?
—Arthur R. Hocker, Fayetteville, Ark.

The stenciling on the uprights is just metallic powders polished onto a coat of tacky varnish. On the uprights, the pattern was usually yellow-gold on a dark background. You can reproduce the pattern from parts of the design that remain, or from other chairs. Make a stencil: trace the design on tracing paper, then transfer the tracing and cut out the design in architects' linen or similar plastic paper, using fine-pointed scissors or an X-acto knife. Make a palette from a piece of fine velour and use silk-backed velvet (stitch or glue the edges to prevent raveling) or a chamois as a polishing cloth. To prepare your palette, rub the gold powder into it.

Touch up or repaint the chair, then pad on one or two coats of varnish with a lintless cloth, wiping most of it off. Begin stenciling as soon as the last coat of varnish is tacky enough that a finger pressed into it won't leave a mark but comes away with a slight click.

Lay the chair on its back with the work area toward you. Hold the stencil in place. Wrap your polishing cloth smoothly over the pad of your first finger, dip it into the powder on the velour and tap off any excess. Use a circular motion to polish the powder onto the tacky varnish. Let this dry thoroughly. For striping around the pattern, use a fine striping brush and a paint color that matches the old chairs. You can mix this paint yourself by adding yellow ochre and raw and burnt umber coloring to a chrome-yellow base. The color should look like mustard or khaki. Mix in a little varnish to get the right consistency. Finish with two coats of varnish tinted with raw or burnt umber to mellow the bright gold color, then two coats of clear varnish, sanded between coats.

Stenciling supplies are sometimes sold by local paint shops, art-supply stores, or sign-writing suppliers, and by mail-order from Crafts Manufacturing Co., 72 Massachusetts Ave., Lunenberg, Mass. 01462. —Florence E. Wright

Joining a chair crest rail

I'm having a problem joining crest rail to back legs of a Queen Anne dining chair. Running the grain either way seems to result in a weak, short-grain joint. What's the best way to make this joint?
—Michael O'Banion, Westminster, Md.

The grain in the crest rail must run horizontally. At the point of joining, both the rear leg and crest rail should be at least 1 3/16 in. thick to provide the most strength possible. If you

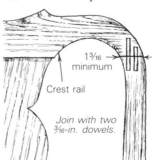

1 3/16 minimum

Crest rail

Join with two 3/16-in. dowels.

start with 2-in.-wide stock for the back leg and confine most of your shaping work to the crest-rail side of the leg, you can include some of the radius in the strong vertical grain of the leg. Use two 3/16-in. dowels instead of one 3/8-in. dowel for this joint. For added strength, run the dowels as high up in the cross grain of the crest rail as you can. Don't make the radius where the crest rail joins the legs too small. I suggest looking through Vol. 2 of Wallace Nutting's *Furniture Treasury* for examples of chairs with traditional lines. —Andy Marlow

Working Woven Cane
Spline holds cane firmly on the frame

by G.A. Michaud

Though hand-caning was a staple project in every industrial-arts program around the turn of the century, the time when caning techniques were common knowledge has long since past. The rebirth of interest in restoring antique furniture and the lovely, sometimes startling application of cane in contemporary furniture, however, has created a demand for practical information about this craft. The easiest, most economical way to learn how to insert cane is to install it on a piece of existing furniture. Inserting machine-woven cane into prepared grooves is the quickest method. The photo below shows a chair seat and the materials you'll need: a pattern, a roll of cane, spline and driving and holding wedges.

Open-woven and close-woven cane are the two styles most frequently available to individual craftsmen, though some upholstery-supply houses sell others. Close-woven cane comes in 18-in. widths and costs about $7 a running foot (all 1980 prices). Open-woven cane comes 12 in. to 24 in. wide, in 2-in. increments, and costs from $5 to $10 a running foot. Spline, the strips used to hold the cane in the grooves, was once available in hickory and reed, but now only reed spline is available. It is classified as light (3/16 in. wide), medium (1/4 in. wide) and heavy (5/16 in. wide).

To begin, remove the old cane and clean the groove of glue, cane and spline. (If the seat frame has a series of small holes drilled around the opening, you'll need to hand-weave individual strands of cane—a different process from what is described here. You could rout a groove 1/4 in. back from the holes, but I think it's easier to learn to hand-weave.) Check the groove for size. It should measure 3/16 in. across by 1/4 in. deep. Sometimes the groove is 1/4 in. or 5/16 in. wide, usually an indication that the frame has been recaned several times—cleaning the groove of old spline and cane widens it. Buy spline in the size closest to the width of the empty groove.

Draw a pattern of the shape of the opening you wish to cover, allowing at least 1/2 in. beyond the groove. Transfer this pattern shape onto the cane webbing, cut it out and soak it in warm water. I have seen formulas for soaking solution: usually 1½ tablespoons of glycerine per gallon of water. I haven't had great success with this because glycerine absorbs water from the air, and in an area such as the damp, river-valley town where I work, it makes the cane feel sticky. If your area is drier than mine try it, but test a patch first.

Establish the amount of spline needed and soak it along with the cane. Don't be afraid of damaging it—soak it at least an hour, longer if you prefer. The more pliable it is, the easier it is to work. The cane and spline will become not limp, but pliable enough so that when bent over on itself the fibers

will not fracture. While the cane is soaking, seal the frame with sanding sealer so the wood is water-repellent—the cane is wet when you insert it into the groove. Next, make a number of hardwood locking wedges and a driving wedge.

Lay out the soaked cane over the opening with its shiny side up and align the weave parallel to the groove most prominent in design, usually the front groove. Woven cane has two sides—a glossy side and a dull side. The shiny surface is the bark of the rattan cane and is the side you wish to display to wear or view.

Pull out the weavers (horizontal members of the weaving) that run over the groove. You don't have to do this all at once but only where you intend to start. With the driving wedge and a mallet, force the cane with light taps into the groove, and lock it in place with the small wedges. Sponge the cane down from time to time to keep it pliable—sponge the dull side, because the shiny side isn't absorbent. To keep the cane flat and parallel to the groove, begin in the center of the

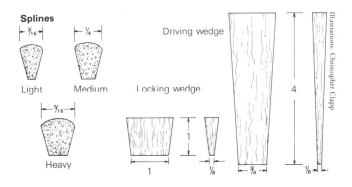

Splines

Light 3/16

Medium 1/4

Heavy 5/16

Driving wedge

Locking wedge

1

1   1/8   3/4   4   1/8

Illustrations: Christopher Clapp

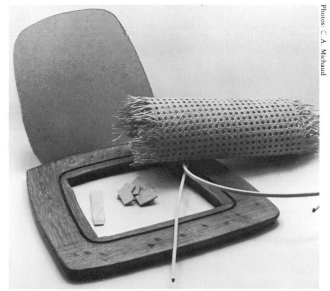

Photos: C.A. Michaud

Materials: Pattern, cane, spline, driving wedge and locking wedges.

EDITOR'S NOTE: Three sources of cane and caning supplies are: Cane and Basket Supply Co., 1283 S. Cochran, Los Angeles, Calif. 90019; Inter-Mares Trading Co., 1064 Route 109, Lindenhurst, N.Y. 11757; and H.H. Perkins and Co., P.O. Box AC, Amity Station, Woodbridge, Conn. 06525.

frame and work out toward the corners evenly on each side. Continue right around the frame, moving from the front to the back, then to each side in turn. The edges of the cane will project up beyond the groove: Cut them off using a mallet and chisel at the outer edge in the bottom of the groove, pulling out the locking wedges as you go. A sharp chisel is a must, for the cane is pliable, stringy and tough.

Traditionally, once the trimming was complete, hot hide glue was run into the groove. For that you have to be fast. I find that aliphatic-resin glue (such as Titebond) works well and gives enough time to force in the spline, the next and final step. Plan where you want the spline joint. Begin there and force it into the groove, wedging the cane in place. Since the spline is soaked and is pliable, it will compress and make room for the cane that shares the same space. Do not expect driving in the spline to take up any great amount of slack in the seat—the seat is drawn taut in the wedging process. Drive the spline down until the crown is just visible, no lower than the frame surface. This way the crown will protect the bent edge of the cane from wear. Use a padding block in driving down the spline and not the face of the mallet, or the spline will be wavy and dimpled. I have read instructions for inserting dry spline into a groove that has untrimmed cane jutting out in order to tighten up slack in the seat. The results are disappointing. The crown of the spline may flatten out or split. In addition, the spline can't be driven all the way into the groove because the cane, while pliable, cannot be compressed to the extent of being invisible. Trimming is also much more difficult because you must cut into the spline and can damage the crown.

When you get around to the back again, lap the spline over itself and cut it with a sharp chisel. Wedge the ends into place. Sponge off the excess glue and allow the cane to dry, about a day. The cane will shrink and tighten, so much so that when tapped it will ring.

Soaking raises whiskers in the cane. A light sanding with fine paper will remove most of them; snip the larger ones with scissors. Another method is to burn off the hairs with a torch, but the possibility of scorching the surface makes this method risky.

If you wish, the cane can be coated. Lacquer sanding sealer plus a lacquer top coat of whatever sheen will work well and change the natural color little. To add color, use a water stain on the damp cane—carefully. Cracks in the cane will accept more dye and the seat will have uneven color. Other methods, such as coloring the top coat or rubbing in a pigmented stain on dry cane, all give different results. Test a sample first. In my experience, oil and varnish finishes are too dark and uneven. Of course, you can always choose not to finish it at all.

Making a caned headboard — My headboard, an ellipse with a major axis of 60 in. and a minor axis of 22 in., is made of elm laminated to a thickness of 1½ in., but ash, hickory and oak would work well, too. The ellipse is formed in two halves about 4 ft. long and joined by a simple scarf joint. Forming the headboard frame in two halves allows for different-width bedsteads and simplifies mold-building to a single all-purpose half. Just trim and join to the appropriate size.

After deciding on the design, I cut hardwood mold blocks 1½ in. thick shaped to the interior curve of the ellipse, and bolt them to a ¾-in. thick plywood base. I then cut follow-up

blocks 1½ in. thick. Laminating itself is straightforward. I slice the elm a little over ⅛ in. thick—I prefer to slice my own veneer rather than use the thinner commercial veneers. Although laminating thin veneers may result in sturdier construction, thicker veneers require fewer laminations and create a finished form that appears bent from solid stock. A band saw fitted out with a hard-edge (not silver-steel) blade is ideal for this work because it cuts a narrow kerf and therefore wastes less stock. On a 14-in. saw I use a ⅜-in., four-tooth-per-inch blade with buttress tooth design. The problem with using these blades is that they come only in bulk-packaged lengths. Some mail-order houses (like Woodcraft, Box 4000, Woburn, Mass. 01888) will cut and weld band-saw blades to size, but a toolmaker who will weld blades to your specifications will give you the greatest selection.

Slice the laminate strips and keep them in order as they come off the plank; a touch with the hand plane and they're ready for gluing. I use an aliphatic-resin glue because of its color, strength and fast cycle time. Coat both sides of each strip using a small, short-haired paint roller and rub the strips together. When the pack is glued up (in this case 13 strips) lay it between 1½-in. wide steel straps and clamp into the mold. Straps keep the fibers from breaking out around sharp bends, smooth out imperfections in the mold, and even out follow-block clamping pressure. I recommend spring steel, but low-carbon steel can be used successfully if all the kinks are flattened out. Paint the steel because the interaction between glue and steel and wood will leave a stain—with aliphatic-resin glues it is usually deep blue-black. Allowing 30 minutes from the beginning of clamp time to mold release is not unreasonable in a warm shop. Then restrain the piece for about 24 hours, wrapping it with string or clamping it around a spare piece of mold, to minimize springback. If you're not in a rush, let the piece sit in the mold under clamp pressure, and little if any springback will occur.

Once the halves are molded, I join them with a simple, long, slender scarf joint. The resulting ellipse is planed flat so the router, used to cut the groove, will ride on a level base.

The usual placement of the groove for the cane is ½ in. back from the interior edge of the frame. In the ellipse headboard, the groove is set back ¾ in. Bevel the surface from the groove to the inside edge so the cane stretches free of the frame. In new construction I prefer the ³⁄₁₆-in. spline for a delicate look, but no matter what size spline you choose, sink the groove ¼ in. deep.

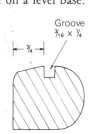

Groove
³⁄₁₆ × ¼

|← ¾ →|

Now laminate the frame legs in the same manner as before, but this time the ellipse frame becomes part of the mold. Fasten the frame down around interior pattern leg blocks, one set for each side. The lower part of each leg is solid lumber and is both form and screw-in block for the bed rails. There is always a gamble with springback and each leg can take an independent set, but this is not too important and won't affect the strength of the finished product.

Once it is dry, shape the final form of the headboard. Since the overall form is curvilinear, I complete it with generous radii. A spokeshave and hand plane, unlike power sanders, which tend to dig in and are somewhat hard to control on light work, allow control and smooth out dips. A 9-in. bench plane works well on long convex surfaces. I use three types of spokeshave: a flat-bottom straight blade, a convex-bottom

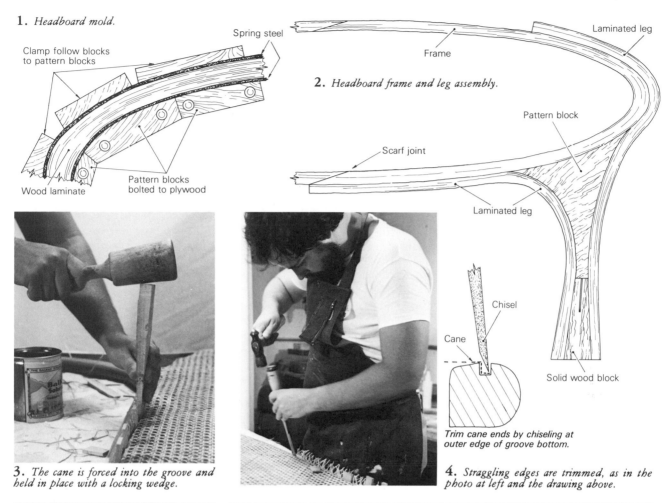

1. *Headboard mold.*

Clamp follow blocks
to pattern blocks

Spring steel

Laminated leg

Frame

2. *Headboard frame and leg assembly.*

Pattern block

Wood laminate

Pattern blocks
bolted to plywood

Scarf joint

Laminated leg

Chisel

Cane

Solid wood block

*Trim cane ends by chiseling at
outer edge of groove bottom.*

3. *The cane is forced into the groove and
held in place with a locking wedge.*

4. *Straggling edges are trimmed, as in the
photo at left and the drawing above.*

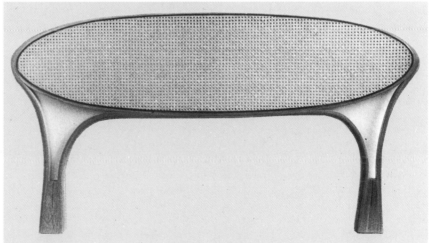

5. *The spline is wedged into the headboard.*   6. *The completed headboard, of laminated elm, is 60 in. by 36 in.*

straight blade and a flat-bottom concave blade. Sand lightly with 150 garnet paper, then with 220.

Finishing is next. I use a lacquer system. The normal sequence is grain-raising, sanding with 220 garnet paper, staining, sealing, filling if necessary, then the top coat. Always seal the frame before inserting the damp cane. The sealer keeps stain from bleeding into the cane and water from the damp cane from soaking into the frame.

The spline shown in the headboard is stained black with an alcohol-soluble aniline dye, which when set won't bleed. Mix

the strength needed and soak the spline until it is saturated with dye, then remove excess solution and dry. Resoak the spline in warm water to soften it, and it's ready to insert.

After cane and spline are installed and dried in the frame, complete finishing. I spray another coat of sealer over all and sand when dry. I only rub out the frame—rubbing out the cane is neither practical nor necessary.   □

Gerry Michaud is assistant professor of industrial design at the University of Cincinnati.

How I Make a Rocker
A master craftsman reveals the details

by Sam Maloof

Of the twelve different basic rocker designs I make, the model with solid wood seat and flat spindles is the most popular, and the most imitated. I don't believe in copying, but if knowing the way I work will help other serious woodworkers develop their own ideas, I'm happy to share my methods. I don't have a formula that I follow, nor do I work out mathematically the way my rocker rocks. Each rocking chair differs somewhat in dimension and also somewhat in the density of its parts, so I just work out its balance along the way. I aim for a rocker that doesn't throw you back or tip

you out, and somehow I'm usually right on.

I begin with the seat, cutting from 8/4 stock usually five boards at least 22 in. long and 3 in. to 7 in. wide—enough to add up to a 20-in. width after glue-up. I buy random width and length, common #1 or #2 walnut because its figure is more interesting than that of firsts and seconds. After milling the wood to size, I arrange the boards for the nicest figure match, regardless of whether this happens to be bark-side up or down. I then take the middle board and draw on its long edge the contour of a dished seat, a gentle curve whose maxi-

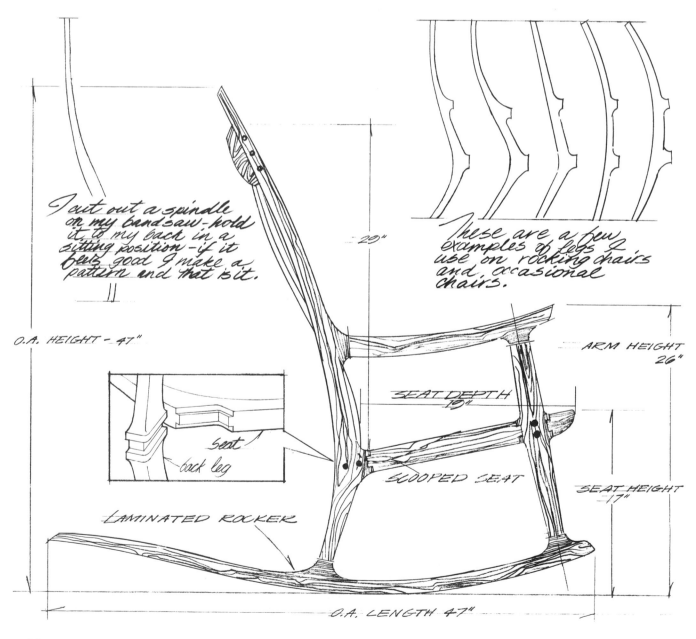

I cut out a spindle on my bandsaw—hold it to my back in a sitting position—if it feels good I make a pattern and that is it.

These are a few examples of legs I use on rocking chairs and occasional chairs.

O.A. HEIGHT - 47"

Seat

back leg

LAMINATED ROCKER

20"

ARM HEIGHT 26"

SEAT DEPTH 19"

SCOOPED SEAT

SEAT HEIGHT 17"

O.A. LENGTH 47"

mum depth leaves ½ in. of thickness about three-quarters of the way back from the front of the seat. I bandsaw this curve, holding the board on edge, then I angle the board through the blade and saw the top of the seat toward the front, to leave a ridge in the middle. I put this middle board back between the two seat boards to which it will be glued, and mark the contour I've just sawn on the edge of each. I bandsaw this contour, and transfer it to the edge of each outer board of the seat. I angle the boards to saw this contour, so that when joined together the five boards form a hollowed-out seat. Before gluing up, I mark and drill for 3-in. long, ½-in. dia. dowels, staggering them about 2 in. apart for ease of assembly, and for strength.

While the seat blank is in the clamps, I lay out both back legs, nesting them on a roughsawn 8/4 board about 7 in. wide and 48 in. long. I look for a curve in the grain to match the curve in the legs. I bandsaw the legs before jointing and thickness-planing them, because flattening the wide blank might result in a leg that is too thin. I get both legs to be the same shape with a 2¼-in. long straight cutter on the spindle shaper, using a template. When I've decided which is the right leg and which the left—by how the grain looks from the back and the front—I saw off the bottom of each leg at a 5° angle. Canted to this degree, each leg will join its rocker properly, giving the chair back a nice splay.

Now I take the clamps off the chair seat and I square up the edges so that the blank is 20 in. wide by 21 in. long. With a 7-in., 16-grit disc on my Milwaukee body grinder, I rough out the bandsawn hollow in the chair seat. I continue shaping and smoothing with 5-in. and then 2-in. discs, up to 150-grit. The top of the seat thus shaped, I cut the notches in the seat to receive the legs. For the back legs, I tablesaw a notch in each rear corner of the seat blank, 3 in. in from the

back and 2½ in. in from the side. For the cuts with the back edge of the seat on the table, I set the miter gauge at 85°, first in one direction, then the other, so that the leg posts will cant outward at their 5° angle. On some chairs I also angle the cuts on the sides, to cant the legs backward or forward, but on the rocker design shown here I make the side cuts at 90°. Now using a router with rabbeting bits—a regular 90° one for the front edges, and custom-made 85° and 95° bits for the side edges—I rabbet the top and bottom edges of these notches, as in the detail of the drawing on the facing page.

The notches for the front legs are less complicated: they're simply dadoed out at 90° and rabbeted, top and bottom, with a 90° rabbeting bit. Having cut the leg joints in the seat, I bandsaw its outline. Then I round over the underedge of the seat along the back and the two sides, using a 5-in. dia., 2-wing router bit that tapers the seat to about a 1-in. thick-

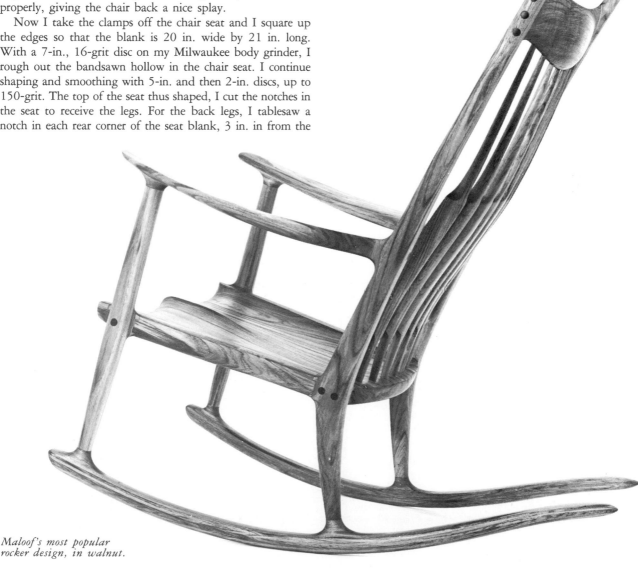

Maloof's most popular rocker design, in walnut.

With assistant Mike Johnson tracing the curve, Maloof demonstrates how he casts the shape of a rocker on the piece of particleboard that will be its gluing form. Also shown is the glued-up blank, with platforms for smoothing the transitions between legs and rocker, ready for shaping.

ness. I leave the area around the joints unshaped, for fairing later. Before fitting the legs, I finish-sand the seat.

With backsaw and chisel I cut the dadoes in the back legs that fit the rabbeted grooves in the seat. I suppose I could jig up and cut these on the tablesaw, but because the back legs are irregularly shaped and because I vary the angles of the back legs in different chair styles, I find the backsaw easier. Next I bandsaw the thickness of the back legs to 1⅜ in., leaving the full 2-in. thickness in the area of the seat joint and the crest-rail joint, for fairing. With the leg still basically rectangular in section, I drill a ½-in. hole in the bottom of the leg to receive the dowel that will connect it to the rocker. To shape the edges of the leg, including the corner that will fit the seat joint, I use a ½-in. roundover bit, but I leave unshaped the area where the arms will attach, and also the outside edges of the leg, because these will be hard-edged. Now I glue the back legs on, clamping across the width of the seat and from back to front.

I make each front leg out of 8/4 stock, 2¾ in. wide and 18 in. long. First I dado it on the tablesaw on three sides to fit the rabbeted notch in the sides of the seat. I then lathe-turn the leg, offsetting the center to the outside of the leg, so that the joint area will be thick enough for fairing into the seat. To complete the leg, I drill a ½-in. hole at each end for attaching the arm and the rocker. I then round over the corners that will fit the rabbet around the seat notch. Now I glue

the front legs on. When the glue is dry, I secure all the leg joints, front and back, to the seat with 4-in. drywall screws, countersunk and plugged with ebony.

At this stage, the chair looks like a seat board with a leg at each corner: no back, no arms, no rockers. I fair the leg joints now, sanding to 150-grit before attaching the arms, so that I have room to work. Each arm requires a piece of 8/4 stock, 6 in. wide and 19 in. long, although I usually cradle two arms on a longer piece. I lay out the arm, locating the dowel hole to attach the arm to the front leg, and saw the flat at the end of the arm to abut the flat on the back leg; this latter joint will be screwed from the back and plugged. Then I freehand-bandsaw the arm, shape it using a Surform, attach it, and fair the joints.

I make the back spindles, seven of them for this rocker, from pieces of 6/4 stock at least 29 in. long. I also use the waste from the back legs, thicknessed to 1⅜ in. I lay out the side profile on the face of the board, being careful to avoid areas where the grain will cross the width or the thickness of the spindle, and bandsaw. I also bandsaw and then spindle-sand the contour of the spindles as seen from the front. I used to shape the spindles, but one day I had two shatter on me, and I said phooey, there must be a safer way. They're just too slender to feed into the shaper, and it doesn't take that much longer to bandsaw them. I round over the back edges of each spindle with a ½-in. roundover bit, and then shape both ends

From *Fine Woodworking* magazine (September 1983) 42:52-55

with a rasp. The end that goes into the seat is ½ in. in diameter; the end that goes into the crest rail is ⅜ in. These dimensions are all eyeballed. I shape the slender parts by hand with a patternmakers' file, leaving hard edges along the front. Most of the front of the spindles remains flat.

Next I make the crest rail out of 10/4 stock, 7 in. wide and 26 in. long. I cut the ends to the 5° angle that will accommodate the splay of the back leg posts, then bandsaw the curve of the front and back faces. This gives me an accurate thickness in which to lay out the spindle holes. I space the hole centers evenly across the length of the crest rail, and then do the same across the width of the back of the seat, which will evenly splay the spindles. I use a yardstick now, aligned between corresponding hole centers in the crest rail and seat, to set my bevel gauge for positioning my drill-press table. I bore the crest-rail spindle holes on the drill press, but the seat spindle holes by eye. All holes drilled, I bandsaw the bottom edge of the crest rail and shape it with a Surform. I glue the spindles into the seat, fit the crest rail on the spindles and glue the rail in place between the back leg posts. When the glue is dry, I screw from the leg posts into the crest rail, countersinking and plugging the 2½-in. screws. I then fair the joint and finish-sand.

I laminate the rockers, beginning with 6/4 stock, thicknessing it to 1⅜ in. and then sawing it into ⅛-in. plies. I use a carbide-tipped blade on the tablesaw, and I don't joint the stock between passes—I find the sawn surface smooth enough for laminating. The rocker consists of seven plies about 48 in. long. To make the form for gluing them up, I bend a strip of wood to a shape that looks right, and have a helper trace this curve on a piece of ¾-in. particleboard. I bandsaw three pieces of particleboard along this line and face-glue them into a clamping form. I add seven more short plies to form two platforms for fairing the rocker into the legs. Then I glue up, using white glue. To ensure flatness, I clean up one edge of the rocker blank on my jointer, the other in the thickness planer. I round over the outside corners with a ½-in. bit, except in the area where the legs will connect. The rockers rough-sanded to shape, I put them on the flattest surface in my shop, my tablesaw, and mount the chair on top. The platforms allow for up to 2 in. of adjustment, forward or back, in the placement of the chair. I shift the chair back and forth until the rockers come to rest contacting the ground at about 2 in. in front of the rear legs. I find this looks best, and rocks best. I mount the chair to the rockers with ½-in. dowels, 4 in. long in the back, 3 in. long in the front. Then I fair the joint with a rasp.

I finish-sand the whole chair to 400-grit and apply three coats (at two-day intervals) of a three-part finish: equal parts of polyurethane varnish, raw tung oil and boiled linseed oil, removing all excess oil after each application. I then apply a final coat of a mixture I mix up on a double boiler: a half-gallon each of tung oil and boiled linseed oil, with a couple of handfuls of beeswax grated in. Do this outdoors and be careful—linseed has a low boiling point. The mixture has a long shelf life (stir before using), and leaves a beautiful sheen when buffed with a soft cloth. □

Sam Maloof has been making furniture for more than 35 years in Alta Loma, Calif. He is author of the book Sam Maloof: Woodworker, *published in 1983 by Kodansha International.*

A Child's Rocker
It's small and straightforward

by William Lavin

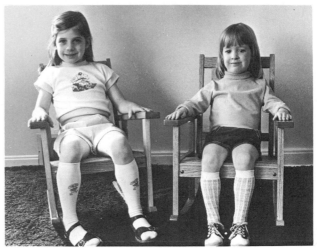

The author's daughters, testing out his project.

Picture an elderly woman knitting, or an old-timer chewing tobacco while playing checkers or whittling, and invariably both are sitting in rocking chairs. The rocking chair stereotypes this age. At the other extreme is the youngster full of unbridled energy that only a rocker can vent. We've all seen it: the elder rocking with gentle, smooth movement in a full-size chair, next to which the child rocks as vigorously as can be in a smaller version. For the average woodworker, a full-size rocker is intimidating to build—too many expectations to fulfill. A child-size chair, however, can inspire freer energies: simple, basic joints and modest proportions demand something reasonable from our abilities.

The idea for this particular chair came from one built more than 50 years ago for my father-in-law by his great uncle, John McCarthy. Originally handcrafted in white oak by a skilled woodworker for an energetic little farm lad, the design yields to simple power tools and a few hand tools. I have toyed with the idea of a short production run, so readily does this design lend itself to a simple router jig for making the mortises.

Construction is divided into three subassemblies: the sides, the backrest and the seat. The sides and backrest are joined similarly: horizontals mortised into verticals, except for the arms, which are mortised to receive the tenons on the front posts. Cut this stock, and lay out and cut the joints. Leave the legs a few inches longer than needed so that you can trace the curve of the rocker and then saw the legs later to fit. Note also that for maximum strength the rockers ought to be bandsawn from stock whose grain follows the rocker curve. Dry-assemble, and when everything fits right, take the assemblies apart and sand, finishing up those surfaces that would otherwise be difficult after assembly. All corners should be chamfered. Drill the holes for the screws that will fasten the

Drawings: Lee Hov

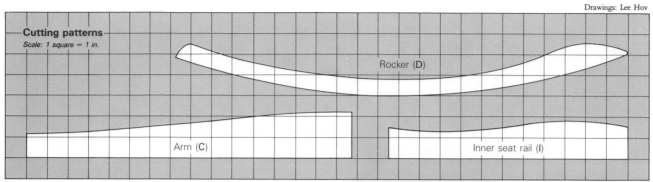

Cutting patterns
Scale: 1 square ≈ 1 in.

Rocker (D)

Arm (C)

Inner seat rail (I)

Making a rocker for a child brings a formidable furniture project down to size. Detail, above, shows where backrest is screwed to seat frame and arms.

arms to the backrest posts and the backrest posts to the seat. The backrest assembly is completed in a like manner. Glue, clamp and allow to set overnight. When the side assemblies have cured, center the legs on the rockers, drill and fasten with 2-in. screws.

The seat assembly is a butt-glued and screwed frame with the slats tacked on top. The top edge of the inner seat rails is sawn to a contour that dishes the seat. The seat frame is tapered in plan, and I find it helpful to draw the full-size plan view, showing the thickness of the seat rails and front and rear crosspieces. Then I cut the pieces oversize, and place them directly on the view for final cutting (at an angle of 3°) and assembly. The front crosspiece is assembled directly with glue and screws (countersunk and plugged), while the rear crosspiece is fastened only temporarily by a couple of pins—I use large cotter pins, because their rounded ends make them easy to remove. The pins keep the seat rails in position while the slats are attached. At final assembly, screws attaching the backrest to the seat will replace the pins.

The seat slats are ripped from a wide piece of ¾-in. thick stock. I shape the edge first using a Stanley #45 fitted with a Record 12H nosing attachment. Another way would be to scribe guidelines about ³⁄₃₂ in. from the edge and block-plane a rounded edge. And, of course, there's always the router with a roundover bit, although you'd only approximate the nosing drawn. Rip a slat (I actually rip two at once, because I use 30-in. long stock and chop the ripping in half), then shape and rip the next slat. Make a couple of extras in case you make a mistake when cutting to the exact length later. I find it easier to finish each strip before assembly, so that finishing material will not fill in the crevices between the slats.

Cut the finished slat lengths individually, scribing directly from the seat frame, and drill a small hole in each end using a jig to ensure that all the holes will be equidistant and aligned. Fasten the slats with glue and brass nails.

Complete the assembly by first gluing and screwing (from the inside) the seat frame to the side crosspieces. Then attach the backrest, screwing from the backrest posts into the seat frame, and through the arm extensions into the backrest posts. Countersink these screws and plug with buttons for a tactile detail. A durable varnish will finish your heirloom chair. □

William Lavin teaches junior high school industrial arts in Camillius, N.Y. Photos by the author.

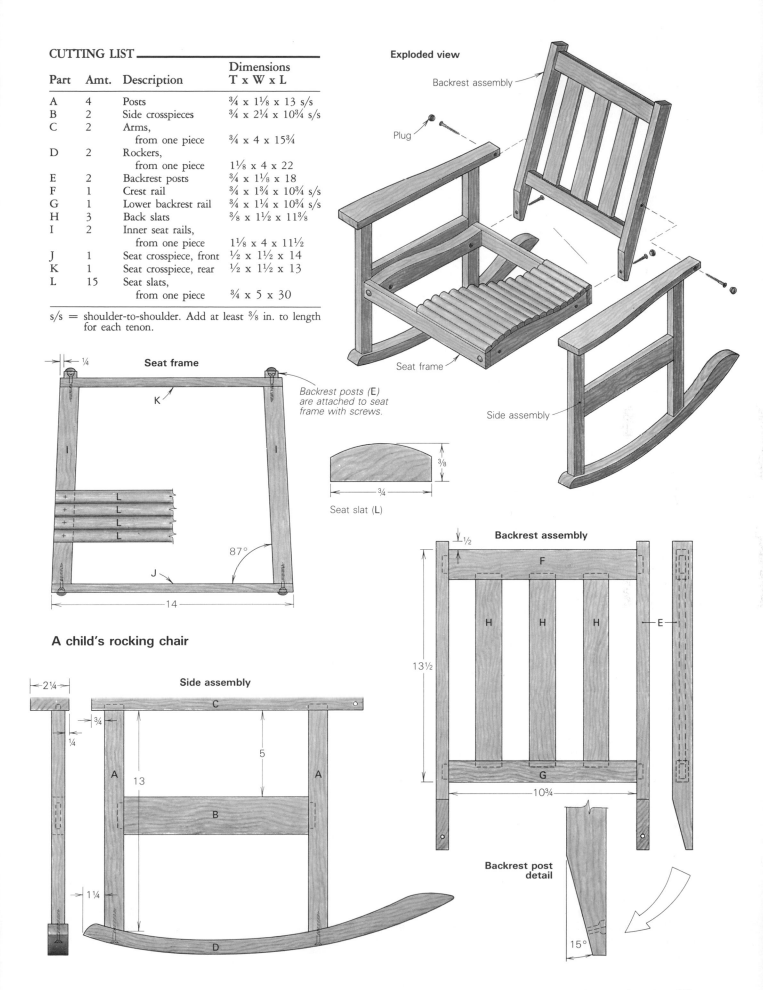

CUTTING LIST

Part	Amt.	Description	Dimensions T x W x L
A	4	Posts	¾ x 1⅛ x 13 s/s
B	2	Side crosspieces	¾ x 2¼ x 10¾ s/s
C	2	Arms, from one piece	¾ x 4 x 15¾
D	2	Rockers, from one piece	1⅛ x 4 x 22
E	2	Backrest posts	¾ x 1⅛ x 18
F	1	Crest rail	¾ x 1¾ x 10¾ s/s
G	1	Lower backrest rail	¾ x 1¼ x 10¾ s/s
H	3	Back slats	⅜ x 1½ x 11⅜
I	2	Inner seat rails, from one piece	1⅛ x 4 x 11½
J	1	Seat crosspiece, front	½ x 1½ x 14
K	1	Seat crosspiece, rear	½ x 1½ x 13
L	15	Seat slats, from one piece	¾ x 5 x 30

s/s = shoulder-to-shoulder. Add at least ⅜ in. to length for each tenon.

Exploded view

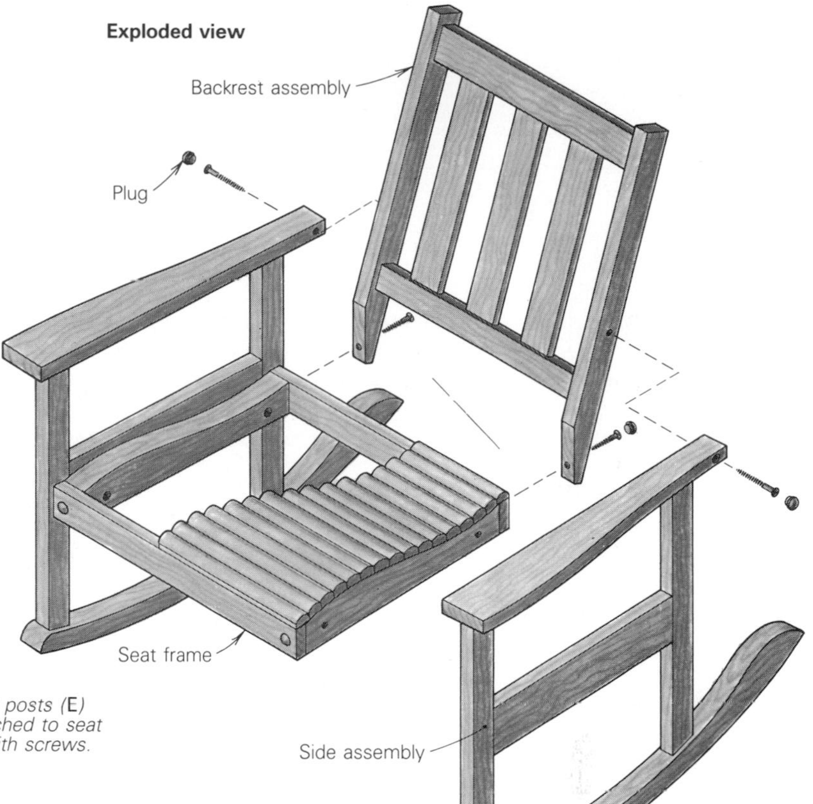

Backrest assembly
Plug
Seat frame
Side assembly

Seat frame

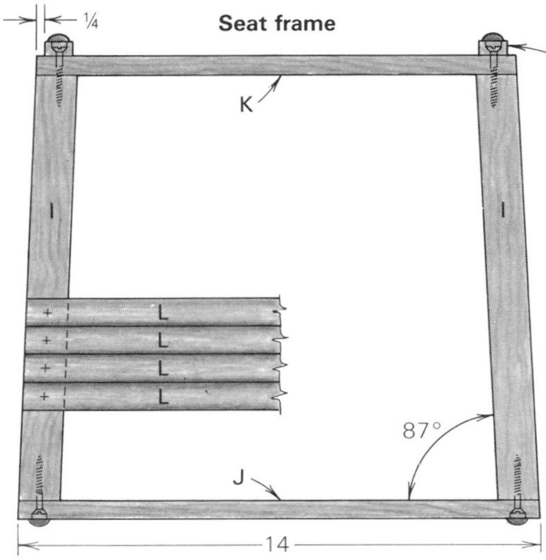

¼
K
I
I
L
L
L
L
87°
J
14
Backrest posts (E) are attached to seat frame with screws.

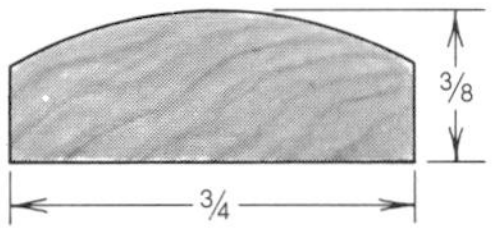

⅜
¾

Seat slat (L)

A child's rocking chair

Side assembly

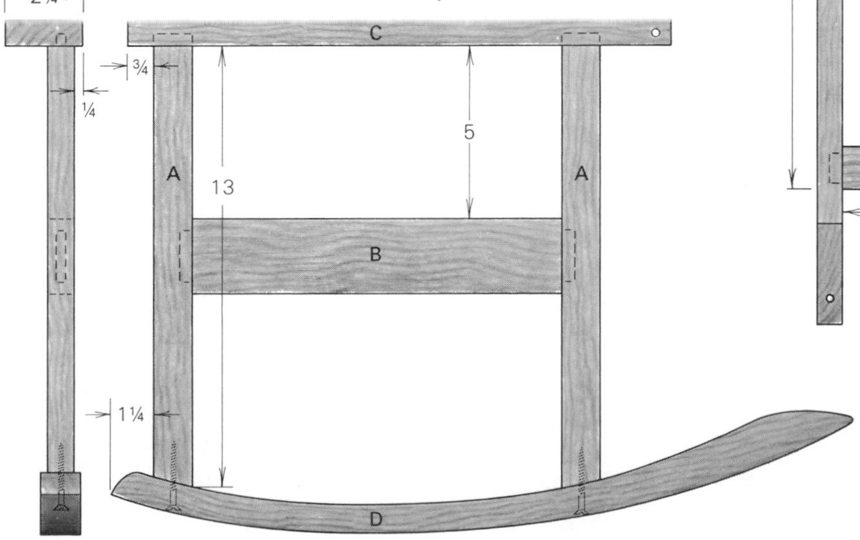

2¼
C
¾
¼
5
A
13
A
B
1¼
D

Backrest assembly

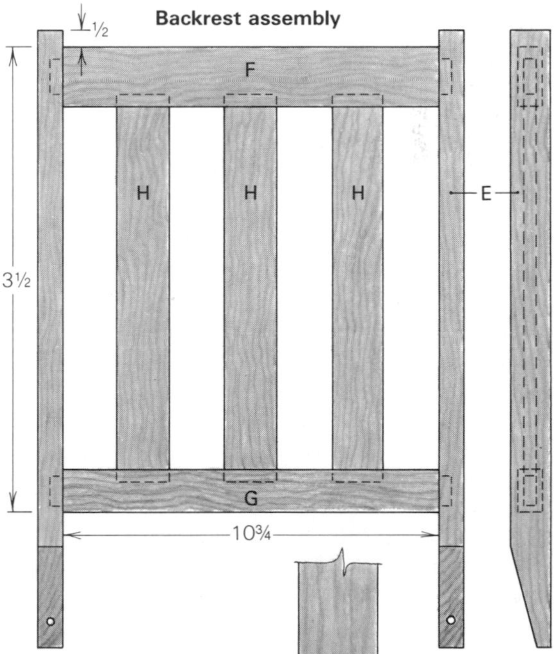

½
F
H
H
H
E
13½
G
10¾

Backrest post detail

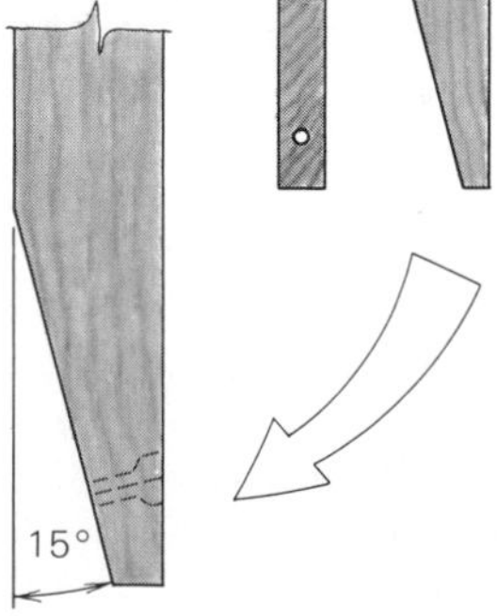

15°

Plans for a High-Chair/Rocker
Two chairs for the price of one

by R.W. Swinyard

"Dad, will you make us a high chair for Aimee?"

A few months after the birth of my first grandchild, my daughter, Linda, made that request in a phone call from Maryland. What proud grandparent would be able to refuse? This maple high-chair/rocker is the result. I built two bases, one for the high chair and another for the rocker, so Aimee will get a few more years' use out of the piece. When either base is detached from the seat, the chair fits easily into the backseat of a small car.

In this article, I'll tell how I use an auxiliary tilted table on my drill press to angle the holes so that all the chair's parts go together. I always test-assemble the parts as I go. Each part in a chair affects the next, and going piece-by-piece gives me a chance to make small changes if necessary.

The auxiliary table is a ramp that tilts the part being drilled to the correct angle. Mine, shown in figure 2 on the facing page, is a piece of plywood about 8 in. by 10 in. I tilt it simply by tacking plywood shims to its back edge. To check the angle, I line up the auxiliary table's centerline under the bit and aim it at the center of the drill-press column. Then I set a T-bevel between the centerline and the column, and verify the angle with a protractor. The various angles at which to tilt the table are shown in the drawings.

Many of the holes are at compound angles, that is, they appear to lean in two directions, one from the front view, the other from the side. I drill such holes in two ways. The cleats at the top of the rocker base illustrate one way. As shown at right, the rocker legs radiate from the cleats at 13° in side view and at 11° in front view. I raise the auxiliary table to the 13° angle by tacking shims under it at the back, then I block up one side of the table to 11°, the second angle. This tilts the workpiece in two directions at once. A second way—which I use to drill the holes in the seat for the back corner

Fig. 1: High chair converts to rocker

The same seat can be screwed to two different bases to extend the life of the chair.

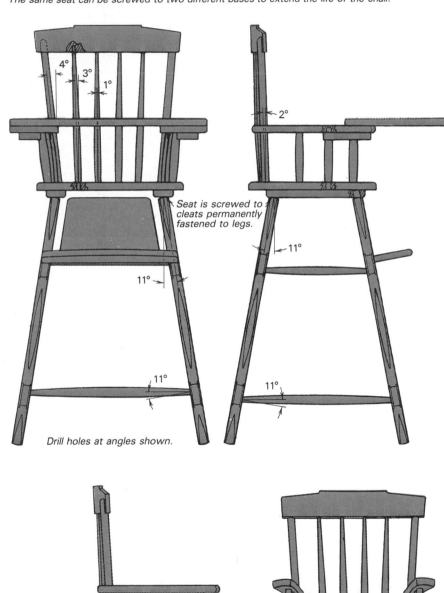

Seat is screwed to cleats permanently fastened to legs.

Drill holes at angles shown.

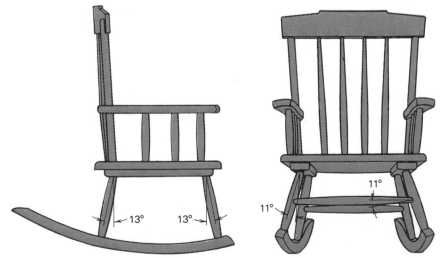

posts—is to determine the axis line along which the "compound angles" actually become a single angle (for more on axis lines, see the article on pp. 6-11). In the finished chair seat, for instance, the back corner posts show a 4° tilt in front view and a 2° tilt in side view. You can get the posts to align with these angles by drilling a 6° hole as shown in figure 2. The axis line is shown as line A on the seat plan in figure 3.

An axis line, whether it be the angled line on the seat or merely the centerline of the part itself—as when drilling the legs—must point in the same direction as the table's centerline, or the angle will not be correct. As an aid in positioning the workpiece, line up the auxiliary table's centerline directly under the bit and point it at the center of the drill-press column. Then when you position the axis line on the workpiece under the bit and point it at the column, the part will be positioned correctly.

Some parts can lie flat on the auxiliary table when being drilled, but others will need extra support. The chair's crest rail can be braced against a block to keep it steady. Round parts, such as the rocker legs, ought to be clamped in a handscrew, and so should the rockers themselves. Spade bits work fine for the through holes, and machine-spur bits or Forstner bits are good for the blind ones.

First lay out the seat as in the drawing and drill the back corner post holes. Next turn the corner posts to the size shown in figure 7 on p. 91, which contains dimensions for most of the other chair turnings as well. The two crucial diameters are the ¾-in. tenon for the seat and the ⅞-in. diameter that fits the hole in the armrest. One way to size tenons is to caliper the diameter of the drill bit that will cut the mortise, then use the calipers to check the size of the tenon while it's still on the lathe. Some experimentation will show you the tolerances you should allow with your particular set of bits. Aim for a snug not a force fit. Set the posts in the seat and make the armrest blanks (oversize for the time being: ¾x3x14½), but don't drill the other holes in the seat yet.

For each armrest to fit over its corner post, the hole in it must be drilled at the correct angle and orientation. In your mind's eye, slide the armrest down the post until it lies flat on the seat and parallel to the seat's edge. Notice that the

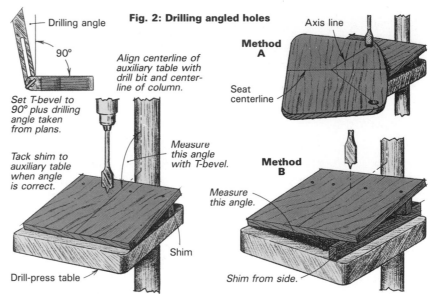

Fig. 2: Drilling angled holes

Drilling angle
90°

Set T-bevel to 90° plus drilling angle taken from plans.

Align centerline of auxiliary table with drill bit and centerline of column.

Tack shim to auxiliary table when angle is correct.

Measure this angle with T-bevel.

Drill-press table

Shim

Method A

Axis line

Seat centerline

Method B

Measure this angle.

Measure this angle.

Shim from side.

When the plans call for a single angle, shim a plywood auxiliary table as required (above left). Compound angles can be drilled in two ways. **Method A:** A single 6° hole drilled on the axis line (line A in the seat plan below) yields an approximate tilt of 2° in side view and 4° in front view. **Method B:** First shim the table up to one angle, then shim the side to the other.

Fig. 3: Seat layout and armrest

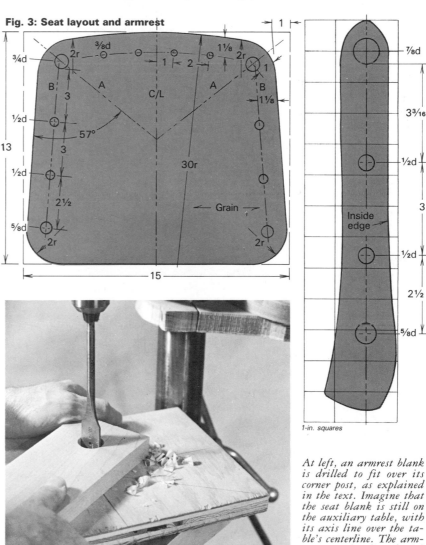

¾d · 2r · ⅜d · 1⅛ · 2r · 1
B · A · C/L · A · B
3 · 1 · 2 · 1⅛
½d · 57° · 3
½d · 2½ · 30r
⅝d · 2r · Grain · 2r
13 · 15

⅞d
3³⁄₁₆
½d · Inside edge
3
½d
2½
⅝d

1-in. squares

At left, an armrest blank is drilled to fit over its corner post, as explained in the text. Imagine that the seat blank is still on the auxiliary table, with its axis line over the table's centerline. The armrest must be aligned with the seat's edge, radiating out at the 57° angle shown in figure 3.

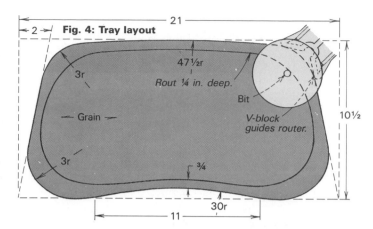

Fig. 4: Tray layout

21
2
47½r
Rout ¼ in. deep.
3r
Bit
Grain
V-block guides router.
10½
3r
¾
11
30r

Cut the tray to shape, then rout the dish's outline with a core-box bit, guiding the router with a V-block as shown in figure 4. Next rout out the center with a straight bit (photo above), leaving bridges to support the router. Then chisel these away and sand.

hole in the armrest lines up exactly with the angle of the hole in the seat. Now imagine that the seat is still on the auxiliary table, and that you have just drilled the corner post hole. If you were to raise the quill and lay the armrest blank in position flat on the seat, you could drill the hole. But this would risk damaging the seat beneath if anything shifted. So, instead, you can mark the correct position for the arm on the auxiliary table, and drill the hole as shown in the photo on p. 89.

To determine where to mark the correct position for the armrest on the table, refer to the seat plan in figure 3. There is a 57° angle marked between the axis line on the seat and the centerline of the armrest. When the back corner post hole was being drilled, the axis line on the seat was directly over the centerline of the auxiliary table. The armrest's centerline must therefore be turned 57° from the auxiliary table's centerline when you drill the hole.

Also, as you slide the armrest up and down the post, the higher it is, the farther it moves back in relation to the seat. Consider the arm spindles. I've designed them to be perpendicular to the seat in side view, as shown in figure 1, not to tilt back the way the back corner posts do. I therefore had to compensate for the armrest's backward displacement by offsetting the arm spindle holes farther forward from the corner post hole in the armrest than they are in the seat. I made a trial assembly and found that the offset, measured along the centerline of the armrest, was 3/16 in., and this is the amount shown in figure 3.

Next verify the angle for the arm

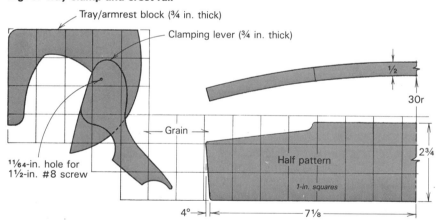

The armrests slip into blocks glued to the bottom of the tray and are locked by clamping levers (photo above, plan below). The legs (bottom of page) are sawn square and centered in the lathe. After the tenon at the tailstock end has been turned, the leg is removed and its corners rounded with the router. Back in the lathe, each leg is then turned to the shape shown, with 'squares' where the rung mortises will be drilled.

Fig. 5: Tray clamp and crest rail

Tray/armrest block (¾ in. thick)
Clamping lever (¾ in. thick)
½
30r
Grain
Half pattern
2¾
11/64-in. hole for 1½-in. #8 screw
1-in. squares
4°
7⅛

Fig. 6: High-chair legs and footrest

Footrest
30r
Round top and bottom.
Leg rest
1⅛
Position of leg rest
5
1
11°
6
Round face only.
11°
¾
10½
¾
Flat
4
2
11½
2
6
1
Leg
¾
26½

spindle holes. I used a T-bevel, with its handle perpendicular to line B in figure 3, to check that the angle of slant of the corner post in that plane was the 4° the drawing indicated it should be. It was, so I shimmed the auxiliary table to suit, drilling all holes in both armrests to a depth of ⅝ in. Then I drilled the matching holes through the seat.

I bandsawed the curves on both armrests according to the pattern in figure 3. Figure 5 and the bottom photo on the facing page show how the tray bottom locks into the front end of the armrest.

To drill the seat for the back center spindles, first shim the auxiliary table to 2°, the backward tilt of the spindles, then block it up to the necessary side angles, which are shown in figure 1. The crest-rail blank should be tilted only toward the sides of the chair when you're drilling the holes in it, so it will follow the 2° backward tilt of the corner posts.

I test-assembled everything, sanded away all machine marks, rounded the edges with the router where appropriate, and plugged the screw heads. Then I made the tray as shown in figure 4 and the photo at the top of the facing page, and I turned the legs as illustrated in figure 6. I made the footrest and the leg rest to the shapes shown.

For the final base assembly, I attached the footrest and the lower front rung to the legs first, so I could drive the screws holding the footrest with a brace and screwdriver bit. I assembled the back next, then the sides, using web clamps to hold the frame together while the glue dried, and checking for squareness with a framing square.

Keep in mind that the chair seat will be screwed to the tops of the cleats. During glue-up, be sure that the top surfaces of both cleats lie in the same flat plane. You can check this by laying a pair of straightedges from cleat to cleat and sighting along them, then working the cleats into proper alignment. The same concern applies to the rocker base.

When all was done, I applied two coats of urethane varnish to the chair, the base and the rocker, and gave the tray three coats of Constantine's Bowl Seal.

There's one necessary item not shown in the drawings—a safety strap that's fastened under the seat. □

R.W. Swinyard is a retired industrial arts teacher from Kinderhook, N.Y. Photos by the author.

Fig. 7: Rockers, spindles, cleats and rungs

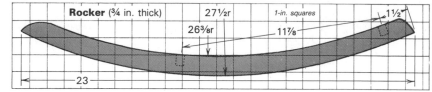

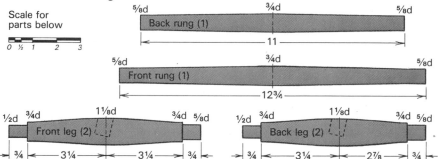

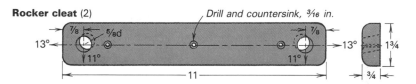

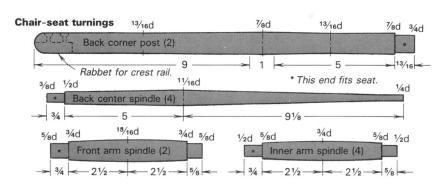

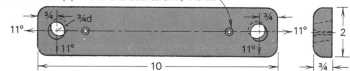

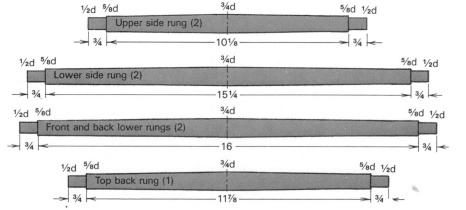

A Spindle Cradle

by Dick Webber

The imminent arrival of our first grandchild recently forced me to put aside other projects and turn my attention to the design and construction of a cradle. An adequate supply of air-dried cherry, purchased eight years ago from a country sawmill, seemed an ideal choice of wood. My problem was the design. I wanted it to be practical, of a style that blended traditional lines, and of a construction that omitted metal parts yet allowed the cradle both to rock and to be removed from its stand. Too, it should be sturdy enough to last several generations. I am an amateur turner, and I got some assistance in designing the spindles for this cradle from a long-time turner, Walker Justice, of Vermillion Bay, Ont. He improved the spindle forms by suggesting more pronounced curves, perfectly semicircular beads and right-angled shoulders, exactly the sort of crispness that is usually missing from a beginner's turnings.

The stand—I wanted the effect of a single-post end support, but needed good lateral strength to withstand the racking stress of a rocking cradle. I decided to fasten two 8/4 turnings together, and left three parts of the turnings square for later gluing. The lower two receive the square tenons of the turned stretchers. The upper one receives the cradle-support pin (of oak, for strength), and is slotted accordingly. The bottom of the larger and smaller diameters of this T-shaped slot must conform to the size and shape of the pin. I started the cut by drilling a hole the size of the small diameter of the support pin into the face of the post where pin meets post. Then I chiseled down into the top the exact width of the diameters of the pin, making sure to position the mortise properly for clearance between post and cradle, and stopping at the centerline of the previously drilled hole. The last task here is to cut out the rounded part of the slot that receives the large diameter of the pin. I roughed out the space with a ¼-in. chisel, and finished by making a slightly smaller copy of the support pin, gluing sandpaper around the large end and turning my sandpaper peg in the slot with an electric drill. Once the cradle was built, I drilled a hole in each end and glued in the support pins, waxing them with paraffin where they fit the T-slot for smooth, quiet operation.

I bandsawed the feet of the stand from 2x3 stock, then mortised for the posts and drilled for caster posts before rasping and sanding the feet to a pleasing rounded shape. Casters are optional, but I figured them in my overall height, so omitting them would necessitate adjusting the length of the posts or the shape of the feet.

The cradle—The construction of the cradle is post and rail, using mortise-and-tenon joints with framed panels at both ends. One-inch dia. spindles with ½-in. round tenons connect the top and bottom rails before they are joined to the corner posts. I laid out the corner posts, then turned the ball at the top and the button at the bottom. I then mortised the posts for rails, and grooved them for the end panels. I joined the rails ⅛ in. from the outside of the posts in order to allow more depth for the tenons and to keep them from meeting.

Instead of molding them, I grooved the outside face of the top side rails and the top of the end rails using a ¼-in. core-box router bit. I sanded the edges of the grooves and rounded over the tops of the side rails to produce a section like that of a handrail.

I made the bottom of the cradle from ½-in. stock, notched to fit around the posts. The bottom rests on ⅜-in. by ½-in. cleats screwed to the inside of the

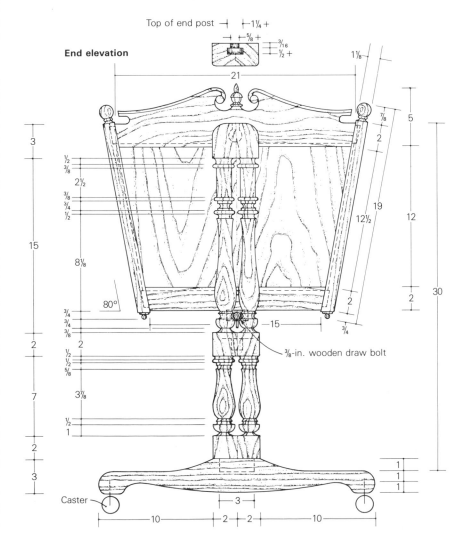

End elevation

Top of end post

³⁄₈-in. wooden draw bolt

Caster

Photos: Mike Hill; author's plans redrawn by Karen Pease

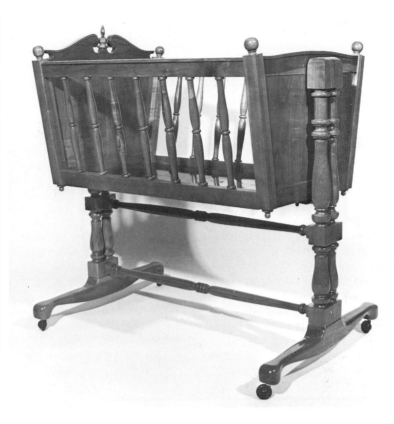

An ideal project for the turner, this cherry cradle uses twin 8/4 spindles for strong, stable posts. Instead of using metal hardware, the cradle pivots on an oak pin in a T-shaped slot, above, cut at the top of the posts. The cradle can thus be lifted easily from its stand.

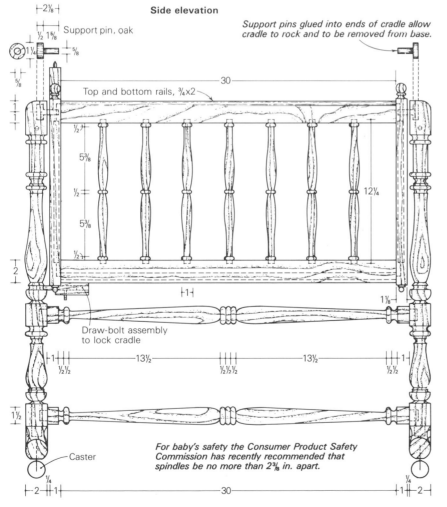

Side elevation

2⅛

Support pin, oak

Support pins glued into ends of cradle allow cradle to rock and to be removed from base.

1¼ ⅝ ⅝

½ 1⅝

⅝

Top and bottom rails, ¾x2

30

½

5⅜

½

12¼

5⅜

½

2

1⅛

1⅛

1

Draw-bolt assembly to lock cradle

1 ½ 1 13½ ½ ½ ½ 13½ ½ ½ 2 1

1½

Caster ¼

For baby's safety the Consumer Product Safety Commission has recently recommended that spindles be no more than 2⅜ in. apart.

¼

2 1 30 1 2

cradle, flush with the bottom of the rails. I chose not to fasten the bottom to the cradle thinking that, given the habits of infants, it might be handy to be able to remove it. A standard-size mattress fits into the bottom of the cradle.

To keep the cradle from rocking when the baby is left unattended, I made a wooden version of a draw bolt and fastened it to the bottom of the cradle. When extended, the bolt slips between the two turnings of the end post.

Finishing—Because so much of this project involved turnings, I finished the parts before assembly. I use Qualasole hand-rubbing lacquer (available from Woodcraft, 41 Atlantic Ave., Box 4000, Woburn, Mass. 01888). I begin by applying a generous amount with a cloth pad, making sure to saturate corners and crevices. As the finish builds, I apply lighter coats, increasing the pressure on the pad as the finish dries. When finishing on the lathe, I stop the lathe occasionally and rub longitudinally to prevent ridges from developing. The final coat should be a light application of Qualasole mixed 50/50 with thinner and rubbed vigorously until dry. □

Dick Webber is a real estate developer in Oklahoma City, Okla.

From *Fine Woodworking* magazine (November 1981) 31:72-73

A Wooden Mechanism for Dropside Cribs

by Kenneth Rower

Cribs are often designed so the sides can be slid down to get the baby in and out. The proper metal parts might be hard to come by, and even then unsatisfying to see and use. But the whole mechanism—pins and grooves that allow the gates to slide and to be removed when the child outgrows the need for them, bolts that stop the gates in several positions, and springs that activate the bolts—all can be wood.

Fit upper and lower guide pins at each end of the gate to run in grooves cut in opposite posts. At the bottom of each groove, cut an escapement for the lower guide pin, to allow the gate to be swung outward. Once in this position, the gate can be removed entirely by tilting it, thus freeing the upper guide pins from the grooves.

Near the top of each leg, deepen the groove into a notch that will receive the spring-loaded bolt. Two such bolts, each passing through a bar and a stile of the gate, support the gate when up. A single-leaf wooden spring, housed in its own groove in the gate and retained at its lower end, presses the bolt outward into the notch. Drill a finger hole in the end of each bolt to make the bolts easier to retract.

Lower down in each groove, cut a notch to hold the gate off the floor. Slope the grooves for a short distance above these lower notches to allow the gate to be raised without having to retract the bolts. Cover the seats of the notches with thin cork to absorb shock.

To prevent a child from withdrawing the bolts, first at one end then the other, and bringing the gate down with resounding effect, fit locks across the bolts where they pass through the bars of the gate. These locks are simply dowel pins notched part way through for the thickness of the bolt, and shaped where they protrude on the outside of the bar to offer a finger-and-thumb grip. In one position the pin allows the bolt to move freely, but if rotated one-quarter to one-half turn, it locks the bolt in the mortise.

While there are no special pitfalls to the construction, groove and notch depth, bolt travel and bar centers in the gate must be carefully planned. The guide pins on the prototype are through-fitted dry, and thus adjustable as to projection, but you can cross-pin them once they are properly located in their grooves. Make the bolts and springs of straight-grained stock, and cut the mortise in the bolt for the spring deep enough so the spring can be pulled up past its retaining pin when installing or removing the mechanism. Mortises in the bars should be cut before the bars are shaped, and the whole system tested before gluing up the gate. The holes for the lock pins can be bored once everything else is in place. Locate them to put just less than half the diameter of the pin in the path of the bolt.

In order for the system to work smoothly, the legs of the crib must be stout enough to resist spreading; otherwise the gate can jam. □

Kenneth Rower is a woodworker in Newbury Village, Vt.

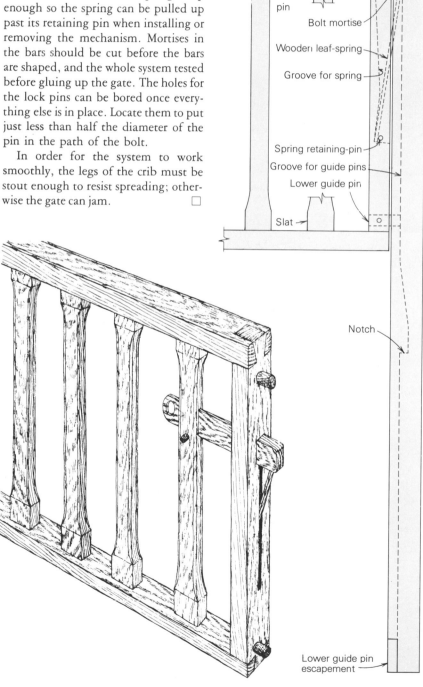

Side view

Bar

Bolt

Upper guide pin

Lock pin

Bolt mortise

Wooden leaf-spring

Groove for spring

Spring retaining-pin

Groove for guide pins

Lower guide pin

Slat

Notch

Lower guide pin escapement

From *Fine Woodworking* magazine (November 1981) 31:74

Making a Pencil-Post Bed
How to shape tapered octagonal posts

by Herbert W. Akers

I knew I was in trouble as soon as we walked out of the furniture store. We had just looked at several king-size pencil-post beds in solid cherry, all priced at about a thousand bucks. Then my wife asked me if I could make one. I took another look at the price tag and naively replied, "Sure." As I walked back to the car, I heard a little voice asking: How in the devil can you shape a 7-ft. long, 3-in. square post into an octagonal section with equal sides and a graceful taper? How do you even hold a post that size securely enough to plane it?

Before I was through making the bed shown here, I had answered those questions myself. Shaping the posts turned out to be easier than I'd thought—I planed them by hand, using a method similar to what boatbuilders employ to make masts and spars. Holding the posts was no problem either, once I had devised a vise made of pipe clamps and 2x4s.

Finding plans for the bed I wanted, however, wasn't so simple. Many country beds of the mid 18th century are called pencil-post because their posts are hexagonal in section, just like a wooden pencil. Others, however, are square posts ta-

Fig. 1: Pencil-post bed

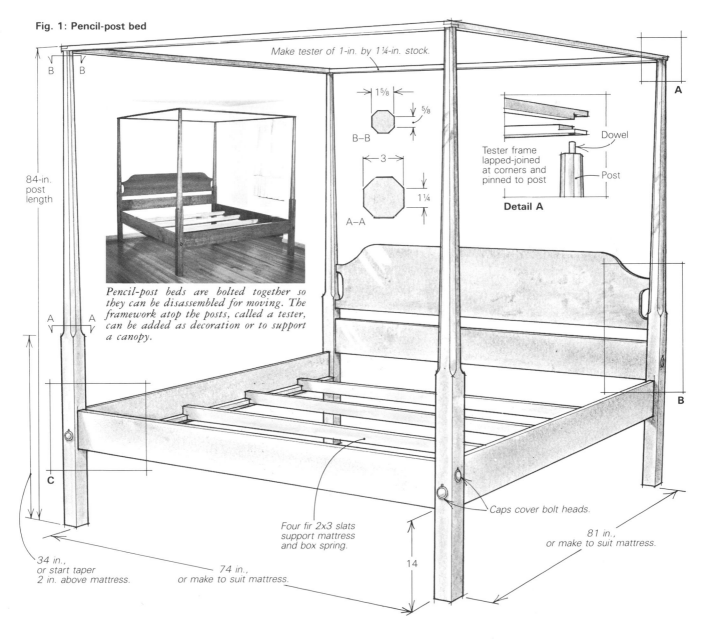

Make tester of 1-in. by 1¼-in. stock.

B–B   1⅝   ⅝

A–A   3   1¼

Tester frame lapped-joined at corners and pinned to post

Dowel

Post

Detail A

84-in. post length

Pencil-post beds are bolted together so they can be disassembled for moving. The framework atop the posts, called a tester, can be added as decoration or to support a canopy.

Caps cover bolt heads.

Four fir 2x3 slats support mattress and box spring.

34 in., or start taper 2 in. above mattress.

74 in., or make to suit mattress.

14

81 in., or make to suit mattress.

pering into eight sides. An exhaustive search at the local library turned up no plans, so in desperation I turned to a stack of old antiques magazines, and I got lucky: I found photos of several beds with octagonal posts.

By contemporary standards, pencil-post beds are quite lofty. Typically, the top of the mattress was 32 in. high, elevating the occupants well above the cold floor and leaving room for a trundle bed beneath. You can design the bed with a lower mattress, but if you do, consider also lowering the point where the taper begins on the posts, which is usually 2 in. above the mattress. Don't forget to measure the mattress and box spring you will actually use, and leave about a 1-in. clearance at the sides and ends for bedclothes. I found it essential to make a full-size drawing of the posts on taped-up sheets of graph paper.

Shaping the posts—Sixteen-quarter lumber is hard to find, and prone to checking anyway, so I laminated two pieces of 1½-in. thick cherry to make my 3x3s, taking care to match the color and grain. I made a quick-action vise consisting of

two Sears pipe clamps threaded into flanges screwed to the benchtop, as shown in figure 2. With this setup, I could securely grip about 27 in. of the post either on its corners or on its flat sides. The rest of the post extended out over the end of the workbench, so I could plane in either direction, depending on the grain of the wood.

Lay out the posts as shown in figure 3. Try to arrange your layout so that you'll be planing with the grain toward the smaller end of the post. You may want to test-plane it first, as grain-reading can be tricky with some woods. You'll be using this method over and over again to determine how much wood to cut away. The idea is to draw the guidelines, cut away material from the adjacent surfaces and then draw more guidelines on the newly cut surfaces. You alternate your shaping work, cutting the post's four corners first, then the four flats, then the corners again and so on. As you progress, the octagon will slowly take shape until each surface measures $\frac{5}{8}$ in. at the top and $1\frac{1}{4}$ in. where the tapers begin. It may be tempting to simply scribe the octagon's final shape on the end of the post and taper down to it, but this would require re-

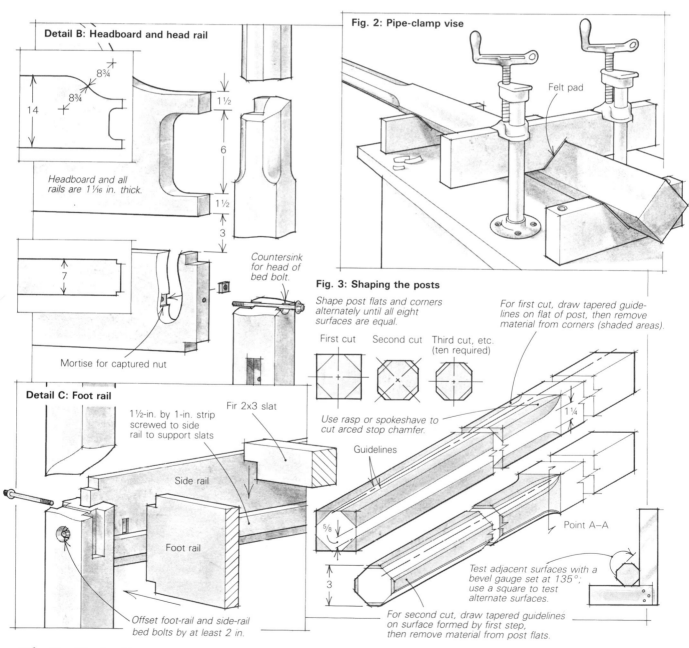

Detail B: Headboard and head rail

14

8¾

8¾

1½

6

1½

3

Headboard and all rails are 1 1/16 in. thick.

7

Mortise for captured nut

Countersink for head of bed bolt.

Detail C: Foot rail

1½-in. by 1-in. strip screwed to side rail to support slats

Fir 2x3 slat

Side rail

Foot rail

Offset foot-rail and side-rail bed bolts by at least 2 in.

Fig. 2: Pipe-clamp vise

Felt pad

Fig. 3: Shaping the posts

Shape post flats and corners alternately until all eight surfaces are equal.

First cut   Second cut   Third cut, etc. (ten required)

Use rasp or spokeshave to cut arced stop chamfer.

Guidelines

For first cut, draw tapered guidelines on flat of post, then remove material from corners (shaded areas).

1¼

5/8

Point A-A

3

Test adjacent surfaces with a bevel gauge set at 135°; use a square to test alternate surfaces.

For second cut, draw tapered guidelines on surface formed by first step, then remove material from post flats.

From *Fine Woodworking* magazine (July 1983) 41:54-56

moving too much material from one face at once, making it difficult to keep the taper uniform and the post straight.

I began shaping by cutting chamfers on the square post. Starting at the bottom of the tapers, I cut toward the top of the post with a sharp chisel until I could switch to a power plane which I'd used this project as an excuse to buy. A hand plane would be fine for this work, but a lot slower. Where the chamfers stop and arc into the square lower portion of the post, I used a ¾-in. rotary rasp chucked in an electric drill, although a spokeshave is the authentic solution. As you plane, keep a long metal straightedge handy to check for scooped-out spots in your tapered surface. Check the accuracy of your work with a square and a bevel gauge, as in figure 3.

As you near the final shape, check the dimensions of your post against the full-size drawing and sight down the post for straightness. On my post drawing, I struck perpendicular lines at 5-in. intervals, and then used dividers to make sure that all the faces were equal and that the width of my taper matched the drawing at these points.

If you end up planing against the grain and you tear out a chunk or two during the first few cuts, reverse your plane. You'll be cutting away enough wood to remove any blemishes as you approach the final shape. Just be sure to keep your plane extra sharp and to set the blade so that it takes a fine shaving.

Assembling the bed—I made a full-size drawing of the curved ends of the headboard and transferred this shape with carbon paper to the two glued-up boards that form the headboard. I mortised the posts first and then cut the headboard to fit. Since I wanted to be able to dismantle the bed for moving, I didn't glue the head-rail and foot-rail mortises and

tenons. They are fastened with ⅜-in. by 7-in. bed bolts threaded into captured nuts, as in detail C (p. 96). A pivoting brass cap hides each bolt head. I got the bolts from Horton Brasses, Box 120F, Cromwell, Conn. 06416. Get the wrench that goes with the bolts, or use a 12mm socket wrench. With no glue holding it together, I didn't want to risk an ill-fitting tenon shoulder where the headboard joins the posts, so I simply didn't cut shoulders, letting the full 1¹⁄₁₆-in. thickness of the headboard fit snugly into the mortises (detail B).

The side rails are stub mortise-and-tenoned into the posts and bolted. For strength, the two bolts that pass through each foot post should be a minimum of 2 in. apart. Most four-poster beds have the bolt for the side rail lower than the bolt for the foot rail, but it could be done either way.

Whether you plan to use a canopy or not, the bed looks better with the traditional bars that commonly join the tops of the posts. These are called the tester (pronounced "tee-ster") and they form the supports for a canopy. The laps that join the tester bars are not glued but are held together by dowels driven into the top of the posts.

I finished the bed with clear Watco oil, which darkened the wood just enough to enhance the grain of the cherry. A month later I followed up with a liberal application of Watco satin oil, and I think the final finish is exquisite.

This is not a small project, but because I drew my own plans and used techniques new to me, it's one of the most satisfying I've ever tackled. Trouble is, my daughter asked me if I could make one for her and I said "sure," again. I'll never learn. I wonder if she'll settle for pine.   □

Herb Akers lives in Rockville, Md., and makes reproduction furniture as a hobby. Photo by the author.

Layout tips from the boatyard

by Michael Podmaniczky

A long straightedge or a chalk line does well for laying out guidelines on square-sectioned stock to be worked into an octagon. But this old sparmakers' marking gauge speeds the job, and you can also use it to mark out a swelled taper, as for a round mast or a boom.

It's made of a scrap that's a few inches longer than the greatest thickness of the taper to be worked. The two dowels that guide the gauge and the nails that do the scribing are inserted according to this geometry: In a square slightly larger than the section of the work, lay out the octagon as shown in the drawing. Then locate the dowels so that the distance between their inside edges equals the length of a side of the square. Position the scribing nails as shown.

To use the gauge, saw or plane the taper "in the square" on four sides of your stock. Then, with the dowels held

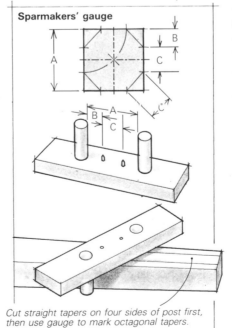

Cut straight tapers on four sides of post first, then use gauge to mark octagonal tapers.

tightly against the edges of the stock, scribe the corners of the octagon by drawing the gauge down the length of the piece. Drawknife down close to the line and finish with a smooth plane. A boatbuilder making a mast or a spar would continue shaping by first eyeballing the octagonal post to 16 sides, eventually planing off all the corners to form a uniform, round section.

For strength and weight, spars have noticeably swelled tapers. I suggest adding a subtler swell to octagonal posts, whether tapered or not. This slight bulging, called entasis, is commonly found in classic Greek columns. Entasis imparts an appealing visual correctness. Adding it will also help you avoid inadvertently hollowing the tapers.   □

Michael Podmaniczky is a boatbuilder and patternmaker who works in Camden, Maine.

Making Period Bedposts
Methods from the Deep South

by Asher Carmichael

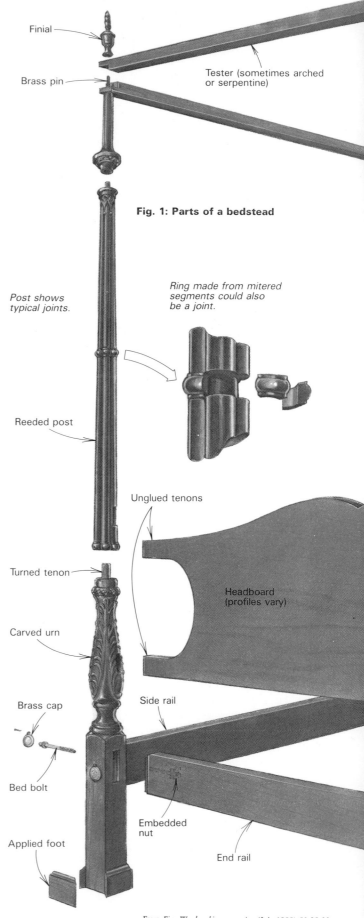

Finial

Brass pin

Tester (sometimes arched or serpentine)

Post shows typical joints.

Ring made from mitered segments could also be a joint.

Fig. 1: Parts of a bedstead

Reeded post

Unglued tenons

Turned tenon

Headboard (profiles vary)

Carved urn

Brass cap

Side rail

Bed bolt

Embedded nut

Applied foot

End rail

A spinning beam 4 in. square and up to 7 ft. long has a lot of inertia, and turning one into a bedpost might seem a frightful task. Yet in the course of visiting several bed makers in the Mobile area, I discovered that proper planning and some ingenious jigs can take the risk and the mystery out of the job. Mobile is a bedmaking center, the home of one major bed manufacturer, Reid Classics, and a few one-man shops as well. The jigs and fixtures shown in this article can be used not only for bedposts, but for any long turnings.

The Reid Classics story began some 50 years ago, when Robert Reid went to work for Roy Blake, a cabinetmaker who specialized in restoring and reproducing the many antiques found in the Mobile area. After WW II, Reid and his brother Julian opened a general woodworking shop that in its early years made everything from horse-drawn carriages to tennis rackets. Because of demand, they eventually specialized in period four-poster beds. Over the years, they have devised machine-production methods that still maintain the uncompromising excellence of detail they had learned from Blake (who in his late seventies still does some work in a one-room shop in his home).

The Reids have, over the years, done their best to perpetuate their methods and the traditions that Blake started. Of the three other bedmakers in the area, two—Milton Collins and Glenn De-Gruy—worked for the Reids for years before starting their own shops, and the third, William Blake, learned his craft from his uncle Roy, the same old master who steered Robert Reid into woodworking so many years before.

Beds are knockdown construction so that they can be moved. A typical four-poster is shown in the photo on the facing page. End rails and side rails—usually 2 in. thick and 5 in. wide—are tenoned to fit into mortises cut in square sections of the posts, as shown in figure 1, then held in place with long bolts and embedded nuts. The standard hardware used in the 18th century is still available today from many local hardware stores, and if not, period-hardware suppliers such as Horton Brasses (Box 120F, Cromwell, Conn. 06416) will have them.

The headboard is never glued in place. It is kept from loosening by the location of the bed bolts—the bolts securing the end rails are above the ones in the side rails, so that they constantly pull in on the posts and the headboard. The tester (pronounced teester, and often spelled that way in old records) is sometimes straight and rectangular, sometimes arched or serpentine. The top of each post carries a brass or steel pin that passes through

From *Fine Woodworking* magazine (July 1985) 53:28-33

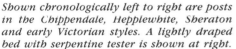

Shown chronologically left to right are posts in the Chippendale, Hepplewhite, Sheraton and early Victorian styles. A lightly draped bed with serpentine tester is shown at right.

the tester to hold it in place. The finial then slides onto the pin to conceal it. In Colonial days, testers carried the weight of voluminous side curtains of expensive imported fabric, which could completely enclose the bed and its occupants. A richly draped bed provided privacy and shelter from drafts, and showed off the family's wealth as well. One old document lists 56 yards of material ordered as bed "furniture," which is what they called the fabric. Today's four-posters are seldom so fully furnished.

Mattresses, filled with up to 40 pounds of down, were at first supported on thick stuffed pads laid directly on the floor, but methods of raising them up on webs of rope and canvas were soon devised, with the ropes secured through holes or pins in the rails. Reproduction beds are usually adapted to take standard box springs in the same ways used for regular beds.

The Reid shop makes scores of period designs by combining about thirty different posts with various headboards and testers. By studying bedposts in museums, and making templates of antique posts that come in for repair, the Reid shop has accumulated authentic patterns that span periods from early Chippendale to late Victorian. As a rough guide, Chippendale's influence shows in cabriole legs with ball-and-claw feet, and also in square posts with applied foot moldings. Hepplewhite's style had reeding instead of the earlier fluted designs and Sheraton introduced round, tapering legs. Such distinctions are not always easy to make because styles and influences overlapped. The tall posts favored up to around 1820 soon gave way to heavier designs with shorter posts, no drapery, and sometimes even fancy foot rails in addition to the structural members. Such changes marked the end of an era. As Wallace Nutting once wryly wrote: "A foot rail did not come in until good styles went out."

The furnituremaker in the 18th century often turned bedposts in one piece except for the finial. In those days, turning a one-

piece post had advantages. For one thing, their boring tools were probably not as efficient as today's, and it would have been difficult to drill accurate dowel holes to join a post made in sections. In addition, turners used manually powered lathes, which allowed them a range of slow speeds that took most of the danger out of turning long, heavy stock. This and the use of a steady rest diminished the tendency of slender work to whip and vibrate.

A few of the shops in the Mobile area have lengthened their lathes to accept longer than usual work. One approach is to remove the headstock and tailstock from a standard lathe, and then make new lathe ways from heavy angle iron. The headstock and tailstock are attached by whatever means is practical, and the whole assembly is raised up on a sturdy wooden stand. Another way to lengthen a lathe is to remove the tailstock from one and the headstock from another, and to bolt the two lathe beds in tandem atop a long support table.

Yet even though they have the means, no one in Mobile regularly turns full-length posts. Instead, area bedmakers have developed methods to join posts turned in shorter sections. These ideas can be used by any turner to join long work such as standing lamps and coat racks as well as bedposts. If you begin with full-length stock, as most bedmakers in Mobile do, you can make the grain in the finished work match from section to section. Yet this isn't absolutely necessary. Shorter stock may be much more available—and economical—and there is usually so much decoration around the joints that the continuity of the wood grain will be somewhat obscured in any case. A big advantage to working in sections is that your present lathe will probably be up to the job. Also, a post turned in sections will turn out straighter than a one-piece post.

The Reid shop rips post stock full length from 4-in. thick planks, and a typical blank will warp a little as it is cut from the

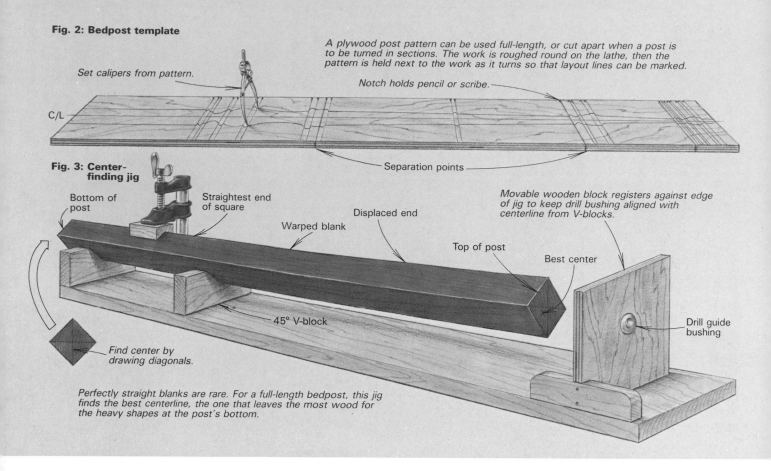

Fig. 2: Bedpost template

Set calipers from pattern.

A plywood post pattern can be used full-length, or cut apart when a post is to be turned in sections. The work is roughed round on the lathe, then the pattern is held next to the work as it turns so that layout lines can be marked.

Notch holds pencil or scribe.

C/L

Separation points

Fig. 3: Center-finding jig

Bottom of post

Straightest end of square

Displaced end

Warped blank

Movable wooden block registers against edge of jig to keep drill bushing aligned with centerline from V-blocks.

Top of post

Best center

Drill guide bushing

45° V-block

Find center by drawing diagonals.

Perfectly straight blanks are rare. For a full-length bedpost, this jig finds the best centerline, the one that leaves the most wood for the heavy shapes at the post's bottom.

board. If you are planning to cut a post into three or four sections, warp will not be too much of a problem, because you can square up the joints on the lathe, undercutting the endgrain a little for a perfect fit.

When working in sections, it's wise to consider which part of the joint should be tenon and which part mortise. There are often deep cove cuts either immediately above or below a joint, and the rule is to bore the mortise through what will be the heavier part in the finished post. It is a good idea to keep any joint mortises well away from the square mortises for the bed rails, in order not to weaken the post at this critical point. Bedposts typically separate as shown in figure 1, and an average tenon might be 1-in. to 1¼-in. dia., and about 3 in. long. Tenons are grooved to allow glue squeeze-out.

A crucial step in making a bedpost is to draw this sort of information, including the separation points, on a full length plywood pattern of the post, as shown in figure 2. If the post is to be turned in sections, the pattern can be cut apart and used to scribe separation points onto the stock, allowing extra length for integral tenons (at upper joints, where strength is not so critical, it is often possible to substitute a dowel, which conserves post stock and makes for better grain matching).

With the work in the lathe, hold the pattern next to it for marking the points where the profiles change. At the base of the post, and with the lathe turned off, mark the point where the square section ends, and scribe the lines around all four faces. Then round off the corners with the point of a skew chisel. Mark the other points on the work after it has been roughed round with a gouge—simply hold the pattern next to the stock as it turns and slide a pencil down the notch in the pattern. Then set calipers according to the pattern and transfer the di-

ameters to the work with a parting tool.

If you cut full-length stock into sections, be sure to mark their orientation on the end grain as soon as you cut the divisions, so that they can be turned and assembled in the correct order. You can mark the matching sections A (for the bottom of the post), then B-B, C-C, etc. These letters will serve to keep you from accidentally reversing a section when you put it in the lathe. These marks will probably be turned away when you square up the joint lines, but you can mark them again at that time so you won't intermix post sections later.

If you have a long-bed lathe and decide to have few separation points in your design, you will have to consider how much the stock is warped. In ordinary turning, a slightly warped piece of wood is simply center-marked at both ends, and the warp is turned away. But in a bedpost, such a procedure may cause problems. It is necessary for the square section of the stock to stand straight and to be perpendicular to the bed rails. This means that the blank must be chucked in the lathe with the square part of the post on-center—any warp in the blank must be confined to the length of the post that will be above the rails. Figure 3 shows a jig that finds the best centers for a full length post. The bottom of the post (the straightest end of the blank) is marked with diagonals to show its center, then is held in a pair of V-blocks. The warped end is allowed to go its own way. A movable wooden block with a drill-guide bushing in it then locates the "center" at the finial end. If you make a jig like this, locate the drill-guide bushing in the block according to the size of the V-blocks and the stock. To check that the bushing is correct, put the block at the base of the post (the end that will remain square); the bushing must align exactly with the marked center. Of course in stock that is too badly warped, you may not

Drawings: David Dann

Robert Reid gauges a bedpost tenon to the right diameter, using calipers and a parting tool at several places along its length.

be able to turn full length without running out of wood.

When the finial center has been drilled, the blank is usually divided into two sections before turning. Because the tenon is turned at the top of the square section of the post, the upper post section must have a mortise at its bottom end as well as one for the finial pin. It is no trick to center a turned tenon, but it would be almost impossible to accurately center the matching mortise if it were drilled after the stock had been turned. The solution is to bore the mortise before turning, then insert a steel plug in the hole, as shown in figure 4. One end of the plug is countersunk to match the 60° live center at the tailstock, which centers the pre-drilled mortise so that the post can be turned around it. When mounting the work in the lathe, the finial end goes at the head-stock, and is driven by a spur center that instead of having a point, has a center pin that fits the finial mortise. Both mortises, therefore, end up centered in the post.

The center-finding jig is also useful if you plan to make a pen-cil post bed, one with octagonal posts instead of turned ones. When the Reids make a pencil post, they first find the center and drill the hole for the finial pin, then they mount the blank on a sliding jig that runs past a commercial shaper, which cuts each face of the tapered octagon in turn. Robert Reid got the basic idea from Roy Blake, whose original jig worked on the bandsaw, as shown in figure 5. The jig indexes the finial mortise on a pin that allows the post to be rotated for successive cuts. The band-saw blade cuts a straight taper from the top of the post, but the taper ends above the square base of the post. Thus, the bottom of the post can be used to index each cut in turn, by resting first on a flat face and then on a corner. In order that the taper end grace-fully, the corner cuts must be stopped before the blade exits the work. The blade is then backed out of the cut and the waste

Fig. 4: Aligning joints

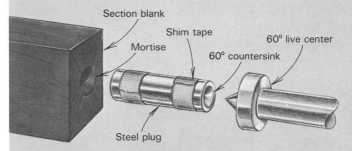

Tenons are turned on the lathe, which ensures that they are perfectly centered and parallel to the section's centerline. Mortises are bored in the square stock, then the post section is turned using a plug in the mortise to ensure that the post is centered around it.

Fig. 5: Bandsaw taper jig

This bandsaw jig can taper a full-length octagonal post. It can also remove excess wood from a blank before turning. The head block indexes the top of the post in the finial-pin mortise (drilled as shown in figure 3), while the base of the post is supported by a block that is sized to register against either the flat sides or the corners, allowing the blank to be rotated for successive cuts.

Detail: Cutting sequence

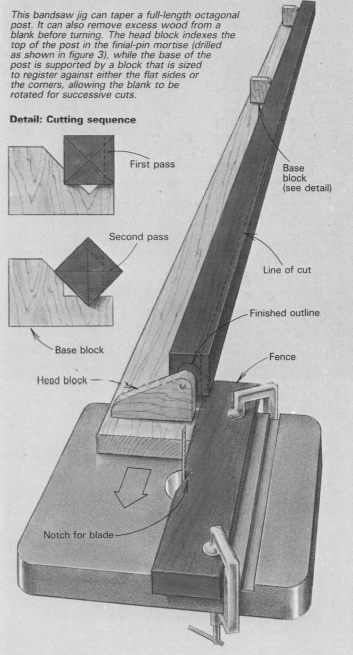

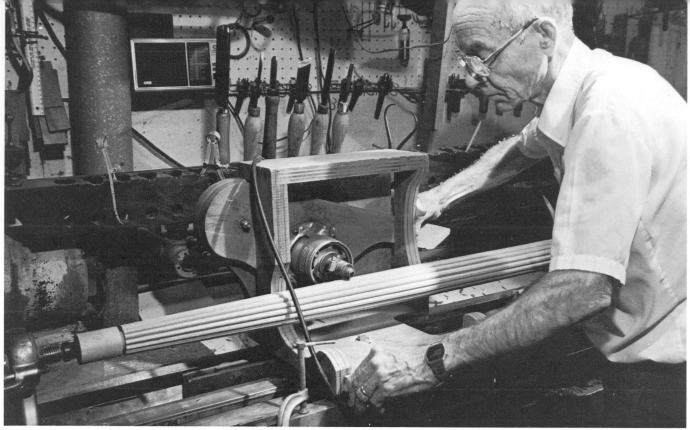

Julian Reid, above, operates a reeding jig—a carriage that rolls along the lathe ways carrying a router mounted on a pivoting arm. A bearing on the bit holder follows the contours of the work, which is locked in position by an indexing plate at the headstock. Mobile bedmaker William Blake, left, demonstrates his similar jig, which uses a simpler solid-pilot bit machined from tool steel (far left). The setscrew visible at the end of the bit locks the V-shaped cutter in place.

Reid's ingenious rope-twist machine, shown below, uses a bit similar to the straight-reeding machine (top), but in this case the carriage is attached to a cable arrangement that hooks up to the headstock spindle. As the operator moves the carriage along the ways, the work rotates a specific, adjustable amount for each inch the carriage moves.

Robert Reid's shopmade duplicating router carves four knees at once, following a pattern mounted in the center.

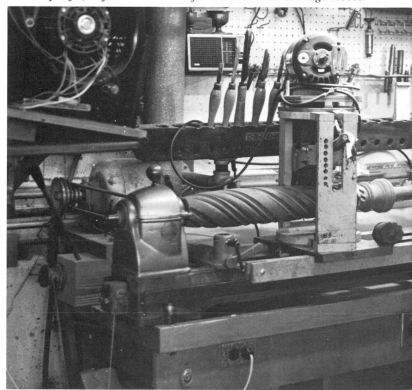

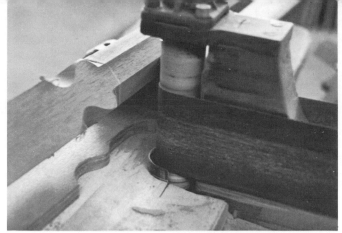

The Reid shop shapes lamb's tongues on a pencil-post by pattern-sanding the curves on a belt-sander.

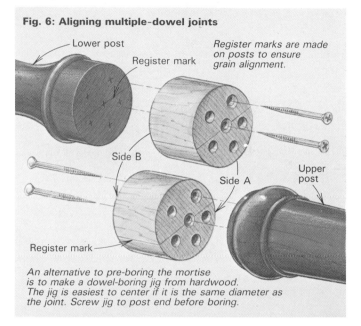

Fig. 6: Aligning multiple-dowel joints

Lower post

Register mark

Register marks are made on posts to ensure grain alignment.

Side B

Side A

Upper post

Register mark

An alternative to pre-boring the mortise is to make a dowel-boring jig from hardwood. The jig is easiest to center if it is the same diameter as the joint. Screw jig to post end before boring.

A bed with cabriole legs must have unusually heavy corner posts to withstand the strain put upon the rails. Note that this section of the post carries the tenon. If the tenon were on the upper section, the corner post would have to be mortised, weakening the construction.

nipped off, leaving enough wood for either a lamb's tongue or a simple cove. The Reid shop makes lamb's tongues by pattern-sanding, as shown in the top photo on this page. Lamb's tongues can also be shaped by hand with spokeshaves, carving tools or drum sanders in an electric drill. The tapered faces can be cleaned up with a few strokes of a plane.

An alternative method for aligning sections of a post is shown in figure 6. The joint is held together by four dowels, which are accurately located by means of a hardwood boring jig screwed to the end of the section. The jig is easiest to center if it is made the same diameter as the finished post. Grain alignment is accomplished by registering the jig on reference lines marked on the stock before it is turned. Posts can be clamped up by jacking them against a ceiling joist or by building an extra long clamp.

The jigs shown thus far are enough to make several authentic bedpost designs. But fancy ones call for reeding, fluting, carving and other decorations. In the old days, these chores were done by hand, but Robert Reid quickly found that handwork was too costly, and he soon invented some production methods. As he says: "Any time a machine can make a perfect duplicate of handwork, a man would be foolish to insist on doing the job by hand. But a 100% machine-produced object that arrives at only a 98% duplication of handwork is a compromise with integrity. What you want is whatever the machine can do—25%, 75%, 98%—plus whatever handwork it takes to finish the job right."

The four-man Reid shop can turn out about 125 beds a year, each one taking about two weeks through the system. Every bed is a custom order—the shop will make any combination of posts, headboard and tester. Machines do most of the roughing out, but the final touches still require handwork. There's a duplicating lathe, for example, that follows a pattern with four ounces of pressure on its stylus, and applies 400 pounds of pressure to cut the wood. The bedpost comes off the lathe clean enough that a lot of factories would then simply sand, stain and lacquer it, but Reid's remounts the work on another lathe and refines the shapes by hand-turning.

Similarly, Reid built a router jig, shown in the top photo on the facing page, for reeding bedposts. The work is locked in position by an indexing plate at the headstock. Then the carriage is moved along the lathe bed by hand, and a router mounted on a pivoting arm follows the contours of the work, piloted by the bit holder. Reid's uses a commercial bit holder, with a ½-in. shank and ball-bearing pilot. Bedmaker William Blake has adapted the idea using a bit machined from steel, with the cutter held in place by a setscrew from the end. Blake's cutter and jig are shown in the photos at far left on the facing page.

Reid also built a duplicating router (bottom left, facing page) that follows a carved leg and makes four simultaneous copies. These also get their share of hand carving before stain and lacquer go on. One of Reid's most ingenious machines (left, center) looks like a great-granddaddy of the Sears Router-Crafter. It's a router setup that makes helical rope-twist bedposts, and he cobbled it up from Model-A parts when he was only nineteen years old. Reid recalls the first Victorian rope-twist bed he made: "I had to carve each post by hand, and it seemed like I would never finish. If there's an easier way to do something, I'm going to do my best to uncover it." But it's a safe bet that he's not going to lower his standards to do so. □

Asher Carmichael works for Emperor Clock Co., in Fairhope, Ala. Photos on pages 102 and 103 (except photo at far left, page 102) by the author.

Index